I0414631

UNGOVERNING

Ungoverning

The Attack on the Administrative State and the Politics of Chaos

Russell Muirhead

Nancy L. Rosenblum

With a new preface by the authors

PRINCETON UNIVERSITY PRESS
PRINCETON AND OXFORD

Copyright © 2024 by Princeton University Press
Preface to the paperback edition copyright © 2026 by Princeton University Press

Princeton University Press is committed to the protection of copyright and
the intellectual property our authors entrust to us. Copyright promotes the
progress and integrity of knowledge created by humans. By engaging with
an authorized copy of this work, you are supporting creators and the global
exchange of ideas. As this work is protected by copyright, any reproduction or
distribution of it in any form for any purpose requires permission; permission
requests should be sent to permissions@press.princeton.edu. Ingestion of
any IP for any AI purposes is strictly prohibited without a license to do so;
licensing requests should be sent to DigitalLicensing@press.princeton.edu.

Published by Princeton University Press
41 William Street, Princeton, New Jersey 08540
99 Banbury Road, Oxford OX2 6JX

press.princeton.edu

GPSR Authorized Representative: Easy Access System Europe - Mustamäe
tee 50, 10621 Tallinn, Estonia, gpsr.requests@easproject.com

All Rights Reserved

First paperback edition, 2026
Paperback ISBN 9780691250533
ISBN (epub) 9780691287775
ISBN (PDF) 9780691283913

LCCN: 2025949308

British Library Cataloging-in-Publication Data is available

Editorial: Rob Tempio, Chloe Coy
Production Editorial: Elizabeth Byrd
Jacket/Cover: Karl Spurzem
Production: Erin Suydam
Publicity: James Schneider (US), Carmen Jimenez (UK)
Copyeditor: Anne Davidson

This book has been composed in Adobe Text Pro and Gotham.

To Hazel and Leo Rosenblum Palmer, who in their young lives have had to face the forces of destruction.

To Margaret, a formidable believer in governing.

CONTENTS

"Ungoverning" names something almost unprecedented in the history of politics: the comprehensive and intentional destruction of state capacity. It is more than an evocative term. Ungoverning is a precise word for willfully undoing the legitimacy and capacity of institutions developed over decades to serve the nation's needs.

We anticipated the scope of ungoverning, but not its speed. We published the book before the 2024 election and could not know how the world would turn. Of course, we hoped that the phenomenon we named would not come to pass—and that by naming it, we might help avoid it. Not so. It is now perhaps an understatement to say that ungoverning defines the second Trump administration.

Ungoverning replaces the policy state with personal rule. To govern by policy is to pass laws that tell the president to marshal the government's resources in certain ways to serve specific goals, such as ensuring everyone has access to health care or that allies can count on US security guarantees. Governing is about effectiveness, but also about legitimacy and the limited authority and power of even the highest offices.

Personal rule, by contrast, is about empowering the president's unpredictable will, which culminates not in policies but instead in capricious commands and unenforceable "deals." In his first term, many of Donald J. Trump's actions were performative: "build the wall!" and "lock her up!" But in Trump's second term, they are imperatives, crystallized in executive orders, which have come at a pace that is likely to exceed that of every previous US president (prior to Trump, the record was set in FDR's first term). Ungoverning is sweeping, concrete, and effective. It goes everywhere and all the way down.

Where Ungoverning Goes

As we have seen it in action during the first year of Trump's second term, the objectives of ungoverning are concentrated in three domains. At the most basic level, it focuses on appointments and the familiar project of combating the "deep state," which includes eliminating the nonpartisan civil service that dates to the 1883 Pendleton Act. Ungoverning goes on to concentrate even more power in the person of the president—exploiting the Supreme Court's recently minted presidential immunity to prosecution. And at its most ambitious, ungoverning is put in the service of redefining US national identity. It aims to reconstitute who we are—and the terms of citizenship. It does this not by legislation but rather by executive order. At each step, reasons are given for why populist authoritarianism requires an authoritarian constitution. All are designed to delegitimate liberal democratic government and policies—to strip them of their meaning, value, and authority.

Appointments

President Trump has had his way with the submissive Republican majority in Congress; his nominations are ensured. They are of a piece. Critical posts such as the director of national intelligence or director of the Federal Bureau of Investigation are assigned to people without experience and expertise.

Appointees do not know what it means to govern. They cannot advise. They cannot manage. They cannot explain. They cannot effectuate. But for this administration, these are not defects; these people were chosen precisely because they were patently inappropriate to the post. To shock. To undo. To ungovern. Their main qualification is not what they know but instead what they are willing to do.

For example, take Department of Health and Human Services secretary Robert F. Kennedy Jr., who fired *every* member of the Centers for Disease Control and Prevention's advisory panel on immunization in June 2025. Or Secretary of War (previously Defense) Peter Hegseth, who shared classified information about US military operations in Yemen in a Signal group chat that included his spouse and his brother. Or Attorney General Pamela Bondi, who is bent on using the Department of Justice to harass, threaten, and remove the president's perceived enemies from positions—not only firing the federal prosecutor, Mike Gordon, who had brought the case against the January 6 insurrectionists, but following Trump's direct instructions to ensure Letitia James (the NY Attorney General who before prosecuted Trump) and James Comey (the former FBI director) were indicted.

At the same time came the wholesale rampage against the federal civil service. The standard for federal workers—qualifications of experience and expertise—was replaced with what it was meant to erase—patronage. Where it was too difficult to sort vital civil servants from others and assess submissiveness, the answer was to fire them all. The conspiracist "deep state" was just the first target. Ravaging extended to departments and agencies of every kind: the National Weather Service, Internal Revenue Service, Health and Human Services, and Bureau of Labor Statistics—deconstruction extended to every cabinet department, every office and bureau. This rampage struck at every independent source of authority and knowledge, from the press and universities to myriad cultural institutions. The rampage goes deep into the associations of civil society with their own independent standards of knowledge and nonpartisanship.

The aim is simple: to destroy expert authority. Sometimes experts have authority because of the office in which they serve. This is especially true for the "independent agencies" like the Federal Reserve Commission that are designed to empower expert authority, and insulate it from partisanship and politics. But expertise has a normative authority independent of office. To know something that is difficult to know—that takes experience and study to understand—and highly relevant to public decision-making is to have a claim to be consulted and listened to. This is intolerable for those who want to realize an unconstrained president's personal will.

Law

The baseline was drawn in a 2023 Supreme Court decision in *Trump v. United States*, granting presidents immunity from indictment for criminal acts conducted during their presidency. With that comes an avalanche of executive orders presented as permissible substitutes for law and policy. In action, the once-fringe doctrine of the "unitary executive" means the president can demolish the Department of Education by fiat—never mind that it was established and is currently funded by Congress. A related claim to enhanced presidential authority is impoundment: the refusal to spend billions of dollars for established public policy ranging from foreign aid to federal research to community investment, thereby in effect nullifying Congress's policymaking and budgetary authority.

Ideologically aligned expert legal analysts developed rationales for disregarding legislative or constitutional constraints. Many are versions of the vague but much-used doctrine of emergency powers. Among them are casting the country as under attack—releasing the president to indulge the enormous powers afforded through his constitutional role as commander in chief. By describing the desire of impoverished migrants to move to the United States as a "foreign invasion," the president was able to invoke the 1798 Alien Act, which gives him authority to apprehend, restrain, secure, and remove all subjects of a "hostile nation." Thus disregarding the objection of a federal judge, the United States removed over two hundred Venezuelans to a gulag in El Salvador, beyond the reach of US law. The president called out the military and put the Washington, DC, police under his authority to "clean out" criminals—and not just them.

These legal maneuvers add up to new justifications for enlarging the realm of executive power and its violent face. They do much more, though: they offer in sometimes veiled form authoritarian reasons for constitutional revision. More is going on than defying constitutional constraints and the judgments of courts, and more than expanding the scope of unchained executive action. The key development is an articulation of the true character of the nation and the constitutional changes demanded by authoritarian populism. We see not just brute violation but also the evolution of authoritarian reasons that appeal to popular will. One crucial attempt to date is "denaturalization."

Denaturalization

Taken literally, the phrase refers to the president's power to strip naturalized citizens of their US citizenship. For revenge or as a dramatic exhibition of power, Trump declared his intent to denaturalize New York City mayoral candidate Zohran Mamdani, declaring him a "Communist lunatic." Denaturalization adds millions of people to the already immense set of political targets defined as un-American. It is plainly a method of intimidation—of silencing. It is the successful prelude to attempts to abolish birthright citizenship.

The aim is a program to redefine what is American and who is an American: to control who enjoys the rights and protections of US citizenship, and what those are. No citizen is immune to being redefined, or enlisted in the program of redefinition. The danger to US values "comes [not] from immigration itself but from immigrant control. . . . [Y]ou cannot control outsiders . . . without controlling insiders (citizens)."

The most shocking extension of militarized intimidation is the growing numbers of US Immigration and Customs Enforcement (ICE) agents (all under the president's personal control) who threaten, arrest, and remove legal residents to distant detention centers with no opportunity for appeal or even contact with an attorney. These agents are masked, anonymous, and heavily armed. They occupy streets, airports, and the corridors of courts. They penetrate civil society, such as stores and workplaces. They occupy neighborhoods, rounding up presumptively undocumented immigrants in front of the startled people who live nearby and try to protect the neighbors next door. Tens of thousands of people—including legal residents and citizens—are caught up in these dragnets, and sent to distant detention centers without reasons or due process. The redefinition of America and

Americans is no longer contained to the level of ideology or rogue violence but instead is enacted everywhere and all the way down.

WHY UNGOVERNING

Ungoverning originates in the desire of one man, Trump, a president like none other: someone who thirsts for power, and the ability not merely to command and direct but rather to dominate and humiliate. That ambitious people might appear who thirst for power is not a recent political insight. The point of constitutional government—the form of government invented in the seventeenth-century English contests over monarchical power that became modern democracy—is to quell, contain, defang, and defeat such ambitions, and redirect the lust for power into a desire to serve the public.

But ungoverning is not only about one person's quest to dominate; it has a constituency. By breaking the authority of the administrative state, ungoverning liberates corporations from regulation. By incapacitating the Internal Revenue Service, it liberates the wealthy from the obligation to pay taxes. And it gives business elites and evangelical Christians the probusiness, proreligion Supreme Court they have always wanted.

The most important reason for ungoverning is a claim that often goes unstated about the kind of power the country needs. On this view, a defiant and largely unaccountable power is necessary to impose the type of change that no leader with a more delicate sensibility or procedural scruples could ever accomplish.

Only a contrary president who threatens the destruction of the North Atlantic Treaty Organization (NATO), in this view, could force NATO allies to pay more for their collective defense. Only a powerful will can disrupt the seventy-year trajectory of trade liberalization and replace it with a new tariff regime. Only a commanding executive, indifferent to constitutional niceties, could bring a stop to sixty years of welcoming immigrants. Disrupting the liberal consensus on cultural issues like "diversity, equity, and inclusion" (DEI) or federal funding of scientific research requires, given this perspective, the same thing as imposing tariffs: a willful president who is free of the constraints of office and powerful enough to impose his way.

And behind ungoverning stands the despairing conviction that the normal processes of government cannot work. We cannot use the tools of governing—policymaking—to get change. We cannot *do*; we can only undo.

Yet Trump and his party may want a government that can do things. For instance, Trump's presidential memorandum directing the Department of Education to collect admissions data on sex, race, GPA, and test scores requires that there be a Department of Education—notwithstanding the president's executive order of March 20, 2025, directing the secretary of education to "facilitate the closure of the Department of Education." In case after case, the president may have to choose whether he wants to govern or ungovern.

If, however, what Trump and the Republican Party want is unconstitutional and unpopular, ungoverning may be the only path. For example, if Trump wants to stay in power after his second term—"Trump 2028" as the hats for sale at Trump Tower say—then ungoverning will prevail. If what MAGA stands for is a conception of national greatness that is religious and racial— the restoration of a white, Christian nation—then in a country where only 41 percent of the population is white and Christian, ungoverning will be the only way.

If we were to assume Trump and his followers want policy change rather than regime change—radical shifts in trade and tariff, military and foreign, and immigration policies, and the policies connected to a range of cultural issues—then the Trump administration will need to be an *administration*. It will need the tools associated with something that Trump has so far set about to destroy: governing.

As we show in this book, to give up on governing is not only to be less effective. It is to convert the coercive power of the state into a personal tool—from the investigatory power of the IRS and Justice Department to the colossal power of the military. If that happens, there is no institution that can prevent the targets of intimidation, threat, and violence from expanding. What starts with those on the margins who do not elicit popular sympathy—those who reside in the country illegally; those whose identities mark them off as vulnerable, above all trans people—expands to include foreign students whose politics offend the regime. And then intellectuals, journalists, and university professors. And lawyers who litigate to protect the opposition. Donors who fund the political opposition. Party operatives and then candidates themselves. Trump talks wistfully of sweeping up US citizens and sending them to a foreign gulag outside the reach of US law. The step from where we are to a much more violent politics is a short one. Ungoverning in the end unleashes fear: intimidation, rogue violence, vigilantism, militias, and an omnipresent militarized state.

Americans disagree about what they want the government to do. The question of the moment is whether notwithstanding their disagreements, they want a government that can govern. If so, we will see in states and cities and local communities, in political parties and voluntary associations, on the street and online, people demanding that officials muster the will and restore the capacity to govern.

We invented the term "ungoverning" early on to jolt readers into grasping the distinct dangers at work in American politics today. Much of what we wrote then in a speculative way—following the logic of ungoverning to violence, for instance—has now come to pass. But the argument about ungoverning remains urgent. Because unless we understand what is happening as a malignant normality, we will not be able to resist it.

Notes

1. "Executive Orders," American Presidency Project, https://www.presidency.ucsb.edu/statistics/data/executive-orders.

2. "Protecting the Meaning and Value of American Citizenship," White House, January 20, 2025, https://www.whitehouse.gov/presidential-actions/2025/01/protecting-the-meaning-and-value-of-american-citizenship/.

3. Surina Venkat, "Trump Accidentally Posted Message To Bondi on Prosecuting Comey, Enemies: Reports," *The Hill,* October 10, 2025, https://thehill.com/homenews/administration/5550406-trump-bondi-prosecution-truth-social-post/

4. *Trump v. United States,* 603 U.S. __ (2024).

5. "Declaring a National Energy Emergency," White House, January 20, 2025, https://www.whitehouse.gov/presidential-actions/2025/01/declaring-a-national-energy-emergency/; "Declaring a National Emergency at the Southern Border of the United States," White House, January 20, 2025, https://www.whitehouse.gov/presidential-actions/2025/01/declaring-a-national-emergency-at-the-southern-border-of-the-united-states/; "Fact Sheet: President Donald J. Trump Declares National Emergency to Increase Our Competitive Edge, Protect Our National Sovereignty and Strengthen Our National and Economic Security," White House, April 2, 2025, https://www.whitehouse.gov/fact-sheets/2025/04/fact-sheet-president-donald-j-trump-declares-national-emergency-to-increase-our-competitive-edge-protect-our-sovereignty-and-strengthen-our-national-and-economic-security/; "Fact Sheet: President Donald J. Trump Declares a Crime Emergency to Restore Safety in the District of Columbia," White House, August 11, 2025, https://www.whitehouse.gov/fact-sheets/2025/08/fact-sheet-president-donald-j-trump-declares-a-crime-emergency-to-restore-safety-in-the-district-of-columbia/.

6. "Protecting the American People Against Invasion," White House, January 20, 2025, https://www.whitehouse.gov/presidential-actions/2025/01/protecting-the-american-people-against-invasion/; "President Trump Delivers Justice to Terrorists, Security for Americans," White House, March 17, 2025, https://www.whitehouse.gov/articles/2025/03/president-trump-delivers-justice-for-terrorists-security-for-americans/;

"Invocation of the Alien Enemies Act Regarding the Invasion of the United States by Tren de Aragua," White House, March 15, 2025, https://www.whitehouse.gov /presidential-actions/2025/03/invocation-of-the-alien-enemies-act-regarding-the -invasion-of-the-united-states-by-tren-de-aragua/. The term "hostile nation" is from the Alien Enemies Act of 1798, https://uscode.house.gov/view.xhtml?path=/prelim@ title50/chapter3&edition=prelim.

7. Juwayriah Wright, "Trump Calls Mamdani a 'Communist Lunatic' a Day After NYC Primary, *Thime*, June 25, 2025, https://time.com/7297832/trump -zohran-mamdani-reaction-communist-lunatic/.

8. Chandram Kukathas, "Trump's Deportation Program Is About Control. Even If You Are a U.S. Citizen," *New York Times*, https://www.nytimes.com/2025/07/01 /opinion/trump-deportation-immigration-control.html.

9. "ICE Contractual Capacity and Number Detained: Overcapacity vs. Overcrowding," TRAC Immigration, July 8, 2025, https://tracreports.org/reports/762/.

10. "US Secretary of Education Linda McMahon Directs National Center for Education Statistics to Collect University Data on Racial Discrimination in Admissions," Department of Education, August 7, 2025, https://www.ed.gov/about/news/press -release/us-secretary-of-education-linda-mcmahon-directs-national-center-education -statistics-collect-universities-data-race-discrimination-admissions; "Improving Education Outcomes by Empowering Parents, States, and Communities," White House, March 20, 2025, https://www.whitehouse.gov/presidential-actions/2025/03/ improving-education-outcomes-by-empowering-parents-states-and-communities/.

11. See Trump Store, accessed August 20, 2025, https://www.trumpstore.com /product/trump-2028-hat/.

12. *2023 PRRI Census of American Religion: County-Level Data on Religious Identity and Diversity*, (Washington, DC: PRRI, December 2024), 3, https://prri.org /wp-content/uploads/2025/05/PRRI_Dec_2024_Religion_final-1.pdf.

"Something happens and we're startled into thought" is the opening line of our 2019 book, *A Lot of People Are Saying: The New Conspiracism and the Assault on Democracy.* Like so many others, we were startled by the waves of conspiracy charges crashing over the nation. We wrote to understand our own disorientation. We wrote to clarify what it means to know something. And we wrote to alert readers to the political consequence of conspiracism: delegitimation of the institutions of liberal democracy.

The wreckage we grapple with here is the attack on governing capacity, on the administrative state. Conspiracism assaults the "machinery of government," what is cast as "the deep state" (Heath 2020). But while conspiracism has become part of the daily drama of politics, degrading government departments and agencies is less often reported and less understood for the danger it is.

Destruction of the administrative state has been openly promoted. "I want to bring everything crashing down" is the manifesto of a master of chaos, Steve Bannon, who was an inspiration to an ungoverning president, a party, and a movement (Moore 2017).

We were drawn to this project because of our appreciation for the vital work of public administration. We call the willful destruction of state capacity ungoverning. We name it, diagnose it, spell out how it works and what it portends, and recommend what needs to be done.

We were primed to recognize the danger of the unantici-pated attack on the capacity for governing.

Rosenblum's first book, *Bentham's Theory of the Modern State* (1978), delved into the philosopher's voluminous writ-ings on the design of political institutions. Some were fantastic imaginings, like his plan for the all-visible prison he called the "panopticon." But others were prescriptions for organizing the nitty-gritty of governing. Bentham proselytized for a respon-sible civil service and for what he called the "statistical function" of government. Almost alone among canonical political thinkers, he gave great weight not only to the high ground of constitutions but to the solid ground of rule-bound procedures and expertise. Bentham understood its necessity for fashioning and implement-ing policy in the public good. Here was an early argument for the modern administrative state.

Not the earliest argument, though. Muirhead came to the project having long contemplated Hamilton's defense of "good administration" in *the Federalist Papers*—an ideal that Hamilton contrasted to the more responsive but less effective rule of state legislatures. Hamilton wanted a federal government that could gather information and resources and marshal them to pursue long-term goals. His emphasis on administration, combined with the participatory ethos of another of the great nationalists at the 1787 constitutional convention, James Wilson, pointed to a new kind of democratic state: one that could *govern*.

The present attack on the business of governing gets public attention when witnesses within the agencies describe how their work at the Department of State or the Department of Justice or the Internal Revenue Service was hijacked, circum-vented, derailed, or degraded. They impress on us all how civil servants are personally excoriated, fired, made targets of threats and violence. It takes more than the best reporting, however, to understand the ongoing string of attacks aimed at the capacity to govern. It also takes more than witnessing to understand why this degradation of governing is a distinct assault on liberal democracy.

We both have been students and faculty in the Department of Government at Harvard University, which was housed in the imposing Littauer Center. Dedicated in 1939, engraved in granite across the front of the building is the donor's name and the mission: "Littauer Center of Public Administration." For some time, public administration has not been a subject of study there. The students who passed under the engraving, including us, didn't stop to ask what public administration was, or pause to consider its value and necessity, or worry about how quickly it can be degraded. Now we know.

We finished this book in the months before the 2024 presidential election. It is tempting to think the future of the phenomenon we call ungoverning depends entirely on that election. But ungoverning is not the project of one person. The objective of deconstructing the administrative state is carried by a reactionary movement, by elected officials in the Republican Party, and by justices of the Supreme Court. Defeating ungoverning is more than the work of one election. It will require rehabilitating the administrative state in the minds of citizens. It will require re-creating a partisanship that contests rival approaches to governing rather than a partisanship that contests whether government should have the capacity to govern. And it will require a nation that is alert to the peril of personal rule.

UNGOVERNING

1

Naming It

Ungoverning is an unfamiliar name for an unfamiliar phenomenon: the attack on the capacity and legitimacy of government, especially the part of government that goes by the term "administrative state." The administrative state consists of a vast array of government agencies that shape, implement, adjudicate, and enforce public policies of every kind. It encompasses all those who carry on the day-to-day work of government: the ordinary and routine, the wars and emergencies. The legislature may pass bills, the executive may sign them, the judiciary may pass judgment on them—but it is the appointed officials and civil servants who translate laws on paper into action. "Administration," or shaping, implementing, and enforcing laws by officials charged specifically with the task, is unavoidable. Every modern state is an administrative state.

Yet, the administrative state is besieged. Not only because of the threat this book explores—willful ungoverning—but because of the full range of forces that undercut the effectiveness of government. Progressives, moderates, conservatives, and even libertarians known for their insistence on minimal government are focused on the question of state capacity. From every political quarter, people doubt whether government can succeed at addressing urgent public problems like global warming, housing and homelessness, education, transportation, and health care, and the problem is compounded when we consider actions that require international cooperation.

At the very moment that building state capacity is most essential, a new force is attacking the administrative state: ungoverning.

Ungoverning exploits the wave of frustration with government bureaucracy and government performance. Its objective is not institutional reform, but "deconstruction." One example crystalizes this—the intention to abolish the Internal Revenue Service; without steady and sufficient revenue, government cannot function. There are innumerable others: sidelining senior officials and diplomats in the State Department even at high-level meetings with adversaries like North Korea's dictator Kim Jong Un (Ward 2019); demanding personal loyalty and special treatment for favorites from the director of the Federal Bureau of Investigation (FBI) (Comey 2017, 3); threatening to deny Covid aid to states whose governors were critical of the president (Cohen 2020).

The atmospherics of acts of deconstruction changed from situation to situation. Some were sudden and insouciant—unplanned. Others followed weeks or months of fury—deliberated threats and firings and disruption of regular business. The motive is animus toward government itself (Lobosco 2023). Ungoverning is the undoing of the administrative state. It is the reversal of already highly developed state capacity. It is a kind of backward evolution. It is a rarity, distinct from state failure due to incapacity or what Francis Fukuyama calls "political decay" because it is chosen (Fukuyama 2014, 455–466). What replaces governing is not more freedom but the arbitrary rule of personal will.

Americans have suffered a close encounter with the unanticipated and dangerous disabling of government during the presidency of Donald Trump. He clarified it as no one else could by forming the first presidential administration that was anti-administration. This was not just provocative talk. Procedures for decision-making were circumvented, experts were silenced or fired, and public purposes were abandoned, without any justification beyond thwarting "enemies" who opposed the president's will. Ungoverning is the intentional disruption of regular order for reasons unrelated to public welfare.

But ungoverning is not just about Donald Trump. Although his presidency clarified it as none other, it did not come out of nowhere. Trump brought decades of cultivated hostility toward government to a crescendo (Campbell 2023, 11–14). Ungoverning has a history before Trump, and it will have a future after him. It is not the work of one person.

Nor do we mean to claim that Trump had no interest in policy or governing at all. There were important domains in which he aimed to change existing policies on trade, immigration, and the war in Afghanistan, for example. And many of the policies his administration set in motion on those subjects were continued by his successor. Ungoverning was not the whole of Trump's administration, even if it was its defining character.

Ungoverning is part of the constellation of actions that make up illiberal, anti-democratic politics and result in "democratic backsliding" (Bermeo 2016). It joins other assaults on the essential securities of liberal democracy: constitutionalism, rule of law, and democratic norms. Like these, ungoverning indicates a new kind of assault: not a military coup but an attack on democratic essentials led by an elected leader with popular support. In some cases, like the disruption of election administration, ungoverning aims directly at the core of democracy. Ungoverning can be more indirect, however; by degrading the machinery of government it creates a state that cannot respond to public needs. Ungoverning can go anywhere. No single agency or program stands alone in its sights. No department, no policy, and no public servant is immune.

The idea that those entrusted with responsibility for governing would intentionally make the state less capable—degrading its ability to collect taxes, to deliver mail, to conduct diplomacy, to prosecute violations of civil rights—is almost unthinkable. It is unthinkable because it seems irrational.

State capacity is simply the "ability of a government-in-place to develop and implement policies that its leaders believe will improve national well-being" (Khosla and Tushnet 2022, 97). Capacity is a matter of degree, and more is not always better. Courts may set boundaries for what states can do for the sake of protecting rights or delineating the proper scope of different branches and levels of government. It might be coherent and convincing for leaders to argue that the state should reduce its activities in particular areas of policy. But destroying state capacity in an errant way is almost without precedent.

There are cases of tyrants like Hugo Chávez in Venezuela who, because of the distorted reality they create all around them, unintentionally destroy the states they rule (Neuman 2022). But even tyrants and authoritarians generally want a state that works (for them). Those hungry for personal power want to command the instrument that conveys power—the machinery of government. Even Marxist revolutionaries who imagined a utopian "withering away of the state" sought in the first instance to take over a functioning state, not to destroy it.

Behind ungoverning in the United States is a tale of two conflicts, intertwined.

The first is a story of substituting personal will for governing. Governing is about the authority that adheres to an office, whereas rule is about empowering the will of a particular person or group. Invoking a medieval image, it is the difference between the crown and the king's head on which the crown sits. The assault on governing and substitution of will is comprehensive.

Our challenge is to understand why a president would declare war on the machinery of government. Our answer: to throw off the constraints that the machinery imposes on the exercise of personal power. In telling this story, we argue that ungoverning grew out of Trump's unchained impulse to command and his need to "own" reality and impose it on the nation. The vehicle is an imagined conspiracy, the malignant "deep state." And because the ethos of ungoverning has come to define the Republican Party, the threat it poses goes beyond one person.

The second story is about a reactionary counterculture movement that wants from politics what no liberal democratic government could deliver: a restoration of America as a Christian nation, a white nation, a nation that subordinates women, a sovereign nation divorced from the "new world order." The deep state conspiracy has a constituency. This constituency got its collective identity as a movement from a magnetic authoritarian leader. Like other movements, it is "presentist." The demand is for change *right now*. Whereas designing and implementing policies takes time, ungoverning can happen immediately. The reactionary counterculture is primed to act right now—to intimidate and threaten and turn to violence.

These two stories come together to produce ungoverning. To understand it, we need to name it, which is why we introduce this term into the political lexicon. Ungoverning has a history; everything does. It has a path forward, too.

As we have said, we should not be tempted to think that ungoverning is exclusive to Donald Trump. It has come to define a reactionary movement and the Republican Party. The shared intention is "a sweeping expansion of presidential power over the machinery of government." Identifying and eliminating "pockets of independence" in the administrative state is the aim. The objective is to dismantle agencies staffed by "the sick political class that hates our country" (Swan, Savage, and Haberman 2023). Unless the reactionary movement is defused and the Republican Party reinvents a philosophy of governing, deconstruction of the administrative state is not safely in the past. Another like-minded president, a Congress controlled by bring-it-all-crashing-down extremists, a Supreme Court that seizes the reins of the administrative state in order to eradicate capacities developed since the New Deal—any of these could carry on the project of ungoverning.

Ungoverning is vandalism, a willful sabotage of the institutions that do the work of government. But it has not yet been entrenched. We are no longer complacent about the robustness of liberal democratic institutions or of popular support for them. Our vigilance, now focused on the high ground of constitutionalism and "the soul of the nation," must extend to the unlovely institutions that do the day-to-day work of governing. The future of liberal democracy depends on many things: the rule of law, the legitimacy of political opposition, accountability, representation. It depends, too, on a government that can govern.

Ungoverning Is Its Own Thing

Any addition to the political lexicon, like "ungoverning," will face challenges. Some new terms are esoteric and do not live outside a narrow sphere of like-minded political theorists and comparative political scientists. But some frame how we think about the political moment at hand and orient our sense of what is to be done. A summary of ungoverning includes the following:

- Degrading existing state capacity by derailing, displacing, hijacking, and circumventing administrative departments and agencies
- Wholesale attacks on administrative experience and specific subject expertise
- Wholesale attacks on regular administrative procedure
- Indiscriminate degradation of state capacity rather than targeted reform of rules, regulations, programs, agencies, or departments

The critical adjectives that mark ungoverning are "wholesale" and "indiscriminate." The critical verbs are "attack" and "degrade." Ungoverning is not an attempt to make government work better. It is an attempt to make government not work.

Our story is about how skepticism about the effectiveness of government and support for small government became freestanding hostility to government and a comprehensive attack on governing institutions. Our purpose is to show how features of U.S. politics that are familiar morphed into a rare kind of threat. The familiar elements are altering the scope of government, deregulation, and obstructing the political opposition. All of these can be deployed in a bounded, purposeful, strategic, and constructive way. Ungoverning is indiscriminate and unbounded, and its principal objective is personal rule. It is important, then, to distinguish ungoverning from these familiar elements of democratic politics.

The Scope of Government

Policy innovation can require undoing the status quo, including sometimes also undoing the departments and agencies responsible for bringing existing policy agendas to life in the world. Throughout two-hundred-plus years, the vicissitudes of history, ideology, politics, and the compounding needs of the nation have prompted leaders to shape and reshape the administrative state. Its reach, organization, and level of funding have changed. Over time, presidents and Congresses create, abolish, alter, and consolidate departments and their agendas.

Undoing policies—a Congress or party reversing its own measures or the opposition's—is standard business and may entail abolishing traditional agency functions, or even shutting down entire departments; the first regulatory agency, the Interstate Commerce Commission, was established in 1887 and abolished in 1995. Departments are also added: the Department of Homeland Security was created in 2002. That involved shuffling the places and work of other agencies, notably putting Immigration and Customs Enforcement (ICE) under its aegis. Sixty-two percent of the agencies created after 1946 had been "terminated or substantially reorganized" by 1997 (Selin and Lewis 2018, 85).

Reducing the scope of government is not on its own the same as ungoverning. Nor is ending policies and programs inherited from the past. The best example from U.S. politics is also the first. Following the election of Thomas Jefferson in 1800—which represented not simply a change of personalities but a comprehensive change, known as "the revolution of 1800"—Jefferson reversed core policies he inherited from Washington and Adams. He ended, for example, Hamilton's excise tax program of 1791, and eliminated the internal revenue administration. And he aimed to restrict the scope of national authority. But Jefferson did not disable the state. He wanted what he called the "machine of government" to work (Cunningham 1978, 24), and he involved himself in the details of administration. He relied on the efficient administration he created, first to incorporate the vast Louisiana Territory—"a test of the administrative capacity of the national government" (118)—and later, to enforce the Embargo of 1807, a policy that created an enormous and ultimately impossible administrative burden.

Andrew Jackson, too, wanted what we would now call "small government," and consistent with this philosophy, he destroyed the Second Bank of the United States in 1833. As a result, he was censured by the opposition Whigs, who saw his corollary decision to move the nation's deposits to state banks as an abuse of presidential power (Wilentz 2005, 398–401). Yet, whatever one thinks in retrospect of the constitutional controversy concerning the federal government's ability to charter a national bank—a controversy that began when Alexander Hamilton first proposed establishing a national bank in 1791—the decision to end the bank was a legitimate if contentious exercise of governmental power. It was not ungoverning.

Eliminating a policy or program takes enormous effort. Undoing anything is difficult, even when the undoing seems to make sense to almost everyone. Ending an agency or a program imposes immediate, concentrated, traceable costs on identifiable constituencies that in turn can organize, lobby, and defend their interests (Arnold 1992). Consider the National Technical Information Service (NTIS), which was created after World War II as a repository to make available scientific studies conducted by the government. By 2010, documents that the NTIS was charging citizens hundreds of dollars to obtain were available for free on the internet. In 2014, senators from both parties co-sponsored legislation to eliminate the NTIS, the Let Me Google That for You Bill (S. 2206, 113th Cong. [2014]). Congress failed to make this change, even though over 90 percent of the documents the agency sold could be found by a simple internet search and downloaded by anyone for free.

But there are cases where the frustration with the difficulty of reform can provoke calls for destruction. Take "Defund the police," the cri de coeur from the grassroots Black Lives Matter movement following the police murder of George Floyd in 2020 by Officer Derek Chauvin in Minneapolis, Minnesota. Taken literally, the slogan suggests we can do away with policing. Police brutality is so intransigent and racism so engrained that the only solution seems to be eradication: "The only way we're going to stop these endless cycles of police violence," advocates of "defund" argue, "is by creating alternatives to policing" (McHarris and McHarris 2020).

Some advocates of "defund" insisted that it stood for a nuanced set of reforms, not abolishing law enforcement. What they wanted was rather "to see the rotten trees of policing chopped down and fresh roots replanted anew" (Ray 2020). The objective was to diminish the scope of the authority of law enforcement, decreasing police resources and increasing funding for public services more appropriately assigned to other professionals. Social workers and medical experts, not police, in this view, are the appropriate responders for problems that stem from social disorder due to homelessness, mental illness, addiction.

But as a slogan, "defund" suggested destruction over reform. Born of rage against repeated episodes of police brutality, it appealed to a sense that no new wave of reform could work, no matter how carefully planned or well intentioned.

When problems go deep, reform is rarely simple, and solutions are rarely fast. For frustrated activists and citizens, any real reform may come to seem impossible. Destruction offers to do what reform cannot. Destruction seems like the only path to change. That is the promise of ungoverning, which is a false promise, as we show. And it is a distortion of what reformers who seek to constrict the scope of government aim for—a government that is more efficient and more effective.

Summing up current controversies surrounding the administrative state, one conservative economist put it this way: "We've been having a debate for decades now about the size of government. The more interesting debate is the scope of government" (Wright 2020, 40). In fact, more disturbing today than the scope of government is the capacity to preserve and to use, as governing requires, a functioning administrative state at all. And it is not just a matter of "interesting debate," but of facing up to the tremendous political damage ungoverning inflicts on liberal democracy.

Deregulation

It is also important to distinguish ungoverning from ordinary policies of deregulation. In many cases, deregulation is justified by arguments that markets serve public needs more effectively than government regulations. For instance, the Airline Deregulation Act of 1978, spearheaded by Senator Edward Kennedy, aimed to make air travel more affordable. Kennedy teamed up with Steven Breyer, then a professor at Harvard Law School, to create a plan that would abolish the Civil Aeronautics Board, which since the 1930s had controlled airline routes and pricing, and even regulated the size of the sandwiches served for lunch on flights (Derchin 2022; Eizenstat 2018). Deregulation was subsequently applied to a range of other industries such as trucking and telecommunication.

But there are other cases that look less like policy reform and more like degrading the agency's capacity to do its work—in other words, ungoverning. At the start of his first term, Ronald Reagan's appointment to head the Environmental Protection Agency (EPA), Anne Gorsuch, set out to incapacitate her own agency. She proposed to cut its budget by over 25 percent and to cut full-time staffing by a similar amount (Mintz 1995, 45). Her principal target was enforcement: agency officials were told to focus their efforts on "informal attempts at encouraging voluntary compliance" (43). Appointments were based on loyalty to Reagan, not on qualifications—or even a candidate's interest in the job. As the deputy associate administrator for enforcement reflected, "I handled Reagan's stop in Youngstown as a candidate and when they were recruiting, they asked for my resume. The EPA was the last agency I wanted to go to, and enforcement was the last job I wanted at the Agency" (42). Constant reorganization of enforcement divisions coupled with an absence of any clear policy goal cultivated pervasive confusion among civil servants charged with implementing environmental laws (51). The aim was not to design a more effective and efficient organization, but to incapacitate it. As one official said, there was "very obviously a deliberate plan to paralyze if not totally dismantle the enforcement program" (43, 254n11)—and to do this quickly and invisibly, before the public noticed (Landy, Roberts, and Thomas 1990, 245). Congress, however, did notice. Gorsuch was forced to resign.

Reagan's attempt to hobble the EPA was not an effort to reform an existing policy regime, as was Carter's dismantling of the Civil Aeronautics Board in 1978. Nor was it a case of "capture," where industries control the agencies that have the authority to regulate them. It was ungoverning—an attempt to comprehensively incapacitate an agency so that it would be unable to serve its statutory mission. Reagan failed at the EPA, but not for lack of effort. He failed only because public opinion and Congress wanted government to require industry to clean its toxic waste and stop poisoning the ground, water, and air. To expose the Reagan administration's effort to undo the agency was enough to defeat it. At that moment, there was no constituency for ungoverning. There was no reactionary movement to celebrate his deconstruction as there would be later under Trump—who revived Reagan's effort to disable the EPA openly and successfully.

In an early act of his presidency, Trump signed an executive order requiring that for every new federal regulation implemented, two must be rescinded (McCaskill and Nussbaum 2017). It had a cost component: the net incremental cost for fiscal 2017 should be "no greater than zero." We call this ungoverning not because deregulation was bad policy, but because it was indiscriminate. It was unclear: the order asks agencies to "'identify' two rules to be revoked and find ways to offset costs of new rules." Its result was not efficiency but confusion. It appeared "arbitrary" and "not implementable" (Plumer 2017). And behind it was a veiled threat to withhold cost of living adjustments for agency personnel until they obeyed the order (Crews 2016). It was careless, confusing, and disabling: "The mere existence of a perplexing directive like this, experts say, could bog down work at various regulatory agencies like the Environmental Protection Agency or Food and Drug Administration." As a Harvard Law School professor told *Vox*, "It is primarily an instrument for hassling the agencies and slowing the regulatory process" (Plumer 2017).

Indiscriminate deregulation is not a targeted strategy. While he was running for the Republican presidential nomination in 2023, Florida governor Ron DeSantis pledged to entirely eliminate a raft of federal agencies, including the Departments of Commerce, Education, and Energy and the Internal Revenue Service. The journal *Government Executive* observed, "The Florida governor did not specify how he would manage the dissolution of those agencies, which collectively employ more than 150,000 workers, nor what would happen to key components such as the Commerce's National Weather Service or Energy's oversight of the nuclear weapons program" (Katz 2023). Nor did DeSantis explain how the government would collect taxes in the absence of the IRS—or whether it would tax at all.

To be sure, the web of overlapping federal regulations can be dysfunctional in various ways. It does not follow, however, that because overregulation can be a problem, even *the* problem, then the regulatory authority of government should be degraded or abolished. The solution is relaxing, rewriting, and reforming regulations. This is what the federal government did to meet the crisis brought by the Covid pandemic. Through the innovation of advance purchase agreements and through "emergency use authorizations," the government both underwrote the discovery of vaccines and made them available to every citizen in less than a year (Frank, Dach, and Lurie 2021). One might call it a miracle. In fact, it was government, doing its work. When nothing can do the job except government—and when government works— citizens notice.

Ungoverning is not a rational response to the inertia that afflicts existing policies, programs, and agencies. Indiscriminate attacks and degradation of the administrative state—as in the two-for-one Trump deregulation policy or the "eliminate four agencies" slogan—will not make government more efficient, only more chaotic. Candidates and parties could develop comprehensive proposals for reforming the administrative state, as Al Gore did when he was vice president under Bill Clinton. Accomplishing comprehensive reform would be enormously difficult. Doing things is extraordinarily difficult in democratic politics. So is undoing them, unless it is by slash and burn.

Obstruction and Delegitimation

Finally, in naming ungoverning as its own thing, we want to distinguish it from the normal politics of obstruction. Partisans often want to obstruct the opposition, and obstruction is an expected part of democratic politics. Obstruction becomes ungoverning when it aims at incapacitating government in a comprehensive way. Obstruction becomes ungoverning when its consequence is degrading the institutions that bring every policy to life. When it offers neither alternative policies nor reasons to think *any* policy is necessary. Obstruction becomes ungoverning when it is a party's entire political agenda. And key to arrant obstruction as ungoverning is disregard for consequences.

Ungoverning obstructionists do not shy from imposing devastating costs on the nation—opposing the Affordable Care Act without offering a substitute plan, for example. Shutting down the government with no purpose and no willingness to negotiate. Baldly refusing to negotiate raising the debt limit and driving the country to default.

It can be difficult to identify the point at which familiar tactics of undoing, deregulation, and obstructionism become ungoverning. All are normal and sometimes appropriate elements of democratic politics. But they can become disjoined from any constructive purpose. Opposition to "big government" can lead to disdain for governing, and then to opposition to government itself: If "government is the problem," as Ronald Reagan said at his first inaugural, why have government? Why try to make it work? Why design policies that aim to solve problems or hammer out compromises with the opposition?

While picking out what counts as ungoverning can in some cases be challenging, in other cases there is dispositive evidence. The arousal and launch of private violence can be seen as the ultimate act of ungoverning because it degrades the defining characteristic of the modern state: the monopoly of legitimate violence and with it the responsibility to protect citizens. That is the message when a candidate or president arouses followers to threaten and intimidate the political opposition—and not just officials, but also private citizens in all sorts of social settings. Or when a president makes an unsubtle death threat against the disloyal Senate leader of his own party (Richards 2022). Or when he mobilizes and calls out private militias and armed followers.

The cumulative effect of ungoverning is delegitimation. Delegitimation is not the equivalent of criticism of bureaucracy or criticism of a particular agency, policy, or goal. It refers to something deeper and more destructive than even the plague of distrust of political institutions. Legitimacy says that an institution has meaning, value, and authority. Delegitimation negates all three. The message of delegitimation is that the workings of departments and agencies have no authority, and their rules and regulations need not be complied with. Legitimacy is a warrant for compliance; ungoverning removes the warrant.

The Administrative State: Unlovely and Unloved

Ungoverning is a recent phenomenon, precipitated by Trump, and many leaders in the Republican Party are poised to continue it into the future. The necessary background condition is the long-standing vulnerability of administrative institutions. This cracks open the door for the forces of deconstruction. In the United States, these vulnerabilities arise from the sheer illegibility of the vast structure of the machinery of government and from its anomalous place among the three constitutionally defined branches of government. Even attentive citizens can seldom specify what the phrase "administrative state" refers to or describe where it sits in the constitutional order. Its illegibility and uncertain constitutional status are fertile ground for ungoverning. And underlying everything is the personal experience of subjection to administrative authority, which—as fictional accounts of bureaucratic power testify—often leaves a residue of fear and frustration.

Disaffection often arises when citizens have close encounters with the offices and civil servants who stand between them and what they need from government. We know this from accounts of experience that span time and place. Because this is so common, it is not surprising that government bureaucracy has inspired enduring cultural representations. In nineteenth-century England, Charles Dickens built drama around the inanity and cruelty of state bureaucracy, yet we can recognize something of our own experience in his description. Under conditions of twentieth-century communism, Václav Havel's theater of the absurd told the story in a different key, but we can recognize our own experience there as well. Literature has given us a mythology about bureaucracy, which revolves around two axes: irrationality and tyranny.

Charles Dickens's novel *Little Dorrit* features the all-powerful Circumlocution Office. "No petitioner, whether attempting to do the plainest right or to undo the plainest wrong, can do so without the express authority of the Circumlocution Office,"

Dickens starts out (Dickens [1857] 2021, 71). And as the name of the office indicates, the civil servants who work there are dedicated to a negative mission: "HOW NOT TO DO IT" (71, all caps in original). The department's output is always "no." In office after office, petitioners get the response "Can't inform you" or "Don't know anything about it." There is no answer, anywhere, to the inquiry "How shall I find out?" (76). Petitioners need the correct forms, but each department refers them to another, and the bureaucrat's accusatory position is that "if the—Public does not approach it according to the official forms the—Public has itself to blame" (75). "Numbers of people were lost in the Circumlocution Office," Dickens writes. "Unfortunates with wrongs, or with projects for the general welfare . . . who in slow lapse of time and agony had passed safely through other public departments . . . got referred at last to the Circumlocution Office . . . and never reappeared in the light of day" (72). In the preface to the 1857 edition, Dickens insists that as regards government, *Little Dorrit* is not pure melodrama; it is a realistic depiction of irrationality. "If I might offer any apology for so exaggerated a fiction as . . . the Circumlocution Office," he wrote, "I would seek it in the common experience of an Englishman" (9).

The twentieth-century bureaucratic state that is often taken as a microcosm of tyranny has a literary form of its own: theater of the absurd. Inefficiency, red tape, and incompetence all register, but the thrust is the sheer unfathomability of bureaucratic thinking and purpose. Here, too, everyone is caught up in the irrational world of administration—both ordinary people and officials themselves.

Václav Havel's 1963 play *The Garden Party* is set in the Czech Communist Office of Inauguration and Liquidation (Havel [1963] 1992). Hugo Pludek, a young man looking for employment, seeks a meeting with a high-level government official who is attending a garden party. Hugo also attends and quickly discovers that the organizing committee of the garden party has mixed up large and small dance floors A, B, C, and D, so that scheduled events don't have adequate venues. He offers helpful advice that would sort things out. It takes just a moment, however, for Hugo to grasp the illogic of the office's enterprise, the impenetrability of its business, for which there can be no sorting things out. And no desire to do so. The work of Inauguration and Liquidation is a closed system with no purpose: "Liquidating a Liquidation Office is no easy matter!" (45). Remote from any practical activity in the world, the enterprise distorts the minds of its officials and the lives of its victims.

Literary portraits of men and women in the maws of bureaucracy have power because they both set and confirm expectations of coercion and unreason. They comprise a mythology that identifies government bureaucracy with irrationality and indifference on one side, tyranny and abuse on the other. The store of literature, along with personal experience, lends credence to distrust and resentment of the machinery of government. The administrative state has few ready defenders. People subject to the administrative state—that is, all people—bring these inherited attitudes to their own close encounters.

Close Encounters

On one hand, the administrative state is an alien entity, its shape and function often illegible. On the other hand, citizens encounter it up close. "Bureaucracy" is not a neutral reference to a form of organization. The term evokes demanding, dispiriting encounters between citizens and civil servants. Applications go unanswered, responses to questions take forever. Remedying errors eats up time and exhausts patience. Waiting is a constant, on hard chairs in dreary Dickensian rooms. We exchange stories of our latest travail: walking in the door of an agency or attempting to talk to a live civil servant on the phone and being ill served or treated disrespectfully, our case misplaced, or pushed aside, or dealt with arbitrarily—or at least without an explanation that makes sense to us. This is as true for the state-run registries of motor vehicles as it is for the Internal Revenue Service. As a practical matter, for most citizens, "the state meets the street" episodically and in bits and pieces—at the post office, the social security office, the unemployment office (Zacka 2017). An experience of being ill-treated or thwarted comes to color views of other departments and offices and services—the whole wide world of the work of government.

Not all encounters where "vulnerability meets authority" are critical for people's day-to-day lives, as they are in state welfare offices, for example (Zacka 2017, 8). But if most administrative failings are mundane and corrigible, others are life-altering, even life-threatening. For some citizens (and noncitizens), the offending department is a site of rank injustice. For some, offices are a site of prejudice and social denigration: registrars and clerks are imperious, impertinent, dismissive, rude, impervious. Demeanor weighs along with outcomes. The quality of close encounters depends on whether each client's business is seen to with respect and care, and whether agencies are supported and staffed so that attention and responsiveness are possible.

This requirement is essential, because dealing with the administrative state demands things of us. We must gather paperwork, document claims, and know our social security number or Medicaid enrollment number, and when we don't, our needs cannot be well served. Functioning bureaucracy depends on cooperation and on a modicum of good faith in the professional efforts of the civil servants who attend to us when we finally arrive at the head of the line. It depends on appreciating that the impersonality of procedures serves fundamental values of fairness—or should. Bureaucracy holds this truth for everyone seeking a license, facing a tax audit, or needing emergency aid; relational values matter. As the political theorist Bernardo Zacka puts it, "The administrative state does not just serve citizens, it also makes them" (Zacka n.d., 38).

The administrative state is vulnerable because citizens often do not see it as necessary or legitimate. A bureaucracy that is experienced as irrational and coercive invites fury. It induces helplessness. When close encounters smack of irrationality and coercion, ground is softened for ungoverning. It matters, then, whether citizens understand the value and purpose of the administrative state—and that its defects call for reform, not destruction.

Legibility

Administration, Woodrow Wilson wrote in 1887, is where laws, which exist only on paper, become real. It is "government in action" (Wilson 1887, 198). We can see government doing some things: filling potholes, rescuing sailors caught in a storm, building bridges, fighting wars. Everything government does, it does by virtue of administration. But if some effects of administration are readily seen, most are not. Administrative institutions are vulnerable because the public cannot see much of the business of government. Often enough, citizens do not recognize benefits and services as the work of government at all. When we inhale, we are not aware of the background of regulation and enforcement that make clean air a reality. Safe drinking water appears to flow naturally; we don't think of it as the product of a complex of physical and administrative infrastructure effectively managing and enforcing control of toxins (at least not until we are sickened: think Detroit). A name for invisibility is "the submerged state" (Mettler 2011).

The textbook picture of government also contributes to the invisibility of administration. Generations of schoolchildren have learned how a bill becomes a law. But they do not learn what follows after Congress says, "Let there be clean water." How is the law translated into specific rules that can be applied to every household in every town and city across the country? The implicit assumption in the textbook view of government is that decisions are self-executing, and all that is necessary is police to enforce laws and judges to decide on violations. But laws are not self-executing. Everything that is required to give laws content and bring them into the world is administration—and much of it is unseen.

Even where the work of administration is visible, the administrative state itself is illegible (Rosanvallon 2018, 146–67). The terms "administrative state" and "public administration" come from the Progressive Era and the New Deal, when administrative institutions were developed in earnest (Waldo [1948] 2007; Dudley 2021, 34). To the extent that these terms convey anything, the takeaway is often negative; the sound of the words conjures an overbearing edifice, a Hobbesian colossus.

The administrative state's illegibility also owes to the fact that it has no moment of founding. It has grown by accretion; it has been altered by accretion, and it still is. Americans can celebrate the founding of their country on July 4, and they can read the Constitution. But when they do, they will not find a description of the machinery of government. The three branches of government are inscribed in the Constitution in Article I (the legislature), Article II (the executive), and Article III (the judiciary). Where does the administrative state fit? Where is the Securities and Exchange Commission? The Central Intelligence Agency?

The institutional location of the administrative is in fact very complicated. There are fifteen cabinet-level departments, ranging from the Department of Agriculture to the Department of Veterans Affairs, that include more familiar ones, such as the Departments of Defense, State, and Treasury. Yet, much of the administrative state lives outside cabinet departments, in the Executive Office of the President or in independent agencies, some of which are in the executive branch and some of which are not (Office of the Federal Register 2022).

The authors of *Sourcebook of United States Executive Agencies*, the U.S. government's own description of executive agencies, concede that they have difficulty describing what the administrative state is. The *Sourcebook* authors refer to the "executive establishment," which, because few others use the term, only functions to make what they describe more elusive. What is the "executive establishment"? The *Sourcebook* lists 457 agencies and cautions that this includes "hundreds of bureaus, administrations, divisions, offices, working groups, and committees" (Selin and Lewis 2018, 15). "There is no authoritative list of government agencies," the authors concede. "Every list of federal agencies in government publications is different" (11, 12).

Over 2.2 million civilian employees work for the federal government, not including employees of the U.S. Postal Service or the uniformed military (Congressional Research Service 2022, 5). It is hard to envision or place 2.2 million people, or even one department—like the Department of State, with over seventy thousand employees. By contrast, in the familiar textbook description the three constitutional branches comprise only 546 people (435 members of Congress, 100 senators, 9 Supreme Court justices, 1 president, and 1 vice president). They can fit in one room—and almost all of them do every year during the State of the Union Address.

Even the number of high-level appointments that require presidential nomination is so large that journalists and scholars can barely keep track of them. The president makes more than a thousand appointments that require Senate confirmations, and several thousand more that do not (Partnership for Public Service 2023; U.S. House of Representatives Committee on Oversight and Reform 2020). The number of "political managers at the top" (and assistants, deputies, and deputy assistants) is growing (Skowronek, Dearborn, and King 2021, 7), and identifying them all at any moment in time may be impossible. Vacancies are common, due in part to the difficulty of Senate confirmation in a divided Congress, and service is generally for brief stints and focused on "short-term political objectives rather than long-term agency capacity" (Lewis 2021, 82).

Adding to illegibility is the way that responsibility for implementing public policy reaches beyond government employees to encompass what political scientist John DiIulio calls "a vast and complex array of public and private institutions, for-profit and non-profit organizations, contractors, agents, and facilitators." His understated observation strikes home: "An accurate measure of government's full scope is thus very difficult to come by" (DiIulio 2012).

Illegibility provides an opening for conspiracism, in the charge that civil servants and disloyal presidential appointees comprise a secret force pursuing an agenda hostile to the public good. The bureaucracy is cast as a nest of liberals, socialists, enemies of the president, and enemies of the people. This powerful cabal of civil servants and appointees constitutes the "deep state." The forces of ungoverning appropriate the term "administrative state" as a term of abuse (Peters 2018b). Trump strategist Steve Bannon famously announced that the new president would appoint cabinet members committed to "the deconstruction of the administrative state" (Morris 2017).

Naming it—the phenomenon of ungoverning—is critical in part because administrative institutions are hard to see. The damage may be publicly announced, but that does not inspire resistance or even concern if the consequences are obscure. When citizens do not know what administrative institutions are or what they do, their work remains opaque. The first step is to identify ungoverning for what it is. The next step is to unpack it—to show what it involves and where it leads.

2

Unpacking It

Leaders intentionally weakening the state that they govern is a phenomenon so unusual in politics that it has no name. We give it the simple name "ungoverning." Legal scholars have parsed the arguments about the constitutional legitimacy of the administrative state, which has become a contested topic of jurisprudence in the U.S. Supreme Court. Scholars of U.S. politics have written about the development of the "policy state" (Orren and Skowronek 2017). Journalists and social scientists have brought attention to Trump's comprehensive attack on the administrative state. As political theorists, we use these works to describe, explain, and diagnose what the phenomenon of ungoverning portends. The world has seen a variety of assaults on liberal democracy over the last two decades. Ungoverning poses a distinct threat. In this chapter, we unpack the elements of this destructive phenomenon.

The meaning of "ungoverning" is dependent on its positive opposite, "governing," whose Latin cognate evokes "to steer." It is about guiding an institution or community. In its modern formulation, the steering function becomes synonymous with administration. That includes collecting information and data, consulting with affected groups, harnessing expert knowledge, and implementing policies. Democracy needs the capacity to govern, and governing needs administration—departments and agencies and civil servants that shape, implement, enforce, and evaluate programs and policies.

When this capacity is undone, the result is chaotic and inhumane.

Zero Tolerance

As we noted in the last chapter, ungoverning was introduced full force during the first Trump administration and touched a number of federal agencies and departments, including the State Department, the Department of Justice, the Postal Service, and even the Defense Department. One case brings the phenomenon of ungoverning into particularly sharp focus: Zero Tolerance. It is the name given to a plan to deter immigration by separating thousands of immigrant families at the southern border in 2017 and 2018. Our account is indebted to Caitlin Dickerson's reporting (Dickerson 2022).

Family separation was not the only proposal for deterring migration. Trump had pushed for "a big deep moat" filled with reptiles, and at his insistence, Secretary of Homeland Security Kirstjen Nielson had to ask her staff for a "back-of-the-envelope estimate for digging a border-long ditch and filling it with snakes and alligators" (Danner 2023, 83).

Family separation was less bloodthirsty, but crueler, and it was put into effect. As it was happening, the practice of family separation had a powerful hold on the nation's attention. Interviews with confused and desperate parents and testimony from those who saw conditions at a Customs and Border Protection facility revealed babies, even a newborn, "covered in nasal mucous, vomit, breast milk, urine" (Kunzru 2021). There were photographs of detention centers where children appeared to be caged and held without adequate food, water, or sanitation. We heard from those charged with explaining to parents when or how they would be reunited with their children. One distraught father committed suicide in detention (Miroff 2018).

The policy exposed the president's willingness to throw aside fundamental rights, U.S. and international law, and the rudiments of humanity. Family separation raises the question, what was driving a policy that "took children away from their parents with no plan to return them" (Dickerson 2022, 41)?

Family separation was a demonstration of willful cruelty, and in that respect, it marked a low point in government irresponsibility. It also stands out for another reason: the criminalization of undocumented border crossing, imprisonment of adults, and seizure of children were simultaneously policy and anti-policy. Zero Tolerance was an attempt to implement the president's priorities on immigration, and in that regard, it was a "policy." But in another sense, it was not a policy at all. Both its means and goals were covert and chaotic. There was no public explanation of why children were being separated from their parents. If the purpose was to cause so much chaos and trauma that people would be dissuaded from illegally crossing the border, that was not said aloud. Still, Zero Tolerance was a policy configured over time. It was fought for within the executive branch in the face of resistance within the agencies involved.

Before Zero Tolerance was initiated, the policy of government detention of undocumented families allowed for separating children only when a parent was jailed for a serious crime.

But Trump and his advisers judged this inadequate to advance the goal of rapidly and radically deterring migration. An alternative plan to separate all families by placing children and parents in different detention centers was rejected in favor of something even more draconian: criminal prosecution of all adults crossing the border illegally (Human Rights Watch 2018). The inevitable result would be removing children from their parents (Dickerson 2022, 72). The Zero Tolerance policy mandating prosecution of all illegal border crossers was designed to shock. Seizing children was the point.

Shaping and implementing this policy would normally involve several departments with responsibility for border control and immigration. In general terms, an idea for a new program proposed by the president or legislature is worked out by career staff knowledgeable about the subject. They are relied on to provide estimates of cost and capacity and the effect on existing resources—in this case, the load on federal prosecutors and immigration courts and the demands on the Department of Justice, the U.S. Marshals Service, and the Bureau of Prisons (Human Rights Watch 2018; Dickerson 2022). Family migration and detention should have brought Health and Human Services into the discussion; the agency had experience creating a shelter system and caring for migrant children who crossed the border alone. But the agency was cut out from the start. Normally, only after studies of expected benefits and costs do plans go to higher-level cabinet appointees—in this case, Kirstjen Nielsen, the head of the Department of Homeland Security (DHS). These procedures are designed to anticipate problems and to ensure communication among all the relevant departments that share authority to implement policy.

Zero Tolerance was conceived by a Trump adviser, immigration "hawk" Stephen Miller, and propelled by the president's fury with ongoing undocumented migration and his certainty that "I alone can fix it" (Jackson 2016). A pilot program was in effect in El Paso, Texas, in 2017, and the plan to apply it to all migrants was developed at secret meetings where participants signed nondisclosure agreements. As agency heads and staff became aware that they were being circumvented, some acquiesced, others resisted. DHS head Nielsen described the questions she put to Miller, to which she got no response: "Did you talk to anyone at HHS [Health and Human Services]? Did you talk to the lawyers? What does [White House Counsel] Don McGahn say? . . . Let's find a process here" (Dickerson 2022, 52). For the Trump team, however, process was the enemy. A member of Miller's team on the White House Domestic Policy Council put it this way: "There's this worship of process. Process, process, process. *Process* is code for 'We can slow down the quick impulses of a fiery political administration with no experts.' Well, that's not what was voted for" (Dickerson 2022, 44). The result was "ambient ignorance" (Dickerson 2022, 58). Implementation was chaotic. But for the policy's advocates, that was not a problem—it was a feature.

As were Trump officials' efforts to mislead Congress and the public about family separation, "refusing even to acknowledge that separating children from their parents was the explicit goal" (Buchanan, Wolgin, and Flores 2021). The policy was first officially announced in June 2018 (Southern Poverty Law Center 2022). The day before the announcement, DHS Secretary Nielsen had tweeted, "We do not have a policy of separating families at the border. Period" (Southern Poverty Law Center 2022).

Zero Tolerance also discarded the most elementary function of administration: record-keeping. The DHS Office of Inspector

General reported the stunning fact that the department had failed to properly track and reunify families, citing "poor data entry, data tracking, information sharing and IT systems capabilities" (Southern Poverty Law Center 2022). "Why doesn't anyone just have an Excel file?" one attorney asked (Dickerson 2022, 64). Jennifer Pahlka later explained that U.S. Border Patrol agents processing and detaining migrants used a computer program that was not equipped to assign case numbers to children that corresponded with the case numbers assigned to parents. "There was simply no official record of which kids belonged to which parents," and "agents found themselves sticking Post-it notes . . . on infants' onesies" (Pahlka 2023, 216, 215).

When the American Civil Liberties Union got an injunction against family separation, the court ordered families to be reunited within thirty days, and in the case of children under five, within two weeks. A class-action lawsuit on behalf of separated families (A.I.I.L. v. Sessions, 4:19-cv-00481 [D. Ariz. Oct. 3, 2019] ECF No. 1) was filed against a series of high-ranking government officials (Buchanan, Wolgin, and Flores 2021; Southern Poverty Law Center 2022). Lee Gelernt, the lead lawyer in the case, put it simply: "It's that parents have no idea where their children are, what's happening to their children or whether they are even going to see their children again" (Dickerson 2022, 65). Without official confirmation that DHS had identified all family separations, the number of families that remain severed and the number of children adrift can never be verified (Kunzru 2021, 2). One judge noted that "for every parent that is not located there will be a permanently orphaned child" (Dickerson 2022, 73).

One mark of ungoverning is the elimination of records and data. Traditionally, authoritarian regimes keep (and keep hidden) meticulous records—the East German Stasi, famously—but absence is the best way of shrouding what authorities have done and insulating them from accountability. Even concealed records are critical: all sorts of actions—violent and subversive, corrupt and criminal—can be ferreted out by a subsequent regime, by courts, and by historians. Without records and data, it is impossible for a government to know whether its policies are effective and for others to hold it accountable. It is no overstatement to say that effective governing depends on data. Record-keeping is future-looking—that is, documentation reveals the purpose and methods of government action. And it is backward looking, in establishing a historical narrative. Here we see that records tether politics to reality; their absence allows for fiction.

In a functioning administration, none of this would have happened. An unvetted idea to deter undocumented immigration by separating families would not have survived either expert approval or public scrutiny. Even if the plan could be implemented, a functioning administration would have kept records. Hapless implementation allowed for willful cruelty. As Dickerson remarks, "It's been said of other Trump-era projects that . . . incompetence mitigated its malevolence; here, the opposite happened. . . . Parents and children were lost to each other, sometimes many states apart. . . . Four years later, some families are still separated—and . . . even many of those who have been reunited suffered irreparable harm" (Dickerson 2022, 39).

When Zero Tolerance stirred public outrage and effective legal opposition, the Trump administration resorted to lies: the children were victims of traffickers or of parents who endangered them. Family separation, on this account, was for the benefit of babies. Trump did reverse course, however; fittingly, the executive order he signed ending family separation contained the contradictory statement that the policy would continue

(Human Rights Watch 2018; Diaz 2021). He never stopped advocating for it. The Justice Department only officially ended the policy under the Biden administration in 2021.

Immigration has long been a touchstone for social and partisan divides. By itself, Trump's pronouncement was nothing new: "Whether it's asylum, whether it's anything you want—it's illegal immigration. . . . We can't take you. Our country is full" (Trump 2019). Actions to stop migration and to deport hated groups have always been marked by aggressive, punitive measures. The origin story of Zero Tolerance begins in violence; it is one unanticipated consequence of the national response to the attack on 9/11—the creation of the Department of Homeland Security and the relocation of Immigration and Naturalization Services to the new department. The militarization of border security also antedated the Trump presidency, fertilizing the ground for his characterization of the flow of "caravans" of immigrants as an alien *invasion*—encouraged, the conspiracy charge goes, by George Soros and liberals. "We have people coming into the country or trying to come in, we're stopping a lot of them, but we're taking people out of the country. You wouldn't believe how bad these people are," Trump said. "These aren't people. These are animals" (Korte and Gomez 2018). The acme of malignant claims: migrants are "poisoning the blood of our country" (Gibson 2023). Children are aliens, not innocents, and "child taking is a 'counterinsurgency tactic'" (Kunzru 2021, 4).

Overturning process, circumventing experienced personnel, disregarding rudimentary record-keeping, misleading the press and even officials—this is ungoverning in action. In what follows we unpack the elements of ungoverning with particular focus on the way it involves an attack on expert knowledge and an attack on regular process.

The Elements of Ungoverning #1: Attacking Expertise

The authority of the machinery of government rests on specialized knowledge and respect for procedures. Other institutions of liberal democracy rest on other claims of authority—representativeness, for one. Expertise and proceduralism are the distinctive claims to the legitimacy of the departments and agencies of the administrative state. Of course, as we detail here and again in chapter 9, there are disagreements about the role of experts in making and implementing public policy, and there are times when administrative organization and procedures need significant reform. But just the same expertise and proceduralism are the distinguishing features of the administrative state.

By regularly disparaging specialized knowledge and standard procedures, ungoverning denies their utility. In doing so, it also denies the legitimacy of the administrative state—its meaning, value, and authority.

Specialized knowledge is essential to governing. For example, citizens want a government that can and will protect them from air pollution. There is no way members of Congress and congressional staff could have detailed standards of air purity for the Environmental Protection Agency in the Clean Air Act of 1970; this task was delegated to the agency. The range of hazards that government must address, or decide whether to address, draws on a wide range of scientific knowledge.

Expertise supplies the administrative state with its capacity to shape, implement, and enforce public policy and, we argue, gives it a distinct authority. Subject-specific experts—economists in the Treasury Department and the Bureau of Labor Statistics, military officers and strategists at the Pentagon, career diplomats at the State Department with language ability and contacts in foreign capitals—bring specialized knowledge and experience to decision-making. The civil service also brings institutional memory, knowledge of procedures, and experience with stakeholder networks, all of which are vital to carrying out the work of the federal government (Heath 2020, 35). Expertise is essential to set overnight interest rates for the central bank, to certify advanced models of airliners, and to approve new pharmaceuticals. The expertise housed in the administrative state is what makes it possible to create rules and regulations that serve public needs in the real world.

This was recognized from the early days of the U.S. republic. Contrary to the myth that nineteenth-century laws were "self-executing," there was never a time when the United States lacked an administrative state (Mashaw 2012; Konczal 2015). Put simply, executive branch officials never just implement the directives of Congress, as the textbook model of the relations between legislature and executive would suggest (Heath 2020, 221). Administrators need discretion to use their expertise. Discretion is needed because to take a general policy goal and to make it specific enough to implement requires adjustments. Unanticipated problems and flaws emerge. Circumstances change, and those who implement programs must respond. New disagreements arise and must be considered. In some cases, the Covid pandemic for example, understanding of the disease emerged incrementally and public health recommendations from the Centers for Disease Control and Prevention changed in response.

Ungoverning is an unrelenting, fantastical assault on specialized knowledge. It takes aim not only when the personal will of the president is frustrated but more broadly delegitimates knowledge by casting experts as part of a cabal; the attack takes the form of a conspiracy charge. Researchers at the

Environmental Protection Agency are said to be producing "secret science." Those who advocate regulating greenhouse gas emissions are said to be plotting to impose despotic measures to extinguish personal freedom: "They want to take your pickup truck, they want to rebuild your home, they want to take away your hamburgers. This is what Stalin dreamed about but never achieved" (Sommerlad 2019).

The Elements of Ungoverning #2: Attacking Regular Process

In August 2022, the FBI seized dozens of government documents marked "classified," "secret," and "top secret" from Mar-a-Lago, former president Trump's residence in Palm Beach, Florida. In an interview for Fox News, Sean Hannity asked Trump whether these documents had been declassified. "What was your process to declassify?" Hannity asked. "There doesn't have to be a process," the former president insisted. "You're the president of the United States. You can declassify just by saying—I'm—'it's declassified.' Even by thinking about it" (Hagstrom 2022).

The claim astonished national security experts. Even if it were the case that a president could declassify government materials by simply saying so, he would have to say so to the relevant authorities. He would need to log the items, and notify the agencies, and begin the *process* of remarking the material.

In bureaucracy, everything is process. There is a process for making decisions, and there is a process for the process of making decisions. There is a process for announcing decisions and for implementing decisions. This process layered over process is what makes bureaucracy what it is, and what sometimes gives it a bad name. "Red tape"—an idiom that goes back to the seventeenth-century English practice of wrapping important official documents in red ribbon—today points to the inevitable frustrations of proceduralism that can make it seem that process has become more important than results.

Process is the antithesis of arbitrariness. The alternative to process is the chaos of personal rule. When people administer processes, they do not impose their private wills. The administrator, the bureaucrat, is the counterforce to the unchecked personal ruler. Process helps ensure equal treatment without favoritism or corruption. Upholding rule of law norms, procedural norms, is protection against unbridled discretion.

Process has other purposes as well, including consultation and participation. A process of decision-making compels more than one person to look at the case, the reasons, and the aims, and invites relevant parties—experts, stakeholders—to weigh in, to formally offer considerations that bear on the merits and demerits of policy decisions. Decisions that follow from a consultative process are more likely to benefit from the situational understanding and expertise of those who have studied other cases or the relevant scientific knowledge, or who understand the specifics of how decisions will be implemented and received. Wide consultation makes decisions more likely to be effective and more likely to be accepted; process endows bureaucratic decisions and regulations with epistemic quality and a degree of legitimacy (Manning and Stephenson 2013, 542–43).

Process is not an adornment or corrective to administration, something brought in to curb excess or minimize error. It defines administration. When many of the current institutions of the administration state were developed during the New Deal, even its advocates were concerned about the specter of "administrative authoritarianism" (Nielson 2017, 4n20). The

Administrative Procedure Act of 1946 (APA) was designed to help allay this concern, and "for more than three-quarters of a century," the act "has provided the legal foundation for the administrative state" (Tushnet 2021, 9). The APA can be considered part of the unofficial constitution because it is fundamental to the operations of government: it is the "statutory constitution of administrative government" (Metzger 2017a).

At the heart of the APA is "notice-and-comment rulemaking," which in the simplest sense means that agencies must publicly post rules and invite public comment before issuing them. The precise process is intricate and the details vary (5 U.S.C. § 553). But apart from the specifics, the general form of "notice and comment" is what makes rulemaking consistent with both rule-of-law norms and democratic accountability. Regulations formulated according to this process are akin to laws, and even to undo them, agencies must follow these procedures.

While procedures are at the heart of rule-of-law norms, they can be counterproductive to the point where they hobble programs. Effective government can be stymied by a "procedure fetish" (Bagley 2019). The legal scholar Nicholas Bagley argues for recovering how "New Deal state-builders embraced a results-oriented, nonlegalistic approach to administrative power," and quotes Franklin D. Roosevelt: "Substantial justice remains a higher aim for our civilization than technical legalism" (349).

This makes sense if "technical legalism" is synonymous with pathologies that obstruct desired outcomes, and both conservatives and progressives offer up examples of "inflexible procedural gauntlets." The paralyzing effect on governing that comes from the intersection of layers upon layers of rules is unintended. Pathologies include duplication of regulations—indeed, conflicting regulations set by federal, state, and local agencies. There is also the invitation to private litigation by parties opposed to whatever project is at hand (Elmendorf 2024). Each of these can result in more than time delays and cost overruns; they can produce stasis. In some cases, these pathologies appear to be the result of self-protectiveness on the part of administrators fearful of blame. And with each publicization of frustrated policy comes antigovernment animus, and beyond that, fuel for the destructive energy of ungoverning.

Changing the procedural status quo to improve capacity is difficult. A name for bureaucratic inertia is "kludgocracy" (Teles 2012). Lamenting the inability of California government to build affordable housing, the journalist Ezra Klein notes, "You might assume that when faced with a problem of overriding public importance, government would use its awesome might to sweep away obstacles that stand in its way. But too often, it does the opposite. It adds goals—many of them laudable—and in doing so, adds obstacles, expenses, and delays. . . . Sometimes it tries to accomplish so much within a single project or policy that it ends up failing to accomplish anything at all." Klein calls this "everything bagel liberalism" (Klein 2023b).

One example: $1.7 million in state funds were allocated to build a 150-square-foot public toilet in the Noe Valley neighborhood of San Francisco. The project was eventually abandoned after it emerged that it would take two or three years to install "because of the city's labyrinthine permitting and building process," including numerous layers of review and the high cost of staff time (Knight 2024). Legal scholar Samuel Issacharoff points to another set of disfunctions that beset renovating a terminal at New York's LaGuardia Airport and constructing the Second Avenue subway extension: "clientelism, cronyism, and corruption" make it almost impossible for government to build, to make, to do what needs doing (Issacharoff 2023, 39–40).

A host of procedural requirements came together in the proposed Clean Electricity and Transmission Acceleration Act of 2023, which would require environmental review for approval of interstate transmission lines ("H.R. 6747" 2023). The act not only is open to community input and legal review but also is loaded with (well-intentioned) procedural concessions to "countless interest groups seeking commitments to hire union workers and local residents, developer-paid 'community benefits' such as parks and transit improvements, below-market housing units," and more. The bill fits the description of an "everything bagel." Legal scholar Christopher S. Elmendorf adds, "Groups angling to stall projects or extract benefits for themselves also gain leverage through legal threats." The end result is giving more power to clean-energy opponents (Elmendorf 2024). Cynicism and exasperation are reasonable responses. Government's reputation for ineffectiveness—for proceduralism run amok—is often earned.

Notwithstanding the "everything bagel" phenomenon, government can work—as it did with the remarkable success of Operation Warp Speed during the Covid pandemic. The project accelerated the federal process for "developing, testing, manufacturing, and deploying" new vaccines to treat Covid-19. The Trump administration initiative—a partnership between Health and Human Services and the Department of Defense—worked with drug makers, factories, and distributors, awarded contracts, cleared away regulatory obstacles, and shaved years off the process of producing vaccines and getting them into the arms of Americans. The achievement was possible because "above all, Operation Warp Speed shunned complexity in favor of simplicity" (Hamel and Zanini 2023).

The statement that "America should be more like Operation Warp Speed" is of course rhetorical (Hamel and Zanini 2023).

But the stunning success of the program shows that procedural reforms can have profound effects. While Operation Warp Speed was quickly and lavishly financed in response to a once-in-a-century public health emergency, its example underlines the inescapable conclusion that sometimes government is the solution—the only solution. Reforms need to center on where, when, and why the regulatory process and civil actions are significant barriers to addressing public problems—for example, whether and where EPA compliance efforts and the need to respond to litigation challenging these efforts is, is fact, a burden on environmental regulation (Ruple and Race 2019).

Under ever-increasing conditions of complexity and uncertainty, there are good reasons for agencies to make rules in a more flexible and tentative way than the formal process of notice-and-comment permits. One alternative is called "guidance." Here, agencies propose provisional rules designed for democratic experimentation and correction (Kessler and Sabel 2021, 189). One example is the part of the Affordable Care Act that invited states to experiment with designs for health insurance exchanges. Guidance can encourage "laboratories of invention" (Sabel 2012, 48–49).

Proceduralism is essential to the legitimacy of the administrative state, for reasons we've set out, but not so essential that it should outweigh the importance of results. This much is certain: ungoverning's attack on procedures is not aimed at reform of rules and processes that have become self-defeating. Ungoverning takes aim anywhere, anytime—generally, it is not targeted. Ungoverning's assaults on proceduralism often rest on conspiracy claims that civil servants are enemies within. It takes aim at the core reasons for procedures: creating conditions for consultation and deliberation and constraints on executive power—above all, personal will. It is unrelated to public benefit, as was revealed when despite his claiming credit for the success of Operation Warp Speed, Trump turned against the vaccines, cast doubt on their unique efficacy, and did not promote vaccination (Spencer 2021). Governing could not compete with cranking up anti-government animus.

Why Should the Administrative State Have Authority?

Knowledge and process are the core of why institutions staffed by unelected officials should have authority. Specialized knowledge entails subject-specific knowledge of areas like economics or atmospheric science, which are essential for addressing certain public problems effectively. Administrative knowledge also comes from the "comment" part of "notice-and-comment," which mandates consultative processes that engage stakeholders. Fairness is also the purpose of settled and regular process—to ensure decisions are based on impartial reasons rather than reflect favoritism or ad hoc pronouncements. The importance of fairness is captured by the "notice" part of "notice-and-comment," which requires that proposed rules be published and promulgated in well-defined ways. Process both harnesses knowledge and embodies rule-of-law norms. In addition to knowledge and process, authority is also a function of accountability: administrative institutions are answerable to both courts and the elected branches. Expertise, consultation, publicity, fairness, and accountability are the bases of the administrative state's authority.

Of these, knowledge is always at the center. Expertise and consultation provide the epistemic core to the claim of administrative authority. Both subject-specific expertise and consultative engagement with stakeholders give actors in the administrative state the knowledge they need to write effective rules. A recent development in political theory emphasizes the epistemic basis for democratic authority. Democratic decision-making is more likely to make decisions in accordance with standards of truth and justice, according to this view (Estlund 2008; Landemore 2017). Most "epistemic democrats" focus on the participatory venues of democracy—legislatures or citizen assemblies that deliberate policy issues or questions of constitutional reform. Whether this is the best way to understand the legitimacy of legislatures is an open question, but regardless, it is a curiosity and a defect of epistemic democratic theory that it overlooks the institution whose authority is emphatically epistemic—the administrative state.

To say that the administrative state's authority centers on knowledge (expertise and consultation) and process (publicity, fairness, accountability) is not to discount arguments for making the administrative state more participatory. We turn to this in chapter 9. While we understand that such reforms can make the machinery of government more legible to ordinary citizens, the purpose of making the administrative state more participatory is not to turn it into a legislature. Participation is the heart of democracy, but democracy also needs to marshal expertise to shape, implement, and enforce the laws the elected branches charge them with bringing into the world.

Liberal democracy needs experts. Yet, we want to underscore that it is not the individual expert but rather the expertise *embedded in a process* that has authority because, to repeat, it is consultative, public, impartial, and accountable. What confers authority is the process of recruiting expertise and harnessing it to public purposes. It is an example of what the philosopher David Estlund calls "epistemic proceduralism" (Estlund 2008, 98–116).

Of course, sometimes experts will be guilty of self-dealing or corruption. Sometimes they will overreach. Sometimes they will prioritize process over results. And sometimes they will make mistakes. The idea that legitimates administrative authority is that the overall process by which expertise is applied to public purposes will result in better rules and decisions and more effective government than alternative processes would produce. That the general process of harnessing expertise has authority does not mean that every specific part of the administrative state is as it should be. Reforms are often needed. Sometimes agencies may need to be dismantled altogether—we have pointed to the elimination of the Civil Aeronautics Board and airline deregulation. In the actual world of governing, something is always in need of reform.

If administrators are not necessarily more public-spirited or virtuous than elected politicians or ordinary citizens, they are, at their best, restrained by professional discipline, which reflects a professional ethos (Wilson 1991, 194). In this, the population of government administrators is like that of other professions—personally and collectively adopting and monitoring self-imposed standards, responsibilities, and constraints. Experts understand that they have something to offer in a defined terrain, and that the domain of their knowledge-based authority is limited. Professionalism also involves a community of practitioners who share knowledge and criticize and correct each other. And it entails a commitment to explain not just what they know, but how they know it (Rosenblum 2020). This professional ethos entails more than specialized knowledge and adherence to regular procedure; it includes commitment to employing expertise in the public interest. For many who do the work of shaping, implementing, enforcing, and assessing public policies, this work is a vocation.

In the best case, professional ethos guides bureaucrats in bringing their specialized knowledge and commitment to process to bear on public problems—and to use both in service to the goals of the elected leadership. At times, what expertise demands and what the elected leadership demands conflict. In these conflicts, the authority conferred by expertise is highly qualified and circumscribed. Neither expertise nor professional ethos are substitutes for oversight by the executive, by Congress, by courts, and by the public. Some agencies of the administrative state are meant to be wholly responsive to elected leadership. When the president or Congress endorses a particular aspect of foreign policy, the State Department is charged with carrying it out. Like any other entity with authority, however circumscribed, the administrative state needs to be held accountable.

Still, notwithstanding the need for accountability, in many cases, expert authority needs to be insulated to an extent from politics if it is to be effective. This is most evident in what are termed the "independent agencies," which include the Federal Reserve Board, the Securities and Exchange Commission (SEC), the Federal Deposit Insurance Commission, the Federal Communications Commission, the Federal Trade Commission, the Environmental Protection Agency, the Central Intelligence Agency, and others. Independent agencies are often led by a multimember commission whose members have staggered terms—and thus cannot be appointed by a single president—and who cannot be removed from office and replaced by the president except for cause. Multimember independent agencies prevent presidents from appointing cronies to the Federal Reserve in order to lower interest rates prior to an election, for example.

To say that certain agencies need independence is not to endorse the more comprehensive ideal of administration as a substitute for politics. Administration has its own place. It can answer the "the inadequacies of the judicial and legislative processes," as James Landis, the New Dealer who was the first head of the SEC wrote (Landis 1938, 46). Or as Woodrow Wilson argued, "Administration lies outside the proper sphere of politics" (Wilson 1887, 210). But to defend the partial independence of administration is not to endorse the exalted ideal of rational administration as a wholesale replacement for contestation, pressure groups, and partisanship (Pestritto 2007). In this ideal, administrators are agents of the rational unfolding of progress in history; they are what the philosopher Georg Wilhelm Friedrich Hegel called the "universal class" (Hegel [1821] 1967, §205c).

One can endorse the authority of specialized knowledge without endorsing the Hegelian universal state. Our defense is even more qualified: bureaucratic authority and value derives from expertise and process, and its necessity lies in making government work. Without it, legislation would never get off the page. An infrastructure bill could never be translated into action—into lists of bridges that need repair, calls for bids, the selection of contractors, the completion of environmental impact studies, the design of detours, the movement of materials and management of construction sites. In the administrative state today, the experts who serve government do so not because they are apolitical or bearers of pure reason, but because they have subject-specific knowledge that is useful in shaping and executing effective public policies (Du Gay 2000, 4).

Appreciation for the administrative state rests on its necessity and its legitimacy. We don't elevate expertise and process as the most critical values of liberal democracy—not at all. Nor would we endorse the excessive valuation of the administrative state, which has it that "only an absolute bureaucracy can save us" (Smith 2022). Absolutism is anathema. We don't claim it is the bureaucrat "who makes the modern, neutral state critically different from its confessional antecedents and totalitarian antagonists" (Smith 2022).

Administration is a pragmatic necessity for a government that can govern.

Creating a Government That Can Govern

Every state, as political theorist Michael Walzer says, is a welfare state—meaning that every state that doesn't depend on terror alone for compliance must attend to the needs of its inhabitants as they understand those needs (Walzer 1984, 68). The scale and complexity of modern economies and societies mean that every successful and stable modern state is also an administrative state. The history and structure of administration, of course, is specific to each country. Administration has a longer history where it grew out of absolute monarchies, such as in France, than it does in common-law countries like the United States and the United Kingdom, where empowered representative legislatures preceded the development of administration (Edling 2003, 49–58; Koh 1991; Suleiman 1974; Eymeri-Douzans 2022). Indeed, the administrative state in the United States was the work of Congress, the most democratic branch of government (Beermann 2018, 1640).

In the United States the historical path to what we now call the administrative state starts with Alexander Hamilton, who explicitly invoked the administrative capacity of the federal government when defending the adoption of the national Constitution in the essays known as the *Federalist Papers*. State governments, he conceded, would be closer to the people, and state legislatures would be better able than the federal government to mirror the attachments and interests of local populations (*Federalist* no. 27). If the purpose of popular government were simply to empower popular views and passions, then state governments would be superior and sufficient.

But the new national government was designed to stand at a distance from local majorities. That is the point of representation in large electoral districts, as Madison wrote in *Federalist* no. 10. In districts that are too large for one local majority to dominate, representatives would focus on the "permanent and aggregate interests of the community" rather than catering to small, local groups. The phrase "permanent and aggregate interests of the community" might seem so general as to be empty, but it is meant to convey broad, commonsense purposes: security, peace, and prosperity. Protecting individual rights, security from invasion, freedom from the fear of premature and violent death, and prosperity—these are ends the people can endorse regardless of their religion or their local context. Pursuing these goals requires governing, or "good administration" (*Federalist* no. 27). For Madison, good administration meant protecting individuals from factious majorities—by defending the rights of conscience, for instance. For Hamilton, it had more to do with managing the national economy and national defense.

Hamilton expected that citizens would in time appreciate the new national government for its good administration. If the government did its job well, and in fact produced protection of individual rights, security from foreign attack, and general prosperity, citizens would value the administrative capacity of the national government. They might not look at it as theirs, as a mirror of their own way of life, as they might do with respect to their church, their town, or their state government. But in a cooler and more rational way, they would see the need for it (*Federalist* no. 27). Hamilton put it emphatically: "I believe it may be laid down as a general rule that their [the people's] confidence in and obedience to a government will commonly be proportioned to the goodness or badness of its administration" (*Federalist* no. 27).

When he assumed the position of secretary of the treasury in 1789, Hamilton initiated new administrative functions. He immediately began collecting data about the national economy, which he laid out in his *Report on the Subject of Manufactures* of 1791. That report contained a plan to create an industrial economy on a national scale. By this point, Hamilton had already issued two reports on the national credit, the first recommending the national assumption of state debts (many of which were accrued in the Revolutionary War) and the second recommending a national bank that would monetize the new national debt. He also had a plan to enable the national government to build a navy that would equip the fledging republic to hold its own against the great European monarchies. Hamilton wanted a state that could fulfill the promise of administration, of *governing*.

It was only in the last decades of the nineteenth century, as the voluntary associations and town governments that Tocqueville celebrated in the 1830s were overwhelmed by great concentrations of economic power, that people like Woodrow Wilson called for developing a comprehensive administrative state. He argued in 1887 that the central political question of the eighteenth century—*Who should rule?*—had been settled in favor of "the people." Now it was time to give the people the *capacity* to govern. And that meant administration. "Administration is the most obvious part of government," Wilson wrote. "It is government in action" (Wilson 1887, 198).

Institution-building followed. The first independent commission was created in 1887 with the Interstate Commerce Act, which established an explicitly regulatory power and an agency to house it (Mashaw 2012, 13; Skowronek 1982, 138–60). A civil service whose members would be employed for their expertise rather than their political loyalties was promoted by the Pendleton Civil Service Act of 1883. These developments set the precedent for a decisive expansion of the administrative state in the twentieth century. It began with the creation of an agency to regulate the safety of the food supply and medicines and it continued in 1914 with the establishment of the Federal Trade Commission, empowered to regulate unfair competition and "bust the trusts."

But the administrative state as we know it owes most to the New Deal, when Roosevelt created an "alphabet soup" of new agencies to meet the challenge of the Great Depression and then World War II. In the 1960s and 1970s, presidents Johnson and Nixon expanded the administrative state further, creating agencies to regulate air and water pollution (the Environmental Protection Agency) and workplace safety (the Occupational Safety and Health Administration). And more recently, after 9/11, the Department of Homeland Security was founded to coordinate domestic security efforts.

From the beginning of national politics to the present, the administrative state was established and developed to "run a constitution" (Rohr 1986). It was built to solve problems that beset people in their everyday lives and to respond to emergencies and crises. In the case of the United States, problems that administration was designed to solve were identified as soon as there was a national government: settling conflicting claims on public lands, implementing Jefferson's embargo on foreign trade, regulating safety on steamships (Mashaw 2012, 188–89). Then and still, citizens expect government to step in where there is a need. They expect their government to protect them from buying meatloaf that has been cut with sawdust. Or from public water supplies poisoned with lead. Or from the risk of losing a leg in an easily avoided workplace accident. Or from being denied an apartment because of their race. This requires not only a government that can legislate, but a government that can design policies and implement them—an administrative state.

Our next chapter illuminates how ungoverning works and its unmistakable purpose: to liberate the president's personal will.

3

Personal Rule and the Dynamics of Destruction

Here we plunge into ungoverning in action. Administrative procedures are trashed. Knowledgeable personnel are embattled—fired or sidelined, vilified and threatened. The institutions of the administrative state are derailed, displaced, hijacked, and circumvented. Ungoverning's animating purpose, again, is to free the president from the constraints of procedure and from dependence on public servants with experience designing and managing massive, complex public programs. And often enough, the derogation of experts and trashing of procedure is done with a public flourish. Deconstruction of the administrative state can proceed secretively, but it can also be dramatic, underscoring its willfulness.

Although ungoverning is not the work of one person, Trump is prominent in this chapter. Unlike every other president in U.S. history, he sought to destroy the machinery of governing and transform the presidential office into personal rule. Once he introduced ungoverning, others followed, and deconstruction of the administrative state has been taken up by members of Congress and appointed heads of departments and agencies. Weakening the capacity of government has become an imperative for leaders of the Republican Party. Republicans in office press for deconstruction, or go along with it, or acquiesce out of fear. Covid showed that even in an emergency, the goal of incapacitating government prevailed. The federal government abandoned the states, leaving them to their own devices to find medical supplies and protective equipment, even pitting them against one another (Cohen 2020). The Centers for Disease Control was impeded from issuing its own public guidance. A pointed moment of demoting expertise came in 2020 when Trump proposed treating Covid infections by irradiating patients' bodies with ultraviolet light and injecting them with bleach. Standing beside him was Dr. Deborah Birx, his own White House coronavirus response coordinator, as he said, "I'm not a doctor," pointing to his head, "but I'm a person who has a good you-know-what" (BBC 2020).

Another ostentatious presidential demand for personal deference and preemption of scientific integrity occurred earlier, in 2019, when on his own authority, Trump altered the National Oceanic and Atmospheric Association's (NOAA) forecast of Hurricane Dorian's path. Out of nowhere, he chose to add Alabama to the regions at risk, pointing to a crudely doctored weather map that took the hurricane forecast into that state. When meteorologists contradicted him, Trump had his homeland security adviser issue a statement defending him, and he attacked "fake news." Meanwhile, his nominee to head NOAA was an advocate of privatizing weather forecasting (Dale and Miller 2019; Zaveri 2019).

To be sure, while ungoverning can strike anywhere, it does not disable administration everywhere. During Trump's presidency, the business of many departments was carried on in regular fashion. He consolidated Republican congressional support by leaving the politics and administration of tax policy and judicial appointments to Congress. In some areas, the president issued policy directives that were carried out by agencies in the usual manner, managed by the usual personnel. Normal processes continued in agencies whose business did not attract the president's personal interest or attention.

And some matters of public business that got Trump's attention did not involve ungoverning at all. In the area of trade, for example, he favored policies and used the Department of Commerce to try to achieve his goals, just as presidents ordinarily do. He advocated heightened national protectionism, raising tariffs and pursuing a trade war with China (which was escalated by the Biden administration). Such major policy changes are not uncommon when a new administration takes control after an election.

Shrugging Off Process and Knowledge

As we detailed in the last chapter, the identifying criteria of ungoverning are disdain for expertise and for regular procedure. "Shrugging off process" means violating the rules for deciding and implementing public policies. It is a frontal attack on proceduralism, which is essential to the administrative state's authority. The rule of law, as well as the law of rules—the ethos of rule-following—is a hard-won feature of the administrative state and of liberalism more generally. "Out with knowledgeable personnel" also damages the capacity of administration and exhibits profound disdain for expertise, another hard-won foundational value. Assaults on process and personnel disable programs. They are unpredictable and nonstrategic, and their effect is to degrade the capacity to govern overall. This is how governing institutions are disabled, hijacked, circumvented, and derailed.

A tour of "out with knowledgeable personnel" would begin shortly after Trump's election, when he tore up New Jersey governor Chris Christie's plans for staffing the new administration. Christie had been charged with the advance work of lining up candidates for appointments to White House offices and to positions in administrative departments. During his first year in office Trump did accede to some suggestions for hiring that came from friendly Republicans who had supported his candidacy. Very soon, however, he began to get rid of early appointees, replacing them with wealthy businesspeople, political loyalists, and disruptors. These choices made a mockery of experience, subject-specific knowledge, and capacity to manage. Over time, Trump's appointments could not be identified by any standard criteria of selection at all; they appeared to be impulsive referrals that reflected presidential whim. Bizarre choices unrelated to the demands of the job at hand that had one unifying factor: subservience.

Making appointments with a view to submissiveness was just one feature of personnel under Trump. Another was humiliation of permanent agency staff, and even the president's own appointees could become targets. Some were acquiescent in the face of abuse because the office and spoils were sufficient compensation. Some were fearful, bullied into violating professional norms and public goals. Some were very publicly attacked and summarily fired or forced to resign. Some were threatened with physical violence.

"Out with knowledgeable personnel" ceased to be surprising given the president's penchant for total control and for revenge. One instance was predictable: an enraged president ended the career of Lieutenant Colonel Alexander Vindman, who served in his National Security Council, after Vindman testified against the president to impeachment investigators. Vindman revealed what he knew about Trump's covert attempt to force Ukraine's government to investigate his election challenger, Joe Biden, and Biden's son. Vindman explained how Trump made his self-serving demand a condition for U.S. military assistance in support of Ukraine's resistance to Russian occupation of Crimea (Ryan and Harris 2020; C-SPAN 2019).

Unsurprising, too, was the removal of Michael Kuperberg, the scientist responsible for the National Climate Assessment, in an overt attempt to thwart the outcome of the work that shapes regulations to limit global warming (Flavelle, Friedman, and Davenport 2020). And the summary dismissal of Christopher Krebs, head of cybersecurity for the 2020 election, after he publicly attested to the fairness of the presidential vote count (Wise 2020).

Not every attack on knowledgeable personnel made the news. The perpetual barrage of firing and hiring based on presumptive (but never sufficient) loyalty and submissiveness showed up in the numbers. The standard category, administrative "turnover," was judged inadequate, suggesting as it does a natural process of exit and replacement. A 2019 Brookings report created a new category, "resigned under pressure," to indicate the actual reason for many departures. The report read: "President George W. Bush lost two Cabinet members in his first three years, President Obama lost three, and—three months into his third year—President Trump has lost eight cabinet members. Turnover in the Trump administration remains record setting, no matter how you slice the data" (Tenpas 2019). A complete accounting of personnel harassed, fired, and displaced at levels lower than cabinet appointees may never be known. The general desolation was evident: a report from August 2021 described the Biden administration's race to hire senior government executives as "a staffing spree aimed at rebuilding agencies rocked by turmoil during Trump's war on the so-called 'deep state'" (Zhao and Lipmann 2021).

Trump went to great lengths to avoid appointments on the basis of professional qualifications. It took deliberate effort to select for subservience. One work-around was to simply leave vacancies in administration unfilled. Another method was to exploit loopholes in the rules of administrative appointment. Senate confirmation could be circumvented by making his chosen heads of departments "acting" and then eluding the rules that limit the time frame of interim appointments. Acting appointments were less likely to make any significant decision without the president's approval. Trump's declaration that "I sort of like 'acting'" was, wittingly or not, a double entendre (Sonmez 2020).

Other instruments for getting rid of unwanted civil servants were more imaginative. When he was inhibited by fixed processes from firing the department's experts, Secretary of Agriculture Sonny Perdue concocted a scheme to move the National Institute of Food and Agriculture and its research arm from Washington, D.C., to Kansas City. The purpose was served: resignations followed (Morris 2021).

In all this, domination and submission were on display. Time and again, the mere presence of an expert in the room seemed to spur Trump to contradict, humiliate, berate, and mock his own appointees, typically in public, as he did with his Covid public health team. When he boasted "I have the best people," he did not mean people recruited for their experience and capacity to administer programs. Appointees were favored for their compliance and for their willingness to pay incessant tribute to the president, kowtowing to his claim to know everything better than anyone, or his need to own reality: "I alone can fix it" (Jackson 2016).

The president considered his appointees to be private servants, meant to cater to his personal will. When he called the heads of the armed forces "my generals," it was not just an awkward but unexceptional statement that military leadership ultimately reports to civilian authority; it was a way to underscore their subservience to him, personally. Claims of ownership—of officials, of official documents—became a feature of Trump's presidency. It is unsurprising that he could not work with his own joint chiefs and that even in critical situations he did not always consult the Department of Defense (DOD). In a one-week period after he was defeated in the election of 2020 Trump fired four Pentagon officials, including the secretary of defense, the undersecretary of defense for policy, the undersecretary of defense for intelligence, and the chief of staff to the secretary of defense. He replaced them with sycophants and loyalists without any experience or relevant expertise. A retired NATO supreme allied commander, James Stavridis, said that the president "decapitated our operational civilian leadership of the military" (Stavridis 2020).

The *Washington Post* editorial board in 2020 was unequivocal: "Throughout its tenure, the Trump administration has performed abysmally in staffing and operating the federal government. Hundreds of key positions have remained vacant or filled by unqualified acting appointees; political hacks have persecuted career staff or devoted themselves to President Trump's personal interests. As the administration staggers toward the end of its term, the degradation and corruption are accelerating" (*Washington Post* 2020).

Dynamics of Deconstruction #1: Disabling

Ungoverning is not a tsunami of destruction that leaves nothing standing. The common element is that the degradation of departments and agencies is willful and difficult to square with any public purpose. We identify a set of moves that propel "out with knowledgeable personnel" and "shrugging off regular process." There may be, as two legal scholars quipped, "thirty ways to kill an agency," but we focus on four principal mechanisms (Freeman and Jacobs 2021, 591). We call them disabling, hijacking, circumventing, and derailing.

First, institutions are *disabled*. They are interfered with in ways calculated to undermine their purposes and operations. When Director of National Intelligence Daniel Coats's annual threat assessment identified climate change as a security threat, the Trump team's response was to form a commission to "reexamine" this unwelcome finding. The National Security Council member appointed to lead the climate review panel was a physicist who was on record pronouncing that "the demonization of carbon dioxide is just like the demonization of the poor Jews under Hitler" (Tabon 2019). As we have discussed, changing or rolling back environmental regulations (and others) is not in itself ungoverning. But we are alerted to deliberate disabling when the charge against the agency is conspiracist—that administrators have reached their conclusions by using "secret science."

That was the case with the "secret science rule" of January 2021, officially called "Strengthening Transparency in Regulatory Science" (Environmental Protection Agency 2021). As the journalist Marianne Lavelle reported, even in 1996, a consultant for the tobacco industry had "suggested a tactic to use against the EPA: attack the science by employing a buzzword like 'transparency' and raise doubts about whether the studies were 'able to be reproduced'" (Lavelle 2020). That strategy cast suspicion on existing regulations and changed the guidelines for the kind of studies that would be relied on for rulemaking. The unexceptional fact is that in crafting regulations, the EPA often uses public health data that ensures patient anonymity. But the new rule, in the name of "transparency," would have discounted key research and undermined "settled conclusions about the health impacts of air pollution." Requiring the use of only those studies that do not veil participants' information "narrowly limits the agency's discretion" in considering scientific research. The secret science rule took specific aim at a key basis for air-quality standards, Harvard University's "Six Cities" study, in which "researchers tracked personal medical, occupational, and home location data for tens of thousands of participants for nearly two decades—on the condition that the participants' personal information would remain confidential" (Perls 2021). The secret science rule threatened both the integrity of the findings and privacy (Banerjee 2020).

The timing of the secret science rule underscored its objective: disabling the Environmental Protection Agency. It was fast-tracked just as questions were being raised about whether air pollution increases susceptibility to Covid-19, which might have strengthened the case for more rigorous air quality standards (Lavelle 2020). The rule proposed in 2018 was finalized in 2021, just as the Biden administration was preparing "aggressive health-based standards for combatting environmental pollution" (Perls 2021).

Dynamics of Deconstruction #2: Hijacking

From the beginning of his administration, the president worked ceaselessly to ensure that the Justice Department and the Federal

Bureau of Investigation (FBI) were personally loyal to him. Seven days into his presidency he summoned the head of the FBI, James Comey, to the Oval Office to extract just such a pledge: "I need loyalty. I expect loyalty" (U.S. Senate Select Committee on Intelligence 2017, 3). The meeting with Comey was to get assurance that he would "go easy" on Michael Flynn in his investigation of the former national security advisor, who had lied about having multiple phone calls with the Russian ambassador during the 2016 presidential campaign. Trump told Comey, "I hope you can see your way clear to letting this thing go, to letting Flynn go" (Schmidt 2017). Trump saw the government law enforcement agencies as a staff of personal attorneys, there to protect his business and political interests, to assist in his vendettas, and to use their authority to attack his political opponents. "Lock her up" was not just a slogan but an expectation.

The pattern of hijacking the Department of Justice and the FBI was repeated as the president attempted to impede investigations of his own conduct in campaigns and in office. He fired his first attorney general, Jeff Sessions, for recusing himself from taking charge of the investigation into the president's connections to Russian interference in the 2016 election. He enlisted the Justice Department in his attempt to prove his claim that FBI surveillance of his campaign was part of a malicious plot by Obama to spy on him in order to keep him from becoming president, describing "Obamagate" as "the biggest political crime in American history, by far" (Stieb 2020). He installed as his new attorney general William Barr, a loyalist who whitewashed Special Counsel Robert Mueller's independent report on Trump's relation to Russia. The president characterized every investigation as "a hoax," every allegation of impropriety and illegality against him a "witch hunt." Trump saw the integrity of the Justice Department as "a direct threat to his political legitimacy" (Skowronek, Dearborn, and King 2021, 83). Similarly, aggressive audits by the IRS and revocations of security clearances were used to punish the president's perceived enemies (Schmidt 2022). In sum, the aim was to hijack the Justice Department.

Dynamics of Deconstruction #3: Circumventing

Institutions were *circumvented*—most dangerously in foreign affairs. The president along with Congress has responsibility for U.S. foreign policy. Directing policy and diplomacy depend on processes coordinated among the military and the State Department, the Commerce Department, and others. Trump diminished state capacity by circumventing the people and processes of foreign policymaking and execution. The *Washington Post* reported, "In its first month, the Trump administration . . . has largely benched the State Department from its long-standing role as the preeminent voice of U.S. foreign policy" (Morello and Gearan 2017). Trump refused to fill appointments, and the title of a Democratic staff report from 2020 was blunt: *Diplomacy in Crisis: The Trump Administration's Decimation of the State Department* (U.S. Senate Committee on Foreign Relations 2020).

Routines at the State Department were circumvented from the start. The daily question-and-answer press briefing initiated in the 1950s and monitored by diplomats around the world was suspended. Secretary of State Rex Tillerson was absent from White House meetings with foreign leaders like Canada's Justin Trudeau and Japan's Shinzo Abe. The State Department itself directed foreign policy questions to the White House. Trump insisted that his many capricious tweets were the authoritative expression of U.S. foreign policy. When Laura Ingraham asked the president in a November 2017 Fox News interview whether he was concerned that there were not enough Trump administration appointees in the State Department to carry out his vision, he responded, "Let me tell you, the one that matters is me. . . . I'm the only one that matters" (Chappell 2017). And he acted on this solipsistic claim with mercurial embraces—followed by rejections—of foreign leaders (Specia 2019). He summarily withdrew from treaties, including the critical Iran nuclear deal (Landler 2018).

A key example of circumventing people and process occurred in June 2018, when the president met with North Korean leader Kim Jong Un in Singapore—the first ever meeting of leaders from the two countries. The meeting was marked by disarray and confusion. No foreign service officers were in the room with him when Trump met with Kim Jong Un and committed the United States to agreements with one of its most dangerous foes. Disturbing reports confirmed the absence of notetakers in Trump's meeting with Kim. This followed occasions where Trump talked with Russian president Vladimir Putin without any record-keeping of their conversations, including a meeting at the 2019 G20 summit at which no other U.S. official was present. He instructed his translator not to share details with presidential staff and seized the translator's notes. As one reporter noted, "This isn't a minor clerical issue." It meant that besides the president's own recounting, there was no account of any agreements he may have entered into (Ward 2019). It meant that after meetings with foreign ministers of Russia, Egypt, and Saudi Arabia, the only public reports of the discussions and outcomes came from what the other countries' own officials told their local reporters. Their accounts went uncorrected and unrebutted by the U.S. government (Morello and Gearan 2017).

A series of impenetrable actions toward North Korea followed Trump's meeting with Kim. The president suggested at a press conference that he might be willing to exit the United States' alliance with South Korea—an alliance dating from the Korean War, and a commitment of importance not only to South Korea but to every U.S. ally. He announced that he was canceling the U.S.-South Korean joint military exercises, which he described in terms one would expect from a North Korean leader as "war games" and "very provocative" (Stallard 2020). And he pronounced, fantastically, "There is no longer a nuclear threat" from North Korea (Sullivan 2018). Circumvention of the Departments of State and Defense has been aptly described as "unilateral diplomatic disarmament" (Burns 2019, 102).

These circumventions of diplomatic process made it impossible for the Pentagon and the State Department to conduct steady foreign policy. No countries, allied or enemy or in between, could understand U.S. priorities and policies, because policy had dissolved into one person's unpredictable will and rogue pronouncements.

Dynamics of Deconstruction #4: Derailing

Finally, institutions are *derailed*. Two compelling instances concerned the Department of Defense and the president's use of military officers and soldiers as props in support of his conspiracy claims. Both showed that by acting out the fantasy that the military was his personal force ("my generals"), the president derailed normal operations and protocols. He attempted to degrade the military's professional ethic, which required distance from domestic politics, including distance from the personal bidding of the commander in chief. When it came to the military, Trump demanded not only total loyalty but total obedience. He asked retired four-star general John Kelly, then his chief of staff, "Why can't you be like the German generals?" and refused to believe Kelly's admonition that Hitler's generals had tried to kill him three times (Shear 2022).

Consider the order diverting military forces from their normal operations and instead moving them to the southern border. The pretext was to use armed troops to deter an "invasion" of MS-13 gang members and migrants carrying diseases, violent criminal intentions, and illegal votes (Trump 2018). The problem was not just Trump's alarmist, unconfirmed warning that a caravan two thousand miles from the border was a threat to national security, but also his determination to send in a force of 5,200 active-duty military to protect against this so-called invasion (Peters 2018a). The National Guard has been used to help with border security, but deploying active-duty troops except for domestic emergencies like floods and hurricanes was extraordinary (Burns and Colvin 2018).

Migrants were designated enemies, and so were political protesters. Military leadership was brought out once again to give credence to the presumptive danger they posed. We saw that in the wake of public demonstrations against the May 2020 police murder of George Floyd, a Black man arrested for buying cigarettes with a counterfeit $20 bill. The Black Lives Matter movement organized a peaceful protest in Lafayette Square near the White House. The president demanded that the military be brought out to clear the protesters and asked his chair of the joint chiefs of staff, General Mark A. Milley, "Why can't you just shoot them? Just shoot them in the legs or something?" (Shear 2022).

Their regrets were well founded, not just because the 82nd Airborne Division is not a police force and infantry battalions do not have the appropriate "skill set" for domestic disturbances (U.S. House Select Committee to Investigate the January 6th Attack on the United States Capitol 2021, 37). At issue too is the principle that citizens are not enemies of the nation simply because the executive brands them as such for his own political purposes.

Disabling, hijacking, circumventing, derailing the people and processes that constitute administration—these are the dynamics of ungoverning. Shows of power can be intoxicating. They stir those who admire the *rawness* of power. These dynamics are how personal rule degrades administration.

Personal Rule versus Governing

Rule, as we define it, is the ability to impose one's will on a political community. The aspiration of liberal democratic politics is to replace rule with governing.

"Rule" is the first verb of politics and *Who rules?* is the most elemental political question (Aristotle [350 B.C.E.] 2013; Markel 2006; Lane 2023). In its plainest sense, rule is the ability of one person or group to dominate others. Rulers appropriate for themselves power, wealth, and honor. But since Plato, as political theorist Melissa Lane shows, political philosophers tried to demarcate a distinction between rule and governing, or office (Lane 2023). Put simply, office is about delineating the domain of authority and tethering it to the well-being of the community.

The distinction between governing and rule is also central to modern political thought. John Locke's seventeenth-century foundational treatise on constitutional government created a framework for politics where ideally no one rules, in the sense that no person or group has the power to impose its private will on the whole. Those with authority are charged not with serving their own interests but with protecting individual rights and advancing broadly shared interests such as prosperity and peace. Where rule is about power, governing is about authority, which is bounded in what it can do and limited to purposes that those subject to authority could be expected to endorse. The difference between rule/power and governing/authority is crystallized in an example from Locke's *Second Treatise*: a military official who on the one hand has authority to send a sergeant into a mission that would almost certainly result in death but on the other hand does not have the authority to take one penny from that sergeant's pocket (Locke [1690] 1961, §139). The promise of constitutional government is that we live according to public rules or laws rather than being subject to the "inconstant, uncertain, unknown, arbitrary will of another" (§22).

In systems of governing, authority adheres to offices, which have purposes, responsibilities, and bounds set by a constitution, laws, or settled norms. The U.S. presidential oath of office illustrates this point (Brettschneider 2018). Offices exist outside of government, of course: the chief executive of a corporation holds a legally circumscribed office, and the dean of a university holds an office with responsibilities and authority that are defined independent of who the dean is. The commonality is that office is an institution, a structure with designated purposes and accountability that individuals inhabit provisionally.

To be sure, there is a fundamental tension inherent in the presidency: it is both office and person. To call it an office refers to a bounded writ of authority that constrains every occupant of the office. And yet the president is also a person, which is to grant significance to the individual character and ambition of the person elected to the office. To fully empower the personal judgment of the president would be to eliminate all bounds that define and constrain the office. And to fully specify all the conditions under which presidential authority can be exercised would be to eliminate the role of character and judgment.

In the case of the U.S. president, this distinction is at once vital and elusive. The complication is that the ambivalence written into the presidency should *not* be permanently resolved (Mansfield 1989). What the ungoverning president tried to do was to resolve it permanently in favor of personal rule and to eradicate the constraints of office. We will encounter this ambivalence again when we take up the doctrine of the unitary executive in chapter 9.

Trump, for his part, saw the presidency simply as personal rule. He acknowledged no limits to his own authority. The presidency as an office was subsumed to Trump "as a natural person" (Lane 2023, 390). He incessantly identified the presidency with himself, with the magic of his person. He also represented his person as the singular instantiation of the people—"Me the people," to quote the title of political theorist Nadia Urbinati's book on populism (Urbinati 2019). By identifying the power of the presidency with himself as a person rather than with the office of the presidency, what was empowered was not an office that others in turn would later inhabit, but personal will. As he saw it, nothing he willed could be outside the scope of the president's authority. No procedure, no purpose, and no mechanism of accountability limited personal will. Willfulness is compelling, unhampered, impulsive, and bent on immediate action. The president "*is* the executive branch," his attorney general informed the Department of Justice in 2018 (Barr 2018, 10).

The distinction between authority vested in an office and personal power is at the core of liberalism, which is defined by rights, laws, and limits. Personal will is the antithesis of laws and limits. It is unpredictable not only because it is the always unknowable will of another, but because will itself is capricious.

Personal rule is also inseparable from theatrics. Democratic politics—all politics—draws on symbols and performances. But personal rulers have an acute and constant need for theatrics, symbolic actions, and stagecraft. Substantive results— policies crafted and implemented—are not the necessary or sufficient proof of personal power, traceable to one will. Rule is expressed most clearly by the performative face of power. Symbolic measures are essential to generating the feeling that things are happening immediately and flowing from one source.

In place of legislative activity and administrative implementation come gestures—Trump's infrastructure week, for example, which was announced but never materialized (Rogers 2019a). Personal rule is accompanied by false claims and faux appearances—staged events that mimic managing the business of government, such as events at factories that were never built and summits that did not take place. The political writer and blogger Steve Benen describes a June 2017 "fake signing ceremony," with loyal Republican members of Congress gathered to witness the president privatizing the air traffic control system—except that what was signed was neither legislation nor an executive order, but a press release (Benen 2017).

Ungoverning favors incessant, potent, easily understood public dramas mocking and abusing opposition figures. Or pronouncements that serve as attention-getting targets: in July 2015, then-candidate Trump said of Republican John McCain, "He's not a war hero. He was a war hero because he was captured. I like people who weren't captured" (Cillizza 2019). Or addressing the addiction crisis by proposing to execute drug dealers (Samuels 2022). And the assertiveness behind malignant dramatics allows the ruler to project himself as a protector and at the same time invite followers to protect him.

As we have noted, the Trump administration did produce policies on immigration, trade, tariffs, and vaccine development. Where the president was effective, it was precisely because of his reliance on the agencies of the administrative state. And where he was ineffective, it was because of his penchant for personal rule. One-off commands do not have a sustained effect; unlike policy, they do not deliver regular results. The point of ungoverning is to liberate the rule of the executive, promising unbridled control. But it paradoxically cripples the ability to affect much at all—least of all, changes that endure. Command creates the illusion of control.

The epitome of personal rule is the reliance on family, who in Trump's case lacked political or administrative experience or specialized knowledge in any area. At times, they substituted not only for cabinet secretaries but for entire departments. Son-in-law Jared Kushner's "portfolios" ranged across domains from Middle East foreign policy to the procurement of Covid supplies during the pandemic. Why family? Personal rule is always tenuous. Treachery is the hallmark of royal courts and tyrannies, with whisperers in the halls of power and murderous successors. And while families, too, can be famously treacherous, they ordinarily have bonds that go beyond self-interest. Family is more accommodating when action is demanded without the constraints of specialized knowledge and regular process.

Personal rule also normalizes corruption. It opens the door wide to opportunities for gain. The icing on the cake of ungoverning is personal enrichment. At the top, Trump commanded the administration to direct business to his personal properties, in apparent violation of the emoluments clause of the Constitution. His loyalists remained loyal, in part because they were invited to use their offices for both petty gains (furnishings, travel) and more substantial benefits like using inside information to buy or sell shares of stock, or commissioning government contracts that increased the value of businesses they owned (Weiss 2018). Every government is vulnerable to graft. Often, a quid pro quo is easy to describe but hard to prove, such as regulatory favors doled out in return for political donations. But Trump's own zeal for personal enrichment encouraged something more comprehensive that looked like a "lawless feeding frenzy." We might see it as incipient kleptocracy (Holmes 2012).

Behind Trump's personal rule was not just a brilliant instinct for the seductive qualities of raw power but a pervasive indifference to the details of public policy and implementation. His inattention was noted early on. Candidate Trump had no experience with policymaking and no interest in it. True, his campaign messages focused on several issues—immigration and free trade, for example—and his acquiescence in Republican tax cuts and conservative judicial appointments kept the Republican Party establishment quiescent. But his fundamental disinterest in legislation, noted by Republicans in Congress accustomed to presidential support, was surpassed only by his indifference to the necessity of able administration. From the start, disinterest in things like daily intelligence briefings had advisers desperately trying to find ways to get his attention.

To be effective on most matters requires more than one-off commands; it requires administration. When Trump wanted to impose a critical change in military policy—withdrawing troops from Afghanistan—he failed. His "order" to withdraw came after his election defeat on November 9, 2020, when his aide John McEntee passed an official in the DOD a one-page note saying that the president wanted to withdraw all U.S. troops from Afghanistan, Syria, Germany, and Africa. Because the note did not follow any procedure for presidential orders (the White House national security advisor did not know about it, for instance), top generals in the Pentagon ignored it. Willfulness is capricious, and personal will is antithetical to governing (Swan and Basu 2021).

My Beautiful Wall

Presidential indifference to administration emerges not only in the universe of areas in which Trump had no interest at all, but also on issues that he had repeatedly spoken of as urgent, such as immigration, which he cast as an existential threat to the nation. We've discussed the failings that marked Zero Tolerance at the border. The signature case of command without control, however, was the wall. "I will build a great, great wall on our southern border" was Trump's campaign promise (Valverde 2020). Without a border, a country is not a country, he told his supporters. Nothing was more urgent than to stop the "invasion" of caravans of migrants carrying disease and crime and taking Americans' jobs. Walls have a place in border control policy, but in this case, the "wall" was a substitute for immigration policy.

At 2016 rallies the chorus was, "Mexico will pay for the wall." But there was no plan to fund the wall. In 2018–19 the longest government shutdown in U.S. history was inflicted on the nation in the name of increasing the budget for "border security," though it ended without funding for the president's wall (Popkin 2021, 179). Beyond paying for the wall, there was no policy to address the resistance by property owners close to the border, or to determine the wall's location, or to manage its construction. There was no study or planning to show that the wall could have a measurable effect on deterring migration. There was no interest in using the administrative capacity of government to answer these questions.

In the end, "only 80 miles of new barriers were built where there were none before—that includes 47 miles of primary wall and 33 miles of secondary wall built to reinforce the initial barrier." According to U.S. Customs and Border Protection, as of January 2021 there were 452 miles of wall on the southern border in total, most of it erected by previous administrations (Giles 2021).

Did it matter that the beautiful wall was not built? Trump expressed frustration but at the same time claimed that it *had* been built. Perhaps his capacity for magical thinking made him indifferent to real outputs: if I say it, it will be done. But what about followers who were persuaded by the drumbeat of talk about "caravans" and invasions, disease, and crime that national security required this wall?

Some people may have been convinced that as a matter of fact, the president's will had been executed, and the barrier was doing its essential work defending the country from alien invasion. There was no failure to be accounted for.

But for others, the reality of the wall was beside the point. "Build the wall" was not only a promise to be fulfilled in real time but also a millennial promise, like "Make America great again." The repetition of the promise as something about to be fulfilled gestures toward a restoration of an imagined homeland. With the wall, Trump promised "absolute 'safety' and, in a sense, national purity" (Lifton 2019, 162). What the wall symbolized mattered more than the physical thing. As we say in the next chapter, we shouldn't underestimate the power of messianism to eclipse concern for actual government "outputs."

4

The Reactionary Counterculture Movement

What appeal can ungoverning have, degrading the administrative state and with it, the people who perform the day-to-day work of making government work? What explains the demand side of ungoverning? And what does the ungoverning party—the supply side of deconstruction—offer to attract followers? Ungoverning seems to fly in the face of the commonsense idea that good government is defined by concrete outputs that improve people's day-to-day lives.

The answer to these questions turns on the millennial promise of the movement Trump brought into being. Trump took the remains of the once-organized Tea Party, which had arisen in opposition to Obama in 2008, and created something new and his own: Make America Great Again (MAGA). He did so by turning the energy of an opposition movement into something more, investing it with millennial promise. As a reactionary movement, it connects the imagined goal of restoration with the social experience of grievance. MAGA looks ahead to restoration and backward at loss.

MAGA confers recognition on those who feel aggrieved by what has been lost. Broadly speaking, politics offers two kinds of goods: concrete deliverables and recognition. The reactionary movement harbors social and economic grievances, some of which could be addressed by real policies, but its ardent desire for recognition cannot be assuaged by "deliverables." Ultimately, the deep aspiration, the political fantasy of restoration, cannot be met by a liberal democracy and indeed not by any government at all.

Government "Outputs"

Delivering results that serve the public interest is widely viewed as key to the stability and legitimacy of governments. Indeed, a familiar claim made by authoritarian regimes is that they are better at delivering results. Recall Hamilton's conviction that "good administration" would make citizens appreciate the federal government even when they don't feel close to it. Even when, unlike local and state governments, their sense of being personally represented is elusive.

Trust in government is linked to results, too. Trust is established by competent governing, the argument goes, and when governments deliver, a "virtuous circle arises. The government is trustworthy, and the citizens recognize it as such and respond with compliance and willing cooperation with its policies and practices." This has become a matter of concern because "establishing trustworthy government is a major problem for contemporary democracies" (Levi 2022, 215).

The centrality of results is at the core of much of political science. Democratic theory depends on the assumption that citizens will support candidates and parties that deliver results they value, whether these have to do with the economy, social issues, or foreign policy (Hochschild 2016; Stoller and Dayen 2023). While there are differences in accounts of how citizens assess results, there is wide agreement that results matter. On one view, judgments turn on prospective expectations about which party will improve their lives; on another view, these assessments are retrospective and rest on firsthand knowledge of how they fared under the previous administration (Fiorina 1981). Both accounts acknowledge that popular judgments often rely on candidates' false claims of credit for past results or promises of results to come (Arnold 1992). Even self-described "realist" scholars concede that popular judgments about outputs should, ideally, direct the actions of elected leaders even though these scholars concede that in practice democracies are often unresponsive (Achen and Bartels 2017; Schumpeter [1943] 2008). Many assume that policy is shaped by the donor class and oriented to elites, not ordinary voters (Gilens and Page 2014). All that said, it is still the case that "the appeal of representative democracy hinges on the responsiveness of elected politicians to the preferences and interests of their constituents" (Bartels 1991, 457).

This assumption about results-oriented democratic politics has consequences. It can induce a ruthless party to obstruct outcomes, however necessary, for which the opposition would have received credit. It can lead to obfuscating who should be credited with a policy. It can produce contesting claims of credit within a party coalition, as seen in the rift between Barack Obama and Hillary Clinton over whether Martin Luther King Jr. or Lyndon Johnson was more responsible for landmark civil rights legislation, which was a topic in one of their primary election debates. And both prospective and retrospective assessments are skewed when voters attribute outcomes to political decisions rather than to events that are in fact beyond any government's control (Achen and Bartels 2017).

One political scientist summed up this conventional wisdom succinctly: "A party's brand depends upon the benefits it delivers on the issues they [voters] care most about" (Popkin 2021, 190). Nothing in this wealth of empirical material and democratic theory helps to explain the existence of a constituency for ungoverning. What results do citizens expect or demand that are consonant with deconstructing the administrative state? With the delegitimation of governing institutions broadly? The question is, what explains "the death of deliverism?" (Bhargava, Shams, and Hanbury 2023).

What Results Matter?

The "deliverables" of government that matter most are often material: economic growth, jobs, infrastructure, and benefits like Social Security and health insurance. Deliverables can also include so-called post-material goods: gun control, civil rights laws that would require selling wedding cakes to same-sex couples. Ronald Inglehart and Pippa Norris argue that material concerns receded as citizens became more affluent during the twentieth century, and they chart a worldwide turn to cultural concerns such as feminism and environmentalism (Inglehart 2016; Norris and Inglehart 2019). Both material and post-material goods are the products of public policy; administrative departments shape and implement programs to produce greater disposable income, or clean air and water.

The second broad category of what politics offers is recognition, a sense on the part of citizens that they are seen and understood by those in power, that their claims register with those in power. The demand for recognition is collective, made on behalf of a self-defined group with a history, values, and social standing, and an insistence on their own inherent worth. Recognition begins with feeling "seen" by officials. This may happen when representation is "descriptive"—that is, when people who share the group's racial, ethnic, religious, or gender identity hold power, as when Catholics saw John F. Kennedy and African Americans saw Barak Obama ascend to the presidency. But the politics of recognition plays out in other ways. Officials may try to signal special empathy for a group's situation, as when Bill Clinton commiserated that "I feel your pain."

Or those in power may represent themselves as akin to the group by casting themselves, too, as victims of a common enemy. Trump excelled at this. An official response to their suffering and grievances, their sense of victimization, and, not least, the group's identification of their victimizers is essential. Recognition gives credibility and authority to members' own designation of their oppressors.

Failure of recognition "can inflict a grievous wound, saddling its victims with a crippling self-hatred" (Gutmann 1994, 26). It can bring humiliation and shame. On the widest view, recognition means that those in power give credibility to the group's perception of social reality. Trump's depiction of a violent society out of control in his "American carnage" inaugural speech did just that.

For many decades, organized demands for recognition in the United States have come mainly from historically disadvantaged racial, ethnic, and religious minorities mobilizing for equal rights and for justice in the distribution of benefits and opportunities. In both democratic theory and in practice, the politics of recognition has been predominately progressive: women's resistance to subordination and sexual oppression in the workplace, at home, in politics—everywhere; Black Lives Matter organizing to publicize and stop police brutality inflicted with impunity on Black men and boys; LGBTQ+ demands for marriage equality. These demands all require substantial public programs, effectively administered.

The politics of recognition presents a huge challenge to a liberal society negotiating pluralism. The aspirational goal is universal inclusion, recognition, and respect. But this is always perilous, because recognition may require differential treatment. That's the case, for example, when officials grant a group special rights or exemptions such as religious exemptions from civil rights laws for business owners opposed to gay marriage on grounds of faith. Then, recognition entails permission to refuse to serve gay customers. These painful dilemmas cannot be avoided in a pluralist society.

But for the forces of reaction, attempts to navigate the rough seas of liberal pluralism are anathema because pluralist society is anathema. Today, we see the full force of a demand for recognition coming from those who see progressive programs as a denial of their own appropriate social standing and values. As the demand for recognition turns aggressive, it takes aim not only at elites who deny them what they deserve, but also at those (the undeserving) who receive recognition, benefits, and opportunities at their expense.

On this view, both deliverables and recognition are awarded to others who, Arlie Russell Hochschild explains, have pushed to the front of the line: women, immigrants, and racial minorities broadly. "And President Obama: how did he rise so high?" (Hochschild 2016, 137). The "front of the line" image points to both the status of being first and to the belief that there is a scarcity of rights and benefits. The image also suggests that recognition and deliverables are rarely separable. Fervent anti-immigrant stands, for example, may have begun with concrete fear that newcomers were taking American jobs and that taxes were being raised to educate undocumented immigrant children, but they turned into an adamant defense of national purity tainted by "invaders."

And with animus, the demand for recognition turns dark. It is set on *denying benefits* to the undeserving. Denial can seem fair when "makers" are not getting their share, when "takers" are getting more. So recognition means withholding advantages from unworthy others—above all, people of color—by eliminating programs, cutting funding, and refusing public gestures of respect. Denying others rather than providing opportunities is at the heart of this politics of recognition. It entails turning immigrants and asylum seekers away, and altering school curricula to constrain teaching the history of African Americans and substituting revived versions of the Confederacy's Lost Cause (Smith 2021). With it come unfettered attacks on the officials and agencies of government that put programs serving the unworthy into practice. Punitive ungoverning becomes a measure of recognition.

At stake for the forces of reaction is the survival of their vulnerable way of life, made exponentially more legitimate and urgent than any other claim because it is cast as *the* American way of life. The stakes for MAGA entail reversing the laws and programs and institutions that in their view deny America as a Christian nation, depreciate America as a white nation, reverse the liberation of women (not least, control of their bodies), and cede sovereignty to a new world order. The aspiration is restoration of a partly real, partly imagined old order in which they felt at home: Make America Great Again.

This is the terrain on which the party of ungoverning engages those primed to support deconstruction. It does not take a majority of citizens or Republican voters, nor does it take opposition to every federal program, to give the party of ungoverning enough enthusiastic support to call deconstruction a political imperative, a popular demand, a democratic demand.

Trump combined deliverables and recognition, the two "results that matter" in an infamous pronouncement on August 15, 2017, when he was asked for his response to the march of neo-Nazis in Charlottesville, Virginia. The rally was attended by extremist David Duke and marked by chants that "Jews will not replace us." The march was a display of hate and intimidation. It was a scene of pandemonium in which a young woman was killed by a car driven into the crowd. In response to the question, the president offered his assessment: "You also had people that were very fine people, on both sides." With this, he signaled recognition of the marchers, and it was neither his first nor his last gesture of solidarity with them. In the same interview, Trump boasted of the material results his administration was delivering: "Look, you take a look. I've created over a million jobs since I'm President. The country is booming. The stock market is setting records. We have the highest employment numbers we've ever had in the history of our country. We're doing record business" (*New York Times* 2017).

The Reactionary Movement: The Act of Creation

MAGA did not exist as a recognizable agent at the center of public life—as a movement—until Trump brought it into being. The Tea Party was a precursor, as we discuss in chapter 5; its "plaintiff call" was "I want my country back," but the group was diffuse and leaderless (Skocpol and Williamson 2012, 7). Trump did not invent the grievances that propelled Americans to distrust, and beyond that, to despise the federal government.

He was not responsible for militia training in backwoods and waving "Don't tread on me" flags, or for the besotted love of guns. But he intuited popular rage, encouraged its untempered expression, and marshaled its elements for electoral purposes and other, violent purposes. And in doing this, he gave the forces of reaction an identity, a "we." He offered men and women with virulent grievances and desperate hopes for recognition a collective identity. He articulated a compelling portrait of "the people," he identified them as the real Americans, and he promised restoration of the country in which they felt at home.

He was the sorcerer, not the overwhelmed apprentice. Out of a diffuse set of resentments and disappointments and organizing models like the Tea Party, a new political agent was formed. Trump did more than unleash resentment, then; he created the movement, MAGA. He was their champion, their avenger. He awarded those in the reactionary movement the great good of recognition. "You're going to have plenty of power; you don't need anybody else. You're going to have somebody representing you very, very, well. Remember that" (Dias 2020). Trump gave them their power; in Hannah Arendt's terms, "Power corresponds to the human ability not just to act but to act in concert. . . . It belongs to a group and remains in existence only so long as the group keeps together" (Arendt 1972, 143).

That Trump did not have the support of established Republican leadership in his 2015–16 run for the presidency only augmented his appeal. Prior to the Republican nominating convention, Trump had fewer endorsements from governors and senators than any candidate since the end of World War II. He took this role on, exuding hostility and disrespect for party leaders. Giving conservative Republicans along with Democratic opponents the proverbial middle finger was a daily event, and thrilling. He slandered and threatened. He modeled disdain for both parties, for regular government business, and for the agencies and departments that make it work. He made "deep state" an everyday charge and deconstruction a promise.

What we call the reactionary movement should be seen not only as the electoral base of an altered Republican Party whose conservatism was in eclipse, but as an untethered political force that would not be contained by the ordinary institutions of political life. During his 2016 campaign Trump recognized this force as more than just a surge of Republican partisanship: "The silent majority is back. . . . The people are speaking. It's an amazing thing. It's like a movement" (Tarrow 2021, 175; Hochschild 2016, 226). Referring to his campaign and followers as a movement signaled that elections were not the only way to power, and that standard governing outputs were not the only reason to hold power. It signaled, too, that not even the office of the president could define and bound him. As one scholar of movements and parties observed, Trump "saw himself as the leader of a movement and not of a party or a government" (Tarrow 2021, 175). His language was not the language of an officeholder: "I am your warrior. I am your justice. And for those who have been wronged and betrayed: I am your avenger" (Arnsdorf and Stein 2023).

When Barack Obama campaigned for the presidency, his enthusiastic followers, too, gathered at huge rallies. "Yes we can!" This wave of Democrats and others, given new political life and hope, made it seem to Obama's followers that they were part of a movement. The moment promised a turning point in U.S. politics and culture—a turn away from racism and toward national unity. The moment seemed to be one of transformational politics. But as president, Obama was a sober negotiator and compromiser. He delivered policy, not ecstasy.

Trump, in contrast, kept his movement alive and active. He served up recognition daily, multiple times a day. His rallies continued. His every act was a spectacle. He rode the movement he had brought to life. Their support was necessary if the deep state was to be eradicated and his will unleashed: "There's never been a movement like this in the history of our country, probably in the history of every country" (Trump 2023c).

With the submissiveness and then increasingly active complicity of the Republican Party, Trump consolidated the supply side of ungoverning. His act of political creativity was to call into existence the demand side, a reactionary movement. To define Trumpism as amounting to a "message of grievance at the right time" (Corn 2022, 294) is accurate as far as it goes. But it omits the dynamic of recognition that bound people to this leader, its countercultural energy, its political project of ungoverning, and its ultimate but elusive goal of restoration. The "Again" in MAGA is a marker as significant as "Great."

Restoration Politics and Apocalypse

The anatomy of the movement Trump called forth and led can be correctly called a social movement and a political movement. But these do not capture what is distinctive about it—its combination of being counterculture and reactionary.

The tag "social movement" puts the focus on measurable characteristics such as class, education, region, rural/urban/suburban, age (this is not the 1960s youth movement!), and race. These characteristics help explain followers' beliefs, attitudes, and goals. To understand what MAGA is, it helps to know that nearly half earn at least $50,000 a year, for instance, and that about a third have a college degree (Blum and Parker 2021). But the "social" in "social movement" goes beyond objective markers; it points, as we've said, to common elements of the demand for recognition. "Social" is apt, too, because the movement's domain of activity is not restricted to formal institutions. Members are an active presence in the public spaces of civil (and "uncivil") society, in neighborhoods and families, on the street, and in the arenas of "social" media—the digital public squares and the dark, encrypted media locations as well. Social movements penetrate society all the way down. At the same time, the movement is, of course, a political movement intent on reshaping the Republican Party, electing people to office at all levels—national, state, and local. It began as a party within a party that succeeded in taking over the larger party altogether.

But MAGA also has to be understood as a cultural movement, or more specifically, a reactionary counterculture movement. It is devoted to eradicating liberal culture, broadly understood. It is a force against pluralism—that is, against feminism in all its shapes, racial diversity, secularism, and embrace of LGBTQ+ identities. Cultural pluralism arouses not only anger but disgust. The heroes of the reactionary movement are those who fight with no holds barred in each new incarnation of culture wars. In a survey of MAGA identifiers, almost all thought that "forces are changing our country for the worse" and "the American way of life is disappearing" (Blum and Parker 2021). These social, political, and cultural aspects of the movement come together in its defining aims: deconstruction as a prelude to restoration.

Visions of restoration of the true America can agitate and despoil, but they cannot be realized through normal democratic politics. Delegitimizing and deconstructing government are seen as necessary steps toward the goal, but by themselves they cannot make America great again. No act by Trump or any like-minded president, no political insurrection or rogue act of violence can reverse the fundamental fact of the United States as a pluralist society whose liberal democratic ethos, while clearly neither universally embraced nor invulnerable, is consolidated in many areas of law and social practice. Specific reversals—undoing a half century of constitutionally protected access to abortion, for example—are immensely significant for the lives of citizens and the deeply divided character of the nation. But from the reactionary standpoint, this is one small step.

Looking back, progressives have won many of the battles in the culture wars. In the 1970s feminism was controversial, but most agree that women should be able to participate as equals in the workforce. On other issues like same-sex marriage, public opinion has shifted emphatically. In 1996, when President Clinton signed the Defense of Marriage Act, only 27 percent of Americans thought same-sex marriages should be recognized on par with traditional marriage. Today, over 70 percent support recognizing same-sex marriages (McCarthy 2021). What once were cutting-edge progressive reforms are now accepted practice. Undoing pluralism would require a countercultural revolution.

The idea that the reactionary movement in power could change the public mind that now accepts same-sex marriage and the principle of gender equality is fantasy. The countercultural project would require acknowledging at the very least that the work of reversal would be uncertain, slow, and long-term, even with allies in friendly Supreme Court justices and public intellectuals. Even with evangelical and now Catholic thinkers who advocate a politico-religious restoration one scholar calls "common good constitutionalism" (Vermeule 2022). Yet for the reactionary movement, academic projects have little purchase, and judicial projects are slow. We know, however, that producing a new regime—even one cast as restoration—entails reeducation and rehabilitation society-wide. It requires generational work. It depends on obsession with institution-building and governing.

Demands for restoration can be roared; they are not unspeakable. The white nationalists who carried Confederate flags and gave the Hitler salute as they marched in Charlottesville did just that. MAGA promises just that. But even if it has the support of perhaps one-third of American voters and a fierce reactionary core, no party or movement can stop demographic change in a multiracial society. The fear broadcast by the "great replacement theory" that casts immigrants as "invaders" cannot be assuaged by border security. The invaders are already here; they are citizens of the United States. Economic and demographic forces across the globe continue to make Western societies pluralist in terms of race, religion, ethnicity, and language. This cannot be stopped dead and cannot be undone by restoration in one country—not without force, terror, and organized violence. And brutal authoritarianism.

This is why the reactionary movement is imbued with apocalypticism. The aura is there in its language and actions. It shapes conspiracist fantasies like QAnon, with its promise of the coming "storm." Apocalypticism entails total destruction. And in apocalyptic visions, restoration rises necessarily and on its own, a phoenix from the ashes.

Americans had a preview of reactionary apocalypticism in the Oklahoma City bomber, Timothy McVeigh, who brought down the Murrah Federal Building on April 19, 1995. The target was chosen because it was a site of the federal government; civil servants were going about the business of processing social security checks and getting aid to farmers. The date was chosen because it was an anniversary of the Waco, Texas, raid, which McVeigh saw as an act of mass murder of the Branch Davidian cult by the FBI. He imagined that his bombing would trigger a race war; the sight of the death and damage would attract more and more whites to violence, resulting finally in restoring a white supremacist nation. He prefigured the present reactionary movement in his identification with the patriots of 1776. Though he had no social media to connect him with kindred terrorists, only gun shows and the rantings of radio personality Rush Limbaugh, he was right to believe there was "an 'Army' of fellow believers somewhere out there" (Toobin 2023b, 56).

As we will come back to in chapter 6, during his 2024 campaign, Trump held a rally in Waco, Texas. The message the choice of location delivered to his followers was not solidarity with the FBI, but solidarity with anti-government violence (Bradner and Sullivan 2023). Trump promised the crowd, "I am your retribution" (Arnsdorf and Stein 2023).

We know what was supposed to follow: reinstating Trump as president and continuing the work of deconstruction. But what about the work of restoration? The conspiracists of January 6, some of whom identified with 1776 and called themselves "patriots," had no founding ideas or plans for restoring the Lost Cause. No proposals, much less deliberation, over what restorative arrangements might be like. No constitutional convention, no new compact. No lessons of history. No Tom Paine or James Madison. The same is true, we'll see in the next chapter, when the reactionary movement flirts with "secession" and harbors a vague idea of becoming founders of their own reconstituted nation. None of this is necessary in apocalypse.

Trump cast his recovery of the presidency not as the first step in what might have been expected to be a long project of restoration, but as the sufficient condition: "2024 is the final battle. It's going to be the big one. If you put me back in the White House, their reign will be over and America will be a free nation again."

And "if we don't win this next election, 2024, I truly believe our country is doomed. I think it's doomed" (Trump 2023c).

Everyday Gratifications

While waiting for apocalypse and restoration, the reactionary movement was less tuned into the slow work of ordinary politics than to immediate gratifications. In identifying these, we don't claim the authority of psychology. Rather, we offer an interpretation that fits with the logic of resentment and grievance and of belonging to a movement. As we've said, the fact that restoration is illusory means that followers must be bolstered by frequent, even everyday rewards, and these reveal a lot about the movement's character.

Foremost is license for performative aggression. Movements are fueled and grow by public performance—in this case, rallies, salutes, marches, displays of weapons and numbers, flags, and uniforms; these are emblems of collective identity and exhibitions of muscle and intimidation. There is the excitement of lashing out, throwing verbal stones, vilification, and not least, provoking incredulity and rage (Muirhead and Rosenblum 2019, 38). There is the frenzied echo of accusations and promises, back and forth between the president and his allies and crowds at rallies. Performative aggression enacts what it is to feel suddenly empowered, to belong to a movement that has to be taken seriously and feared.

Transgression of public norms brings its own satisfaction, in shocking unruliness and language (public vulgarity, obscene gestures and boasts, verbal bombardment) and hate speech (racist, antisemitic, anti-Muslim, anti-gay slurs, and attacks on trans children) joined by officials at the highest levels. "Transgressive" applies to the crowd's applause for roughing up dissenters, urged on by Trump when he spotted a protester at a rally and announced, "I'd like to punch him in the face," directing followers to "knock the crap out of him" (Diamond 2016; *Washington Post* 2016). Threats to shoot and kill appear in the ads of reactionary candidates for office (Center for American Progress 2022). There is no value to self-control, and no apologies for episodes like Trump's publicized 2022 pre-Thanksgiving dinner with the white nationalist, antisemitic, pro-Putin figure Nick Fuentes.

The reactionary movement trades in conspiracy, and this too has its rewards. The alternative reality pronounced—the assertions of a corrupt "deep state," the "rigged election," and depictions of Democrats as treasonous pedophiles—arouses feelings of righteous indignation. Gratifying, too, is that the barrage of conspiracy claims confuses and disorients everyone outside the movement. Bare assertion and incessant repetition—("Rigged!") replace evidence and argument, erasing shared grounds of understanding. And ordinary citizens experience this "conspiracy without the theory" for what it is—an assault on what it means to know something. This schism runs deeper than any other divergence and disagreement, deeper than political polarization. It is unbridgeable. We have been unwillingly drafted by the reactionary movement into a contest over who owns reality (Muirhead and Rosenblum 2019, 123).

For movement members, this brings its own special gratification beyond the infliction of disorientation: the pride of knowingness. Movement followers see themselves as a cognoscenti, an esoteric group, an elite. Their "evidence" of the deep state comes in code. Their certainty of a stolen election rests on elusive, ever-changing signals. They can read the signs of QAnon and anticipate the coming "storm." The status of esoteric knowers may come from "emancipation from reality"

(Villa 2021, 84), but it is a shared emancipation and a point of pride.

There is one more gratification served up to reactionary movement followers: the comradery on full show at Trump rallies. Commentator David French described it in "The Rage and Joy of MAGA America": "Can something be cheerful and dark at the same time?" he asks (French 2023). This mix of comradery and anger also marks activists in other social movements; the difference here is the magnetic force of a leader who directs the rage toward vituperation, institutional destruction, and violence.

These gratifications are vital. They are the day-to-day material of collective identity and mutual recognition. In the end, though, they are compensatory, because reactionary politics comes with the implicit understanding that no actual program or policy can deliver what the movement craves: reinstating white supremacy and ensuring permanent rule by their leader. No border wall or violent assault on responsible public officials transforms social and cultural backlash into restoration.

What *is* possible is deconstruction, ungoverning itself. One conservative scholar of public policy put it well: "This is not conservative. This is Lenin dismantling the institutions" (Peters 2018b). A Republican from Alabama, the chair of the Armed Services Committee, declared, "These are legislative terrorists" (Edsall 2023). Years before MAGA, House Speaker John Boehner described the Freedom Caucus as "anarchists" who want to "tear it all down and start over" (Nguyen 2017). The problem arises with starting over: historian Sean Wilentz tried to imagine what starting over would look like. What would follow from the 2020 coup d'état? He envisioned "a counter-government, administered by tweets, propped up by Fox News . . . a kind of Trumpian government in exile, run from Mar-a-Lago" (Edsall 2020).

The Anti-politics of "Right Now"

The reactionary movement is anti-party, anti-political, and demands satisfaction "right now!" It is anti-party because it is incapable of seeing any political opposition—or indeed, the practice of opposition—as legitimate. As the word "partisan" suggests, democratic representation depends on acknowledging that we are only a part and not the whole, and accepting that every victory is partial and temporary, valid only until the next election (Muirhead and Rosenblum 2019, 86). It takes political discipline to acknowledge partiality and to resist claiming the mantle of the nation, or claiming to represent all "real" Americans. For the forces of reaction, opposition must be rendered impotent and neutralized, its proponents disenfranchised. Party and elections are a useful tool until they are not.

The anti-political character of reaction broadens out with its second feature: demand for action *right now*. "The norms of governing are obstacles to the politics of immediacy" (Issacharoff 2023, 85). Electoral politics operates within a formal time frame, in the U.S. cycles of election every two and four years. When the imperative is immediate attack and immediate victory, however, political time is collapsed. Election cycles are intolerable impediments to "right now." Elections themselves are intolerably drawn-out affairs: long campaigns, time and place requirements, ballots, laborious vote counting, certification. The whole business is a highly administered process. "Right now" is imperative. When every action is a saving action, a sense of emergency displaces the constraints of democratic political time.

In democratic politics, nothing is "right now." Republicans boasted that they would get rid of Obamacare "on day one." Nothing happens on day one. Every political institution channels and checks decision-making and implementation so that with few exceptions (the clearest being response to a military attack), governing is slow, results even slower. For the reactionary movement, however, anything drawn out by procedures or incremental by design is anathema.

The intemperate demand for immediacy helps explain the incessant, abrupt designations of new targets. Day to day, hour by hour, in tweets and by innuendo, new enemies are identified and the reactionary movement's fever for immediacy is momentarily satisfied.

Symbolic measures are also important in generating a feeling that things are happening "right now." Shows of action pretend to produce something immediately. In place of legislative activity and administrative implementation come gestures like addressing a complex legal and economic policy such as immigration by offering up a wall.

In 2016, for the first time in its existence, the Republican Party eliminated its party platform. Platforms are a way to address the many demands of a political coalition and to guide and constrain elected officials. The message delivered by this omission was that the president personally would make decisions "right now." The hunger for immediate action can be realized by substituting personal will for governing.

Platforms, by contrast, stand for the idea that parties are more than the expression of one candidate's will. Parties are coalitions joined by shared purposes. In this respect, the transformation of the Republican Party into an ungoverning party is critical. As a movement, MAGA may not last beyond Trump's moment in American political life. But when a movement takes over a major political institution like the Republican Party, its force is poised to endure. We take this up in the next chapter.

5

The Ungoverning Party

In May 2023, long before the Republican presidential primaries, Trump performed at a CNN-sponsored town hall. The *New York Times* described him signaling "an escalation of his bid to bend the government to his wishes . . . only this time with a greater command of the Republican Party's pressure points and a plan to demolish the federal bureaucracy" (Goldmacher et al. 2023). The plan was not subtle: "I will totally obliterate the Deep State" (Trump 2023b).

It might seem as if ungoverning is inextricably bound up with Trump. Yet, the future of ungoverning does not depend solely on the former president. Whether ungoverning continues depends ultimately on whether it is institutionalized within and comes to define the Republican Party. It is ironic to imagine that anti-institutionalism can be institutionalized. But that is what any project or program—or even revolution—requires to outlast those who began it.

Because Trump commanded a movement, and because members of that movement vote in large numbers in Republican primary elections, almost all candidates who vied to defeat Trump in 2024 also emulated him. They did not want him, but they wanted his movement. One candidate for the Republican nomination, Vivek Ramaswamy, cut to the heart of ungoverning: "I will shut down the fourth branch of government, the administrative state. You cannot tame that beast. You must end it" (Ramaswamy 2023). Did that mean that Ramaswamy, as president, would have denied the post-hurricane emergency aid that another Trump emulator, Florida governor Ron DeSantis, urgently requested in 2022?

How did we arrive at the point where the Republican Party has become and indeed defines itself as an ungoverning party? Let's reverse the usual question "How do parties build government institutions capable of handling pandemics and all the challenges of a modern economy in a global system?" (Popkin 2021, 198). How can they *not* build them? What if they don't try?

In schematic outline, the Republican Party has followed a path from small-government conservatism to unyielding political obstruction, provoking the now-familiar charge that the Republican Party is no longer "a governing party" (Kabaservice 2012). The party's obstructionism fueled increasingly vociferous anti-government ideology: "Don't tread on me." And eventually, the Republican Party took the step from obstructionism to the deconstruction of the administrative state—to ungoverning. This step was accompanied by the conspiracist claim that the administrative state is captured by a malignant "deep state," which makes the party's willful incapacitation of government both thinkable and celebrated by its core support: the reactionary counterculture. By the time Trump pushed anti-governmental ideology over the edge into ungoverning, there were no resources left in the Republican outlook that could be harnessed to defend governing institutions. Party officials and elected representatives fell in line; if they were not MAGA enthusiasts, they were mute and submissive.

To underline how foreign grasp of the necessity of administration has become within the Republican Party, consider how unlikely it would be today for any member of the party leadership to echo what former Republican Speaker of the House John Boehner wrote in his 2021 memoir: bureaucrats "can be annoying as hell, but many of them actually do important jobs. They keep the machinery going—getting out Social Security checks and tax refunds, putting together scientific studies, paying and caring for servicemembers, tracking the weather—and we need them" (Boehner 2021, 191).

Reagan's Ambivalent Legacy

The recent history of the Republican Party is one of a long, troubled transformation from small-government conservatism into anti-government ungoverning. Parts of the story we tell here have been told in greater detail by political scientists and historians (Tarrow 2021; Milibank 2022; Peters 2022; Kabaservice 2012; Zelizer 2020; Fried and Harris 2021; Janda 2022; Popkin 2021; Richardson 2014; Stevens 2020). Our account is designed to highlight the key turning points in the path to ungoverning.

The Republican Party of Abraham Lincoln and Theodore Roosevelt built the modern state. Lincoln, the founder of the party, inscribed not only a rejection of slavery but a positive commitment to equality and opportunity at the core of its definition. This required both programmatic legislation like the Homestead Act (1862) and the Morrill Act (1862) establishing state universities, and constitutional refounding crystallized in the Thirteenth, Fourteenth, and Fifteenth Amendments

(Richardson 2014, 25–54). A generation later, Theodore Roosevelt built administrative institutions such as the Food and Drug Administration of 1906 that could regulate corporate power on behalf of consumers and workers. The Republican Party was the party of state-building; it inherited the mission of the Federalists and Whigs before it, "to make the nation more of a nation" (Beer 1966, 71). But in one of the great inversions of U.S. party politics, the Democratic Party—which had been for over a century the party of states' rights and slavery—adopted that cause as its own. In 1932, Franklin Roosevelt radically expanded the administrative state in order to meet the twin threats of economic depression in the 1930s and fascism in the 1940s.

Roosevelt's radical reformulation of the national government was fueled by an electoral coalition that endured for half a century—a fusion of southern whites and northern laborers. It lasted until the 1960s, when southern whites, enraged by the Democratic Party's embrace of civil rights, began migrating out of the party. They gravitated to the Republican Party led by Richard Nixon, who pursued the "southern strategy" of recruiting white voters in the South and embracing states' rights as the "new federalism" (Phillips 1969; Katz 2014). The canonical proclamation of the end of the New Deal formula for solving public problems was Ronald Reagan's at his 1981 inauguration: "Government is not the solution to our problems. Government is the problem" (Reagan 1981).

It is hard, looking back decades later, to convey the force of the moment when Reagan uttered these words. Conservatives hadn't held control of any of the branches of the national government for half a century—since Herbert Hoover countered the Great Depression with nothing but a commitment to small government and rugged individualism. Following FDR and the New Deal, no one could win national elections who opposed an active, interventionist state. The New Deal state alleviated poverty among the nation's elderly with signature policies like Social Security, a policy that even Republicans like Eisenhower supported. Eisenhower used a military justification to advance the largest construction project in human history, the building of the interstate highway system. Both parties came to endorse state management of the macroeconomy with a view to balancing inflation and unemployment. The scope of the administrative state that FDR built was expanded to encompass civil rights in the 1960s, cleaned America's rivers, protected its wilderness, and extended health care guarantees to the nation's elderly.

This is why people called opposition to these developments the "Reagan revolution." To be sure, "it was less a revolution than a consolidation of trends that began over the previous three decades" (Tarrow 2021, 128). Still, Reagan's 1980 victory empowered the ideal of small-government conservatism, and his forty-nine-state reelection victory in 1984 signaled that if the New Deal was not exactly over, its momentum had been arrested. Would it replace New Deal liberalism with a new public philosophy, or would it merely arrest it?

One step toward a new public philosophy was the equation of government regulation with tyranny. Reagan's small-government stance was focused on deregulation—"get the government off the backs of the great American people," meaning off the backs of business (Oreskes and Conway 2023, 333). He had honed this message during his stint as host for *General Electric Theater*, which brought his face and voice into households across the nation and engrained in the public the idea that political and economic freedom were "indivisible." Regulated markets lead to the destruction of other freedoms was the mantra. In this, Reagan was simplifying an argument promulgated by economic theorists that by the 1980s had a profound effect on public attitudes: "In the 1920s, Americans hated 'Big Business'; Reagan would persuade us to hate 'Big Government'" (187). As historians Naomi Oreskes and Erik M. Conway put it, the key element of Reagan's political speeches "was equating market-forward economic policies with freedom and, conversely, reducing freedom to market-oriented policies" (358).

Yet even Reagan was selective in his small government project: he wanted to use big government (i.e., the military) to deter Soviet expansion across the globe. Nor did he aim to eliminate the entitlement at the heart of the New Deal, Social Security. And philosophically, he suggested he had a personal affinity for Roosevelt and the New Deal, even insisting, "I did not leave the Democratic Party. The Democratic Party left me." His famous inaugural proclamation was tempered by an introductory qualification: "*In the present crisis* . . . government is not the solution to our problems" (Reagan 1981; emphasis added). He left open the possibility that in some contexts, government *is* the solution.

This is Reagan's ambivalent legacy. Would small-government conservatism be an alternative or merely a corrective to what conservatives saw as the excesses of liberalism? Was Reagan's legacy a pragmatic conservatism that said go slow? Or was it something more radical—an implicit call to go back rather than to go slow? Which reading of Reagan's legacy would shape the Republican Party's orientation to governing?

Republicans Govern: The Bush Presidencies

The two Bush presidents, George H. W. and George W., stood for a Republican Party that would govern, but their efforts were ultimately defeated. Reagan's immediate successor, George H. W. Bush, was a conservative by ancestry, wealth, and temperament; he was conservative by character, not ideology. The word "prudent" summed him up. During his presidency, the comedian Dana Carvey's imitations of Bush on *Saturday Night Live* gave rise to the satirical catchphrase "Not gonna do it— wouldn't be prudent" (Von Drehle 2018).

But Bush was unable to solicit the loyalties of a newer breed of radical and pugnacious Republicans such as Georgia congressman Newt Gingrich, who was less interested in prudence than in political combat. Bush was never at home with "the right wing of his party or Reaganite ideology" (Kabaservice 2012, 372). His 1990 compromise with Democrats in Congress to increase taxes in exchange for spending cuts laid the foundation for a balanced budget, but because his budget deal contained a tax increase, it was viewed by his fellow Republicans as apostasy. The betrayal was underscored by the memorable campaign promise Bush had made back in 1988: "Read my lips: no new taxes!" When Bush lost to Clinton in 1992, the lesson to Republicans was never raise taxes and never compromise.

The second Bush president, George W., arrived in the White House eight years after the first one left (with Bill Clinton sandwiched in between). He and his strategist Karl Rove set their sights on forging a "long-lasting, dominant Republican majority" (Lemann 2003). Within six years, this ambition would be lost in the sands in Iraq. Still, in the moment of his inauguration, Bush aimed to do what no Republican had done since the beginning of the New Deal: adapt Reagan's small-government ideology into a set of policies and programs that would prove so popular that they would, he hoped, propel Republican majorities into the House and Senate and elect Republican presidents for generations.

The durable governing majority that Bush sought brought conservatism toward the center by adopting a value ordinarily associated with liberal Democrats—compassion. "Compassionate conservatism" would address popular concerns about education with policies like No Child Left Behind. It would address the rising cost of pharmaceuticals with a new Medicare prescription drug entitlement. It would champion comprehensive immigration reform.

Perhaps Bush could have succeeded were not for the terrorist attack of 9/11, which was his provocation to first invade Afghanistan in 2001 and then Iraq in 2003. These resulted in military failures that were evident by 2006, when voters put the Democrats back in control of the U.S. House for the first time since 1994. Two comprehensive military debacles consumed Bush's presidency, and "endless wars" bedeviled the next three presidents.

Both Bush presidents attempted to solidify Reagan's revival of the Republican Party. For George H. W. Bush, fiscal probity was at the heart of a genuinely conservative approach to government: balanced budgets, even at the cost of tax hikes. For George W., the way to make conservativism a governing philosophy was to show that a conservative party could offer public policies addressing broad public needs. Neither Bush succeeded. After them, the party that still called itself "conservative" would constitute an unyielding oppositional force everywhere and all the time, but one lacking an "ability to govern" (Kabaservice 2012, xix).

A Party against Governing

No post-Reagan Republican personifies the spirit of pure opposition and obstruction like former Speaker of the House Newt Gingrich. It was Gingrich who brought House Republicans to the majority in 1992. When he entered Congress in 1979,

Republicans had been in the minority for almost all of the previous fifty-five years. He itched to find new ways of disrupting the entrenched Democratic majority. Irreverent and bombastic, shredding settled norms came naturally to him. He was the first to see the potential of playing to the C-SPAN cameras, giving speeches to an empty chamber, knowing that the speeches would rally true believers. In response, Democratic Speaker of the House Tip O'Neill ordered the cameras to pan the empty room and reveal the sham. Gingrich first came to national attention in a fracas with O'Neill over his charge that Democrats were unpatriotic. This taught him that picking fights was a better path to publicity than policy lectures. The lesson was clear: "You don't get any benefit from cooperation or compromise, only confrontation" (Draper 2023b).

Yet, Gingrich was also something of a policy wonk. He led House Republicans to victory in 1992 by uniting them behind a legislative platform that detailed ten bills, called the Contract with America, which Republicans promised to pass in the first hundred days in office (Gingrich 1994). It seemed for a moment that if Gingrich had been a "political wrecking ball" in opposition, as leader of the House majority he might govern—and even restore to Congress the capacity for policy initiative that long had been relegated to the executive (Zelizer 2020, 38). Yet he failed to enact his promised agenda. Even today, Gingrich is touted instead as the originator of a "no-holds-barred style of partisan warfare where . . . it was fair game to shatter routine legislative processes in pursuit of power" (Zelizer 2020, 6). He "began the zero-sum politics that mutated into the brand of the Tea Party and Trump M.A.G.A. Republicans" (Draper 2023b).

This obstructionist style of politics, fatal to governing, was amplified in 2009 with the election of Barack Obama as president. Texas attorney general (later to become governor) Greg

Abbott said, "What I really do for fun is I go into the office [and] sue the Obama Administration" (Kettl 2020, 165). For many Americans, not Republicans only, the Obama presidency was "scary." The elevation of an African American with an unusual name portended a nation in which whites were no longer the dominant group (Skocpol and Williamson 2012, 48, 78). Immediately after Obama's victory, an unanticipated oppositional movement arose full force.

The Tea Party was a "hybrid"—simultaneously a grassroots movement with over one thousand local organizations and at the same time, one that would attract money from "billionaire-funded political action committees and long-time free market advocacy organizations" (Skocpol and Williamson 2012, 12; Tarrow 2021, 162). Supporters comprised a mix of fiscal conservatives intent on tax cuts and social reactionaries moved by animus toward Obama (tagged a foreign-born Muslim) and toward Black and brown Americans broadly. Amateur political activists were commingled with professional politicos and a network of conservative donors associated with the Koch brothers and the battery of organizations they funded. These forces collaborated for purposes of lobbying, advertising, mobilizing, and creating associations of students and legal professionals that became central to the aim of "whittling down the regulatory state" (Tarrow 2021, 169). With this, the Tea Party "presaged the merger of populism and plutocracy" (160).

Tea Partiers wanted to defeat not just Democrats but also any Republican who would cooperate with the Obama administration. Their mission was to purge the party of RINOs (Republicans in Name Only), using weapons that had once been reserved for defeating the Democratic opposition—raising money to unseat their own colleagues and humiliating their own party leaders (Popkin 2021, 6). They were insurgents within the party. These insurgents "laid the foundation for a new and even more disruptive movement/party interaction" (Tarrow 2021, 165).

But the Tea Party was largely a spent force by 2016 (Jossey 2016). Trump seized on the spirit that had animated its grass roots: "I want my country back." From its spirit and energy, he conjured something new. He fired up the fury and imagination of aggrieved but unorganized haters of government. He fused them all with the Republican Party, a party that would become known not for governing but for obstruction—and then for ungoverning.

Harbingers of Ungoverning

The Republican Party's move to intractable obstruction is crystallized in three episodes: the vote against the Troubled Asset Relief Program (TARP) in 2008, the debt limit crisis of 2013, and the inability to offer a substitute for Obamacare in 2016. Importantly, all these episodes also illustrate the ungovernability of the party itself.

In the late summer of 2008, George W. Bush's treasury secretary, Henry Paulson, was so worried about a collapse of the global financial system that he had rushed away from meetings with recurrent bouts of dry heaves. The national economy—and the economies of countries around the world—depended on government intervention to allay investors' panic by arresting what some worried would become a cascade of bank failures. Paulson hammered out a plan known as TARP, a $700 billion plan that would allow the Treasury Department to take bad asserts off the balance sheets of systemically important financial institutions. Paulson negotiated the specifics of the plan with the Bush White House and senators and members of

Congress from both parties, and vetted it with both presidential candidates, Barack Obama and John McCain. Vice President Dick Cheney traveled to Capitol Hill to advocate for the plan. Republican party leaders, Bush and McCain, unambiguously supported it. Democratic leadership was willing to deliver their votes to pass the program, but when it came up for a vote in the House, two-thirds of Republicans defeated it. They offered no alternative plan. Their position was to do nothing.

The consequences were immediate: in response to TARP's defeat, the stock market crashed and the Dow had its largest one-day decline in history. That was a harbinger of the damage that would come with a party that abdicated responsibility for governing. The jolt was sufficient to prompt just enough Republicans to change their minds when the measure was reintroduced and finally passed (Paulson 2010, 316–21; Isidore 2008).

The second episode crystallizes the destructive energy that defined the Republican Party after Obama came to office. In 2013, the House Republican majority used the "debt ceiling" to try to force the president to defund his signature Affordable Care Act. As the moment approached when the United States would default on its debt, it became clear that many Republicans in the House welcomed the catastrophe. Finally, Congress passed legislation to raise the debt limit and avert default with a bill most Republicans in the House voted against. Destruction was more important than a functioning government and economy (Popkin 2021, 231). As former House Speaker John Boehner wrote in his 2021 memoir,

> I would see it played out over and over again. . . . It wasn't about any so-called principles—it was about chaos. But it was chaos that developed in a predictable pattern: the far-right knuckleheads would refuse to back the House

leadership no matter what, but because they were "insurgents" they never had the responsibility of trying to actually fix things themselves. So they got to "burn it all down" and screw up the legislative process, which of course allowed them to continue to complain loudly about how Washington's spending problem never got solved. (Boehner 2021, 159)

The third episode also concerns the policy Republicans most yearned to defeat: the Affordable Care Act, Obama's greatest legislative achievement, which had passed in 2010 without a single GOP vote. By 2016, overturning "Obamacare" (a term Republicans invented, which Democrats came to embrace) became the highest priority of the Republican Party. In the four years after Republicans won a majority in the House in 2011, they voted fifty-four times to repeal the Affordable Care Act (O'Keefe 2014). By early 2016, the House had voted to repeal the act sixty times, all in vain (Reuters 2016). They finally got their chance after Trump was elected and Republicans had majorities in both the House and the Senate. As a candidate in 2016, Trump had insisted that ending Obamacare would be easy. "My first day in office, I am going to ask Congress to put a bill on my desk getting rid of this disastrous law and replacing it with reforms that expand choice, freedom, affordability," he said weeks before the November election. "You're going to have such great health care at a tiny fraction of the cost. And it's going to be so easy" (Donovan and Kelly 2017).

Trump's promise—"great health care at a tiny fraction of the cost"—was all bombast, no plan. There was no diagnosis of the failings of the Affordable Care Act, and no policy proposals to remedy those failings. When the critical vote to repeal Obamacare finally came up in July 2017, it failed only because Republican senator John McCain cast the decisive vote against it. McCain opposed Obamacare but voted against the Republican bill because it contained "no replacement to actually reform our health care system and deliver affordable quality health care" (Davis and Domenico 2017). McCain wanted more than opposition and obstruction; he wanted the Republican Party to govern.

The Ungovernable Party Embraces Ungoverning

By 2018 it was understood that the party had given up on governing. This was not just an assessment from outside, it was a boast. One of the few remaining moderate Republicans put it well: "As a member of the governing wing of the Republican Party, I've worked to instill stability, certainty, and predictability in Washington. I've fought to fulfill the basic functions of government, like keeping the lights on and preventing default. Regrettably, that has not been easy" (Cillizza 2018).

The Republican Party came to be at war with itself as well. The war went way beyond the usual language and decibels of dissent that characterize any coalition party (Klein 2023a). Its internal chaos was televised hour by hour in 2023 when it took fifteen rounds of voting to elect a Republican Speaker of the House. The issue dividing the holdouts from the majority that favored Representative Kevin McCarthy was neither ideology nor policy. They were promised rules changes and House committee assignments that would give them platforms for obstruction and guarantee that Congress could not function as a governing body. Even after electing the Speaker, Republicans could not negotiate raising the debt ceiling with President Biden in 2023 because they could not agree on or explain what they wanted. Yet the party that took fifteen votes to elect a speaker was able to speedily agree to order the removal of metal detectors installed after the January 6 coup attempt at the Capitol. Increasingly, the GOP was described, even by some officials, as "ungovernable." Former Speaker Gingrich approvingly observed of the new 2023 Republican majority that they were "essentially bringing 'Lord of the Flies' to the House of Representatives" (Draper 2023b). The party could not govern itself, and it did not intend to govern the country.

The regression from Reagan's Republican Party to Trump's— from opposition to big government to incessant obstruction, and then to active ungoverning—was marked by a change in content as well as political strategy. Reagan's small government conservatism aimed at freeing markets to ensure prosperity and freedom. The charge of "government tyranny" had metastasized. The Republican Party, now fueled by a reactionary movement, was animated by revulsion at the entire panoply of liberal political, social, and cultural aims: controlling guns, enforcing civil rights, and tolerating and accommodating religious, racial, and cultural pluralism. The tone of anti-government sentiment had moved far from Reagan's sunny optimism to fury and conspiracism—to "bring it all crashing down."

The Reactionary Movement Meets the Ungoverning Party

Once the reactionary movement was given a collective identity and mobilized by Trump, it fused with the Republican Party, or rather, the party fused with the movement. The president was the axis of both. This fusion of major political party and reactionary movement is unusual—extraordinary, in fact. It's said that "it is hard to turn political campaigns into movements; it is just as difficult to turn movements into party campaigns" (Judis 2016, 86). Parties are coalitions ultimately constructed for electoral purposes; movements are mission-driven. Each can benefit from the other (Schlozman 2015). Movements offer parties connections to the activated grass roots; parties offer movements access to political office, which they need to accomplish their goals (Milkis and Tichenor 2019). And yet, there is tension between the two. Building a large electoral coalition requires compromise, but movements are built on passions, not compromises. In the past, the Democratic Party's root and energy was the labor movement; the Republican Party's was evangelical churches; and parties and movements were entwined in a complex dance (Schlozman 2015).

The new fusion of Republican Party and reactionary movement is a remarkably "potent hybrid" (Tarrow 2021, 6). Trump created a movement of his own and with it, he took over the party. Both elements—the reactionary movement and the remade Republican Party—were uninterested not only in compromise but in governing.

Its failure to accomplish the first necessity of running Congress was televised in 2023, when after the Republican Party had narrowly won the House, it could not agree on electing a Speaker. The moment before the election of a Speaker, the body is constitutionally anarchic; absent someone in the office of Speaker, the majority is unable to act. And things got worse: shortly after narrowly agreeing to elevate Kevin McCarthy to Speaker, his caucus ousted him but was unable to agree on a replacement. For over three weeks in 2023, Congress could not function, during which time the country faced another debt limit crisis and the necessity of responding to Hamas's attack on Israel. Eventually, the exhausted Republican caucus settled on Mike Johnson, a little-known representative from Louisiana who called for "biblically sanctioned government" (Corn 2023a). Johnson had played a significant part in Trump's ploys to overturn the election in 2023 (Motion to Leave to File Brief as Amicus Curiae, Texas v. Pennsylvania, 592 U.S.___ [2020] [No. 155, Orig.]). His first act as Speaker was to make the passage of a critical foreign aid bill in support of U.S. allies Israel and Ukraine conditional on a $14.3 billion cut in funding for the IRS—a move that was sure to fail and to paralyze Congress's capacity to act.

The fusion of the Republican Party and the MAGA movement altered what had once been a conservative party, and more recently an obstructionist party disinterested in governing, into a reactionary party bent on deconstruction. MAGA Republicans slough off conservative ideology as an establishment concern. For them, the malignancy of liberal pluralism and Democratic treason cannot be met with fiscal restraint or family values. What reversal and restoration require is destruction. And the demand is for destruction 'right now'! The movement's leader promises just that.

A governing party depends on elected office and state capacity. An ungoverning party attacks the administrative state and gives satisfaction right now to the movement that lives outside institutions. The reactionary movement's natural habitat is at large and online. It lives by marches, rallies, a blizzard of tweets, and brandishing guns that display its numbers, force and intensity. It lives by intimidation, and ultimately, violence.

6

Violence

Undoing the administrative state incapacitates whole swaths of government. Defunding the Internal Revenue Service curtails the government's ability to collect taxes; upending diplomatic protocols at the State Department sows national and international confusion and invites avoidable conflict; cultivating chaos at the U.S. Postal Service prevents the timely delivery of absentee ballots during elections. Ungoverning in the extreme goes further. It corrodes the essential state capacity to maintain a peaceful civil society. Ungoverning leads to violence–not simply infractions committed by individuals against other individuals, but violence by groups seeking to impose their own imagined social order on the nation. And when those in office incite or exploit rogue violence by individuals and organized violence by armed groups, ungoverning has reached its nadir.

Weak states are marked by the inability to fulfill the essential function of eliminating organized violence by insurgent groups. Historically, the United States has had its share of political

uprisings and armed insurgencies. Even strong states have diffi-
culties maintaining and enforcing a monopoly of organized use
of violence. Consider the ongoing efforts to eradicate organized
crime. Ungoverning is, once again, something else—the abdication of government's "monopoly of the legitimate use of force,"
a phrase that comes from Max Weber's classic definition of the
state.

The state is the *only* entity that can legitimately claim the
right to forcibly deprive people of their liberty by imprisoning
them, take their property by fining them, conscript them to fight
a war, and impose a death sentence and execute them (Weber
[1921] 1946, §278). Criminal gangs may do all these things, but
only the state claims the legitimate authority to do them. In a
liberal democracy, what makes it legitimate is that the government is founded on consent and is constitutionally limited.

When the state is constrained by due process and rule of
law, as it is in liberal democracies, the monopoly on violence
is what keeps citizens safe. It reflects the classic Lockean trade
in the state of nature, in which men and women give up the
right to individually defend themselves by assigning the punishment of infractions to government. Government assures them
that others will be deterred from violence against their person
and property, and in exchange, they do not need to fear each
other or a war of all against all. In Hannah Arendt's words, a
state uses violence to "assure its own survival and the survival
of lawfulness" (Arendt [1963] 1994, 291).

Violence in the Shadows

Although every state claims a monopoly of violence, the liberal democratic state bears a distinct relationship to it, for
revolutionary violence is always potentially justified, and that

justification is explicit, built into democratic theory. If the state turns against the people and uses violence to oppress, citizens are justified in taking up arms against it. In John Locke's foundational account, "If a long train of abuses, prevarications, and artifices, all tending the same way, make the design visible to the people . . . 'tis not to be wondered they should then rouse themselves, and endeavor to put the rule into such hands, which may secure to them the ends for which government was at first erected" (Locke [1690] 1961). Jefferson echoed this a hundred years later in the Declaration of Independence: "A long train of abuses and usurpations, pursuing invariably the same Object evinces a design to reduce them under absolute Despotism, it is their right, it is their duty, to throw off such Government" (Jefferson [1776] 1975, 236). Resistance to the state is both principled and legitimate.

This specter of justified violence used *against* the state is always in the shadows. It is always thinkable. To be willing to contemplate it is not to be seditious, but vigilant; citizens stand ready to defend rights and liberty with their own arms. The constitutional right to bear arms was originally understood as necessary to defend liberty against a potentially tyrannical state. The anti-government militia movement that has moved from the fringes to the center of American political life is a distorted extreme in its imaginings of tyranny everywhere, but it is not anomalous in a culture that reveres personal freedom and idolizes guns: a militiaman "is a stranger of a strange land, warped not against his culture but by it, and the curve of his warp follows the curve of the culture; it is only steeper and continues farther, off the edge of the graph" (Kelly 1995).

The ever-present possibility of revolution makes political violence thinkable in a liberal democracy. What would be seditious in other states is patriotic in a liberal state, at least in theory. This in turn can make partisan political violence think-able as well, if partisans view their rivals as bent on pursuing a path that would lead the country to ruin. Then they see the prospect of the opposition party in office as not only risky or unwise but catastrophic; the opposition in power would change the country irretrievably. It would sacrifice constitutional essentials, violate individual rights, weaken national security, destroy the economy, and alter—that is, pollute—the character of the nation. This is not purely conceptual. In the United States today, over 60 percent of both Democrats and Republicans see the other as "a serious threat," and about 40 percent of each party see the other as "downright evil" (Kalmoe and Mason 2022, 47).

When violence stays in the shadows, it is in part because leaders work intentionally to keep it there. Responsible politi-cal leaders can see into the shadows where revolutionary and partisan violence lurk, knowing that domestic political vio-lence has bloodied the past and could again. They do what they can to keep politics peaceful. They concede when they lose elections. In the public interest, they ratchet down passions after hard-fought political campaigns and harsh conflicts over policies. They speak with restraint when talking to or about the opposition, "my colleagues." They set an example for their supporters because they know what passionate partisans might be goaded into doing.

On the other hand, the forces of "uncivil society" are brought to life and take center stage by the abdication of government responsibility to keep the peace. Violence, threat, and intimida-tion provide the most provocative and frightening evidence of democracy in danger, and licensing these is a form of ungov-erning. Violence is a different order of degradation from every-thing else. Waves of threat and intimidation galvanize citizens not only to fear where democracy is heading but also to make them suffer insecurity right now.

We are going to follow the connection between ungoverning and violence to its many locations. We understand that in the aggregate, popular support for political violence is low. Both Democrats and Republicans oppose violence against their opponents—according to one study, "fewer than 4% of Americans support violent crimes like assault or arson against political opponents" (Polarization Research Lab 2024). Still, we attend to the way ungoverning calls violence out of the shadows because "even small numbers of people who encourage or engage in violence can have dangerous and destabilizing effects on our political system" (Bright Line Watch 2021). And they can bring fear and insecurity to everyday life.

Violence out of the Shadows

When leaders issue invitations to violence, however subtle, they abdicate the fundamental responsibility of governing. These invitations include sending messages that violence against the opposition is acceptable, galvanizing private militias that execute what are effectively commands from elected officials, and redeploying captured state institutions responsible for keeping the peace—the military, the FBI, and other security agencies. Threats of physical violence against not only the opposition but also Republican senators and their families intimidated them from voting to convict Trump after his second impeachment (Benen 2023).

Today, invitations to violence often accompany the overthrow of norms that were thought to constrain threats against political opponents. Instead of a regulated rivalry, officials call on their followers to intimidate and assault the opposition.

In February 2016, Trump was told by his security team prior to a campaign rally in Cedar Rapids, Iowa, to be prepared for someone in the audience throwing tomatoes: "If you see somebody getting ready to throw a tomato, knock the crap out of them, would you? Seriously. Just knock the hell out of them. I promise you, I will pay for the legal fees. I promise." This scene was repeated often enough to stir up perpetual rage in crowds prepared to fight. At a 2016 campaign rally in Las Vegas, Trump said of a protester, "I'd like to punch him in the face." As security guards escorted the protester out of the rally, Trump reminisced, "I love the old days. You know what they used to do to guys like that when they were in a place like this? They'd be carried out on a stretcher, folks" (Fabiola 2021).

The startling thing is how overt these calls for intimidation and violence have become. And how they have been taken up by Republican officials in the states. Florida governor Ron DeSantis excels in this, promising, for example, that migrants smuggling drugs across the southern border would be shot and left "stone cold dead." He did not explain how law enforcement would identify them, saying, "Same way somebody operating in Iraq would know. . . . These people in Iraq . . . they all looked the same. . . . Guys have to make judgments" (Goodman and Nehamas 2023). Campaigning for president in New Hampshire in 2023, the governor promised, "All of these deep-state people, you know, we are going to start slitting throats on Day 1" (Medina 2023).

Excusing violence has become standard for many Republican Party officials. Looking back at the January 6 insurrection, Republicans continue to defend it. Campaigning for the 2024 presidential election, Trump received applause when he said he would pardon the now-imprisoned attackers, which would include Proud Boys convicted of seditious conspiracy (Terkel

2023). He called them "hostages": "They ought to release the J6 hostages," he said. "They suffered enough" (CTV News 2024). Congresswoman Marjorie Taylor Greene boasted that if she had been in charge of the attack on the Capitol, "we would have won . . . not to mention, it would've been armed" (Duster 2022). Other Republicans remain mute, which licenses angry followers to threaten, intimidate, and kill. Disavowals of violence have to be coaxed out of Republican leaders, and then they are erratic and unconvincing. The common thread is this: when threats, intimidation, and violence are not opposed by elected officials, silence as well as provocation amounts to support for ungoverning in this, its most extreme form. Silence cedes government's monopoly on legitimate violence to reactionary forces operating outside of and against the law.

The call to violence has become a normal part of political talk. In March 2023, Trump held a campaign rally in Waco, Texas, which in 1993 had been the site of the violent clash between federal agents and an extremist religious sect called the Branch Davidians. The clash left eighty-two members of the cult and four agents dead. For Timothy McVeigh and militant groups today like the Proud Boys and Oath Keepers, Waco was the animating representation of a tyrannical government bent on imposing martial law (Homans 2023). Trump used this stage to send a message to movement supporters by casting himself, and them, as targets of tyrants: "The Biden regime's weaponization of law enforcement against their political opponent is something straight out of the Stalinist Russia Horror Show"; and "Under Joe Biden, American Patriots are being arrested and held in captivity like animals." His allies in the party were just as ferocious. Senator Rick Scott called the FBI investigation of Trump's theft of classified documents "acting like the Gestapo." Death threats against Democrats figured in campaign literature and in videos for candidates for Congress and governorships (Toobin 2020, 372).

In 2023, the four-time indicted former president urged followers to take action to defend him against the judicial system, calling the prosecutor in two federal cases, Jack Smith, "deranged" and a "thug," and Judge Tanya S. Chutkan, who presided over *United States of America v. Donald J. Trump*, "a biased, Trump Hating Judge" (Polantz 2023). Trump cast himself as a martyr, persecuted by a politicized justice system: "Every time the radical-left-Democrats, Marxists, communists, and fascists indict me, I consider it a great badge of courage. . . . I'm being indicted for you. . . . They're not coming after me, they're coming after you. And I'm just standing in their way" (Dixon 2023).

Judge Chutkan saw this for what it was—a thinly veiled call for violence and imposed a partial gag order. The judge aimed "to ensure that extrajudicial statements do not prejudice these proceedings." She observed, "When Defendant has publicly attacked individuals, including on matters related to this case, those individuals are consequently threatened and harassed," among them "potential witnesses, prosecutors, and court staff." She continued, "Defendant has made those statements to national audiences using language communicating not merely that he believes the process to be illegitimate, but also that particular individuals involved in it are liars, or "thugs," or deserve death" (United States of America v. Donald J. Trump, Opinion and Order, Criminal Action No. 23-257 [TSC], Document 105 [Aug. 1, 2023]). Another close follower of the proceedings was blunt: "Donald Trump is going to get someone killed" (Toobin 2023a).

In fact, invitations to violence go beyond roiling followers to threaten and intimidate. They provide concrete opportunities for violence by effectively deputizing armed followers to act as enforcers of presidential directives—marshaling citizens to travel to border areas to stop undocumented migrants, for example. Or directing followers to intimidate poll workers. Or urging organized militia groups to violently interrupt the certification of Electoral College votes.

Once threats and intimidation are condoned from the top, the picture of degraded state capacity we painted in earlier chapters darkens. Its anti-liberal, anti-democratic character sharpens. Ungoverning is the abdication of the defining responsibility of government to enforce the law and keep the peace. We see political violence today as a defining part of a broad, reactionary political movement comprised of organized followers of a national political leader who provokes violence with the support or acquiescence of many representatives of the Republican Party. Ultimately, ungoverning weakens the democratic state's monopoly of the legitimate use of violence and stimulates errant violence by the forces of illiberalism and anti-democracy. And this is not occasional or incidental; the specter of political violence has come to cast a pall over American life.

Violence is a strategy that substitutes for governing. Many of the targets were despised civil society groups—Democratic Party offices and Planned Parenthood, for instance (Vakil 2021; Chabria 2021; U.S. Department of Justice 2022). Threats and intimidation migrate from targeting a deep state in the recesses of the federal government and the enemies who rig elections. There is no place violence cannot go. The sites of violence extend to federal and state officials, local school boards, journalists, health workers, and classroom teachers. Intimidation and violence take place in workplaces and neighborhoods, in families and circles of friends.

Several scenes of violence stand out. Against the background of diverging judgments regarding economic shutdowns and masking during the pandemic, intimidation became an everyday affair. A second scene of violence is elections, where every official and volunteer, including poll workers, had to worry about their safety. And there was violence as a way to proclaim, if not secure, malignant goals, chief among them white supremacy, which as we have discussed, cannot be won through democratic means. With all this, it becomes clear that threats and intimidation and violence permeate society. Condoned from the top, they go anywhere and all the way down.

Liberate Michigan

The Centers for Disease Control was under unrelenting pressure during the Covid crisis, made worse by pressure from the White House to alter its public guidance and by its own missteps. In 2023 the new head of the Centers for Disease Control (CDC) was working to repair the damage caused not only by partisan delegitimation of the agency but also by "serious weaknesses in areas ranging from testing to data collection to communications" (Stolberg 2023). To be sure, there was room for reasonable doubt about official recommendations and mandates. But at the time, considered disagreement about the efficacy of policies like masking requirements and shutdowns of businesses and schools was in short supply. Mistrust was not. Physical menace was not.

As president, Trump insisted that the virus was intentionally unleashed by China, that it was not caused by a laboratory accident or the result of natural transmission. He repeated the phrase "China virus" endlessly, instigating arrant violence against Asian Americans (as he had reason to know it would). After belittling his own public health advisers and suggesting that medical experts at the CDC were conspiring against him, healthcare workers across the country suffered threats and assaults from aroused militants who saw every health measure as another act of tyranny. Abuse of state officials who were trying to control the spread of the disease was commonplace. "Our staff have been cursed at, screamed at, threatened with bodily harm and even had knives pulled on them," read one hospital statement; another hospital set up a corps of six "mental health peace officers" to protect staff (Harper 2021). The *Journal of the American Medical Association* did meta-analyses of the harms (Mello, Greene, and Scharfstein 2020). Masking and vaccine policy accelerated these assaults. Airline workers were assaulted; flight attendants took self-defense classes (Harper 2021). Workers and even customers in stores were assaulted (Vives and Smith 2021). Masking in schools was represented as the work of despotic school boards or teachers' unions whose purported aim was to subvert personal liberty and parental authority (Haelle 2021). This is the atmosphere in which "Parent Attacks Teacher after Mask Dispute on First Day of School in California" became a headline.

After Trump directed followers to "liberate Michigan" from the public health measures put in place by Governor Gretchen Whitmer, a plot to kidnap her was detected and foiled (Solender 2020). The family of Josh Green, a medical doctor who was then serving as Hawaii's lieutenant governor, was threatened, and flyers of him were posted reading "Jew" and "Fraud" (Kelleher, Tang, and Rodriguez 2021).

Targeting Election Workers

Covid was one occasion for scenes of intimidation and violence nationwide; elections were another, and the threat of violence aimed at disrupting elections became common after the 2020 election. The infamous January 6 insurrection, during which

Trump refused to call out National Guard troops to reinforce the embattled Capitol Police, stands out as the final step in a complicated set of plans to reverse the 2020 election results (Mazzetti and Haberman 2022). It was, however, only the most dramatic instance of violence surrounding elections.

Widespread threats of violence around elections can be effective in part because elections in the United States are frequent and are local affairs, run largely by ordinary citizens in a volunteer capacity. Scapegoated and threatened, poll workers in many states feared violence as the midterm elections of 2022 approached. As early voting began in November 2022, self-styled "protectors" of elections camped out around ballot drop boxes, filming voters and taking down voters' license-plate numbers and posting them on social media. Proud Boys signed up as poll workers in Miami-Dade County (Grenoble 2022). State after state suffered a "brain drain" of local election officials; experienced election supervisors "left in droves," driven from their jobs by "burnout, stress, [and] a blizzard of time-consuming public records requests from election deniers" (Puzzanghera 2022). And by fear. A Brennan Center for Justice poll revealed "that nearly a third of those polled had been harassed or threatened" since the 2020 election (Jouvenal 2023; Edlin and Norden 2023). An analysis by the *Boston Globe* found that 30 percent of top local election officials left their jobs between 2020 and 2022. One official pointed to the consequence: "It's the institutional knowledge that walks out the door that you can't really replace for years" (Puzzanghera 2022).

A much-publicized case involved Georgia volunteer poll workers Ruby Freeman and her daughter Shaye Moss. Trump's lawyer and fixer Rudy Giuliani testified to the Georgia legislature that the two women had violated election laws while working at the State Farm Arena, where votes were being counted. Freeman was "quite obviously passing around USB ports [*sic*] as if they're vials of heroin or cocaine" in order to "infiltrate the crooked Dominion voting machines" (State of Georgia v. Donald John Trump, et al., Act 56 at 34). Trump allies went to Freeman's home to tell her that she would likely need protection—from Trump's own supporters, from themselves— in hopes of intimidating her into submission. The two women were forced into hiding (Edelman 2022). Eventually, Freeman and Moss brought a civil suit against Giuliani and were awarded almost $150 million by a Georgia jury (ABC News 2023). But vindication took years.

The civil case was exceptional, but the harassment suffered was not. Harrowing incidents of intimidation and violence had lasting repercussions for the men and women at the center of the storm who did not have police protection and who lived (and continue to live) in fear of enraged fellow citizens. For instance, Christine Gibbons, registrar in Lynchburg, Virginia, after having been accused of siphoning votes to Biden in the 2020 election, was fired by the Republican-controlled local election board. Although she was just "another low-profile bureaucrat in rural America" (and the sole support of her family), Gibbons found herself at the center of her local stolen election storm. A sign was hung in front of her house: #LOCKHERUP. Gibbons installed security cameras at home to protect her children. As of 2023, she was still seeking to be returned to office as registrar and had brought suit against the members of the electoral board who fired her and refused to reinstate her (Jouvenal 2023). This is how ungoverning—unraveling election administration—goes.

Trump personally participated in this kind of intimidation. During his 2020 phone call to Georgia secretary of state Brad

Raffensperger, the president said, "I just want to find, uh, 11,780 votes, which is one more than we have" (Trump's margin of loss was 11,779 votes). He then falsely suggested that Raffensperger could have committed a criminal offense—implying that he had better comply, or else (Gardener and Firozi 2021; Sullivan and Martina 2021; Walker, Youd, and Sanchez 2021).

In the years after January 6, 2021, Trump continued to call out to his followers and to prepare them to take up arms in his defense. In December 2022, he rallied his "great patriots" by declaring that he was prepared to forcefully overthrow the Constitution: "A Massive Fraud of this type and magnitude allows for the termination of all rules, regulations, and articles, even those found in the Constitution. Our great 'Founders' did not want, and would not condone, False & Fraudulent Elections!" (Howie 2022). We return to the project of deconstructing election administration in the next chapter.

Racial Violence and Guns

Then there is violence to upend social order, especially racial violence by reactionary extremists committed to white supremacy. After a twenty-one-year-old white supremacist with a swastika painted on his rifle murdered three Black citizens at a Dollar General store in Jacksonville, Florida, one commentator reflected, "America is living through a reign of white supremacist terror" (Kurtz 2023). The United States has a history of reigns of terror, including organized mob violence and lynchings undertaken by groups like the Ku Klux Klan to enforce legal segregation. Since the 1980s, however, there has been at least a nominal commitment by the national government to protect Blacks and other minority groups from hate crimes (Naidoo 2016). While state-sponsored racial violence persists in policing and in policies like mass incarceration of Black citizens, public officials have generally professed commitment to equal protection of the law.

Ungoverning today seeks to reverse this commitment. Calling for rogue violence is sheer abdication of the core responsibility to protect the public. Until political leaders began to collaborate with militias and racist groups like the Proud Boys, perpetrators of racial and anti-government violence were seen as extremists, as terrorists like the Unabomber and the Oklahoma City bomber. Until recently, white supremacists and militias were seen as "more a law-and-order problem than a political threat" (Paxton 2004, 205). Racists and anti-government militia had not assumed the collective identity of a reactionary movement affiliated with a major political party and its leader. Until recently, elected officials at the federal level did not actively look for and embrace allies willing to engage in overt racism, intimidation, and violence.

Yet, by 2023, racial extremists posed a more lethal threat than Islamist terrorists, according to the Annual Threat Assessment issued by the Office of the Director of National Intelligence. The assessment describes a "decentralized movement of adherents to an ideology that espouses the use of violence to advance white supremacy, neo-Nazism, and other exclusionary cultural-nationalist beliefs . . . [that seeks] to sow social divisions, support fascist-style governments, and attack government institutions." The report continues, they are recruiting "military members . . . [to] help them organize cells for attacks against minorities or institutions that oppose their ideology" (Office of the Director of National Intelligence 2023).

Instead of working to keep violence in the shadows, political leaders call it out into the streets. The incendiary potential has been escalated by the American culture of guns—a celebration that has become a core element of the identity of the Republican Party. The symbolic first act of the 2022 Republican Congress was to try to end the ban on carrying weapons into the legislative chambers. Some Republicans began to sport AR-15 assault rifle pins, a flagrant act coming as it did immediately after the 2023 mass shooting at Club Q in Colorado Springs and another at a dance studio in Monterey Park, California, favored by LGBTQ+ patrons (Henry 2023; Lin et al. 2023). Referencing the contemptuous acronym for moderate Republicans, or "Republicans in name only," one 2022 Senate campaign ad featuring a candidate with a shotgun read "Get a RINO hunting permit. There's no bagging limit, no tagging limit, and it doesn't expire until we save our country" (Gregorian 2022).

The AR-15 holds a special place among gun fanatics in the United States: designed for war, it has become the armament of choice. It is the weapon used in some of most gruesome mass shootings that have traumatized U.S. communities, including the 2012 massacre of twenty schoolchildren and six staff members at the Sandy Hook Elementary School in Newtown, Connecticut. In context, assault weapons cannot be seen as a necessity for citizens who want to be prepared to defend themselves against a tyrannical government. On the contrary, the weapon stands for killing and instills terror. Fear is diffuse, and more and more guns are bought for self-protection. Private security is visible at churches and synagogues, at schools, in stores, and in affluent neighborhoods. Crime is one reason, of course, but for many the rationale is a measurable increase in hate crime and political violence. The Anti-Defamation League released a report in February 2023 on the great increase in domestic extremist mass killings over the past twelve years. All the extremist killings in 2022 were committed by right-wing adherents, and twenty-one of twenty-five of these killings were linked to white supremacists (Anti-Defamation League 2023).

Think back to Locke and government's monopoly on legitimate violence. This monopoly, which includes the lawful processes of prosecution, trial, and punishment, is just what Locke said it is—taking the right to punish away from individuals. It is "not just a matter of protecting society against its deviant members but of protecting all the members of society against themselves, against the corrosive effects of their own passion for vengeance" (Shklar [1964] 1986, 158). At its most basic, this is what governing is for. And at its most basic, it is what the ungoverning undoes.

"My Generals"

The institution with the greatest potential for violence is the military, and that is why nothing is more central to governing than properly bounding the authority of military officers. As president, Trump behaved as if he owned the military and could appropriate this immense coercive state institution for his own ends. As he had with other officials like his attorneys general, he expected personal loyalty. He boasted in self-regarding rather than constitutional terms of "my generals": "Believe me . . . if I say, 'Do it,' they're going to do it" (Brooks 2016; Ryan 2020). With this, the military joins the Justice Department as handmaiden to personal will.

Degrading and coopting civil-military relations are definitive marks of anti-democratic intent, and at the heart of ungoverning. The military is by far the largest part of the administrative state, and every president and Congress, in wartime and peace, has grappled with the constitutional bounds of this difficult relation. The classic corruption of the military is the degradation of civilian control, with officers wresting control from the elected leadership. Presidential command of the armed forces is firmly established in the United States; constitutional democracy, settled practice, and historical experience all argue for civilian control and for the military ethic of obedience to civilian government (Huntington [1957] 1981, cited in Ben Sasson-Gordis 2023, 8). The justification for civilian control is rooted in and appreciation of the military's capacity to seize power, effect coups, and replace elected representatives with generals or a leader of their own choosing. These are among the familiar causes of the fall of democratic government. Military coups are an ever-present threat. The antidote to military takeover is civilian control. Ungoverning distorts civilian control by treating the military as the personal possession of the commander in chief. This parallels the way ungoverning distorts presidential control of the administrative state broadly by converting it into an instrument of personal will. It is most venomous when the military is ordered to treat citizens as enemies.

Trump called on military leaders for show, to demonstrate that from the chair of the joint chiefs of staff to enlisted soldiers, the armed forces backed him not because of the authority vested in the office of the president, but personally and individually. Photo ops with generals and the appointment of officers to his cabinet were meant to signal the military's approval of his politics and his command, for Trump acted as if his command of the military was unbounded by law or settled practice. As a candidate, he declared that he would bring back waterboarding and order the military to torture prisoners and "take out" terrorists' families (Lobianco 2015; Phelps 2015). He appointed General James Mattis secretary of defense even though he had not been retired from the military for seven years, as mandated by Congress. He intervened in internal military matters; with no notice to military leadership, for example, he reversed the Obama administration's decision to allow transgender men and women to serve. He ordered the deployment of troops to border areas, fanning fear of violent migrants and demonstrating the intention to use military force against "invaders."

Just as some public servants in the administrative state balked at the president's demands, so did active military officers when asked to employ troops for domestic political purposes. Senior officers not only argued with the president and his staff about many of his directives and raised their objections in memos, they also "slow-walked" orders. Secretary of Defense Mark Esper was fired for opposing the president's order to use U.S. forces to put down riots outside the White House (U.S. House Select Committee to Investigate the January 6th Attack on the United States Capitol 2021, 91).

What could justify this resistance—what might be called "military disobedience"? The military oath is to preserve, protect, and defend the Constitution of the United States against all enemies, foreign and domestic. Legal doctrine rooted in domestic and international law, including the Geneva Convention, also requires the military to oppose unlawful orders. Soldiers can be court-martialed for complying with unlawful orders. Disobedience by the military over decisions of war and peace is not justifiable; neither is refusal to enforce decisions in international affairs, even if there is disagreement about whether they serve or endanger national security (Ben Sasson-Gordis 2022). But here was something else: a president who pushed the bounds of civilian control beyond the breaking point—not in a foreign war, but against his political enemies at home. For Trump, to be commander in chief meant that he could use the armed forces against political opponents. When governing devolves into personal rule, the president's political opponents become the nation's enemies—and "my generals" are there to be deployed against both.

Identifying protesters as enemies was the point of the president's response to public demonstrations against the brutal police murder of George Floyd in the summer of 2020. The president told governors across the nation to call out the National Guard to suppress peaceful demonstrators. In Washington, D.C., he appeared in a photo op taken near Lafayette Square, which on his orders had been cleared of protesters by uniformed army personnel. General Mark A. Milley appeared with him in full battle fatigues and Trump identified him as "a fighter, a warrior," and as head of the operation. Milley later regretted his appearance there with the president. Defense Secretary Esper, who had called on governors to mobilize National Guard units to "dominate the battle space," later regretted his words and his participation in this display, too (Ryan 2020). The principle is that citizens are not enemies simply because the president brands them as such (Schmitt, Gibbons-Neff, and Baker 2020).

In fact, Milley authored a memorandum on June 2, 2020, to the chief of staff of the Army, the commandant of the Marine Corps, the chief of naval operations, the chief of staff of the Air Force, the chief of the National Guard Bureau, the commandant of the Coast Guard, the chief of space operations, and the commanders of the combatant commands advising that one of the values embedded in the Constitution is the "right to freedom of speech and peaceful assembly." He added a handwritten note to the memorandum: "We all committed our lives to the idea that is America. We will stay true to that oath and the American people" (Milley 2020).

Later, in testimony before the January 6 Committee, Milley adamantly disclaimed a role for the military on the streets of the United States, even in response to riots, violence, looting, flipping of police cars, destruction of property, and other criminal domestic upheavals—and even when "it looks like the whole place is burning up" (U.S. House Select Committee to Investigate the January 6th Attack on the United States Capitol 2021, 41). The former secretary of defense corrected course, too, and refused to approve a request from the National Park Police for a D.C. National Guard response force during planned demonstrations around Election Day.

The ultimate expression of "my generals" was the scheme to use the military to reverse the results of the 2020 election. Retired lieutenant general and former national security advisor Michael Flynn was a stalwart advocate of seizing voting machines and declaring martial law under the Insurrection Act (Altman et al. 2020). Military leaders were prepared to resist Flynn's plans (Cohen 2021). General Milley made the norms of military action explicit in testimony before the January 6 Select Committee: a contested election had to be decided in the courts. "The military doesn't have a role in determining the outcome of elections. That is the prerogative of the American people" (U.S. House Select Committee to Investigate the January 6th Attack on the United States Capitol 2021, 8). He was emphatic: "We don't have a role in domestic politics, and that's that" (50).

In the end, Trump's attempt to extract personal loyalty and to convert the military into his private army was thwarted. On January 3, 2021, "all 10 living former defense secretaries signed a *Washington Post* op-ed warning that efforts to involve the U.S. armed forces in resolving election disputes would take us into dangerous, unlawful and unconstitutional territory." They were exhorting their colleagues in the military to resist any plan by the president to invoke martial law to stay in power (Carter et al. 2021).

Because he couldn't use his generals to overturn the 2020 election, Trump relied on political allies and the forces of the reactionary movement. The organized elements in the January 6 insurrection had the character of a private army. There were militia groups—the Proud Boys, the Oath Keepers, the Three Percenters, phalanxes of the president's most ardent followers adhering to what they knew to be his wishes, answering his call to arms. We know that Trump intended to join the assault in person (Debonis 2022). The chairman of the joint chiefs offered the January 6 Committee his own impressions of that insurrection: "And then you start looking at what they are wearing . . . helmets and they're wearing flak vests and they have radios." He elaborated, "You look at the shirts they're wearing, 6 million not enough . . . written in German, work will make you free. Waving neo-Nazi flags, the green and white flags with the runes from the Nazi SS" (U.S. House Select Committee to Investigate the January 6th Attack on the United States Capitol 2021, 197). Milley described the "Million MAGA March" as a fascist movement. "These guys look like brownshirts to me. This looks like a Reichstag moment" (198).

Deconstructing the Union: Secession

Violence—in the context of Covid, a storm on the Capitol, even a military coup—promises the reactionary counterculture the change it seeks, *right now*. The movement is excited by apocalyptic scenarios in which violence is required. Secession is one such fantasy extreme. It promises to destroy the hated administrative state by deconstructing the federal government entirely.

Exit, Voice, and Loyalty is social theorist Albert Hirschman's famous typology of choices available to consumers in a market economy, to voters in a party system, and, by extension, to the leaders of states in a federal system when they find their product, party, or national government unsatisfactory. "Loyalty" indicates a decision not to alter the relationship—to be resigned and hope for improvement. "Voice" is oppositional, sometimes radically so—for example, organizing a boycott of a faulty consumer product, or speaking up against a party candidate or program, or civil disobedience. "Exit" is leaving—changing one's own consumer habits, voting for the partisan opposition, and in this case, seceding from the union (Hirschman 1970).

"Sovereign Texas" is not widely proposed in earnest. For most Republicans who flirt with secession, leaving the union is rhetorical. It is aimed not against this or that hated agency or policy or political enemy, but against federal authority altogether. Secession-talk aims to rally partisans for a final showdown. But even as a symbolic gesture, flirting with secession is important because it clarifies just how profound disregard for governing and appetite for ungoverning are. As ungoverning creates chaos, so "the central idea of secession," Lincoln wrote, "is the essence of anarchy" (Lincoln 1861).

In March 2023 Manhattan District Attorney Alvin Bragg brought a thirty-four-count indictment against Trump, the first charge of criminal conduct against the former president. The district attorney alleged "that Donald J. Trump repeatedly and fraudulently falsified New York business records to conceal crimes that hid damaging information from the voting public during the 2016 presidential election" (District Attorney New York County 2023). Immediately, Florida governor DeSantis vowed to block extradition of citizen Trump from his home in Mar-a-Lago to New York for arraignment. The governor was not tested; Trump went to the arraignment voluntarily.

Still, this bizarre vow is significant. It is more than a declaration of Republican solidarity with Trump (at the time, DeSantis was preparing for a primary challenge in the 2024 presidential election). It threatened noncompliance with established law. It asserts that the governor can suspend the U.S. Constitution when he pleases, although according to Article IV, Section 2, Clause 2 of the Constitution, no state has the right to decline an extradition request from another state. It was not just another instance of thumbing the nose at national policy, as when DeSantis flew migrants to Democratic Martha's Vineyard in Massachusetts. The pretense was that Florida is sovereign, and this makes the governor's vow worthy of attention. In threatening to refuse to extradite Trump to prosecutors in New York state, and in asserting the supremacy of state sovereignty, DeSantis approached the edge of the cliff: secession. Perhaps repeated, excited talk of secession will make it acceptable.

In 2009 former Texas governor Rick Perry had asserted, "When we came into the nation, in 1845, we were a republic: we were a stand-alone nation . . . and one of the deals was, we can leave anytime we want. So, we're kind of thinking about it again" (Holley 2022). Following President Obama's reelection in 2012, Texas and other states became home to secessionist movements. Organizations like the Texas Nationalist Movement were formed to campaign to "sever the Lone Star State from the United States" (Holley 2022). In 2022 the Texas Republican Party inserted into its platform a call for a voter referendum on "whether or not the State of Texas should reassert its status as an independent nation." A state representative introduced a bill to place on the 2024 ballot a referendum on investigating the possibility of Texas secession (*Texas Tribune* 2022). While insisting that he opposed secession at that moment, Texas senator Ted Cruz said, "If there comes a point where it's hopeless, then I think we take NASA, we take the military, we take the oil" (Rai 2021).

In *Texas v. White*, the Supreme Court had made clear that states cannot unilaterally secede from the union. In 2006 Justice Antonin Scalia asserted, "If there was any constitutional issue resolved by the Civil War, it is that there is no right to secede" (Holley 2022). Yet, some provocative officials and activists speak of secession as if it were a legal option they might reasonably exercise (Gurley 2021). But dry legal reasoning cannot speak to the zeal to bring it all crashing down. When a group insists that it and only it is the real America, their insistence functions as permission to disenfranchise "fake" Americans. It functions as a justification for permanent rule. It denies the idea of a legitimate opposition. An insurrection like January 6 would seem an essential duty if you are the only group that represents "true Americans." So would secession.

Evoking the Lost Cause and implying that there is a need to prepare for violent confrontation is at the same time a brief for separation. Representative Marjorie Taylor Greene predicted another civil war unless there is a "national divorce" between red and blue states (Pettypiece 2023). But the real significance of flirtation with the fantasy of secession is what it reveals about ungoverning.

Talk of secession, fueled by anti-government passion, is wildly dismissive of, even oblivious to the governing apparatus that joins states and the federal government in getting public business done. It is flagrantly unserious. In very basic terms, independent Texas would have to create "a postal service, an aviation administration to oversee air traffic control, and a border patrol to enforce immigration and trade" (Holley 2022). Texas nation would require a national defense. It would have to be able to take on its share of the national debt. Disregard for the requirements of governing is amplified when the secession fantasy extends to a confederation of non contiguous red states disparate in state capacity, many of them poor southern states with large populations of people of color. The real point is not impracticality, however, but capricious inattention to the requirements for governing. Secession talk also demonstrates that it is not only the Republican Party in Washington but also reactionary governors and state legislators who have ideas for deconstruction all their own.

Volume 137

7

The States of Ungoverning

In classic federalism, states are potential counterweights to the national government. With partisan federalism, things change, and the states become tools and accomplices of the national parties (Bulman-Pozen 2014). Partisan federalism distorts traditional federalism and moves ungoverning to the states.

In the ideal described by Justice Louis Brandeis, states are "laboratories of democracy" (Grumbach 2022). The states can use their independent authority to experiment with policies that the national government for some reason has not adopted. States can "plug gaps in federal policy" by, for example, pursuing anti-poverty initiatives or expanding labor rights (Kuttner 2023). States can also resist and impede national policy that citizens or special interests in the states oppose, by refusing to expand Medicaid, for example. In some instances, states defend individual rights that the national government betrays. An early instance of federalism at work is Madison's and Jefferson's enlistment of state legislatures in Virginia and Kentucky to remonstrate against President John Adams's Alien and Sedition Acts of 1798.

In classic federalism, the states retain independence and invoke their checking function when necessary. In partisan federalism, the checking function is subsumed by national partisanship; state parties are a central feature of national partisan conflict. In classic federalism, Republicans in state governments might resist the actions of Republicans in the national government; the same would be true of Democrats. With partisan federalism, partisans in the states side with co-partisans at the national level. When the party that controls state government is distinct from the president's party, state officials use everything in their power to thwart the president's agenda. When they are the same party, states act as agents of the national party.

Partisan federalism reverses Tip O'Neill's nostrum that "all politics is local" (Hopkins 2018). It generates "thick ties between state and national politicians," and "party politics means that state opposition [to national government] need not be based on something essentially 'state' rather than 'national'" (Bulman-Pozen 2014, 1090). Partisan federalism carries ungoverning into and out from the states, enlisting them in disabling the administrative machinery at the heart of governing. That extends to the deconstruction of election administration, which we will come to shortly. One election-law expert put it well, calling states "laboratories of autocracy" (Pepper 2022). Another titled his book *Laboratories against Democracy* (Grumbach 2022).

In U.S. politics, we often refer to "red" Republican states and "blue" Democratic states, after the colors television networks use on their election-night maps. The informal designations are meaningful, and not only in terms of election night outcomes. As of 2023, over 80 percent of Americans lived in "trifecta" states, where one party controls the governorship, the state senate, and the state house of representatives. Only eleven states have divided party control (Ballotpedia 2023).

Most states today have an emphatically partisan orientation. And many salient policies are now hammered out at the state level, not least, since the overturning of *Roe*, policy on abortion. This makes states sites of intense, salient, and highly contested politics. It also makes states potent agents of national partisan agendas. And in turn, this takes ungoverning out of Washington, D.C., to state capitals, counties, cities, and towns all over the country.

To be sure, federalism has always engaged states in national conflicts. In the United States it is more than a matter of variations in welfare policy or clean air or taxation. American history has seen critical clashes between national and state authorities, with states refusing to obey, much less to enforce federal laws, and even going to the extreme of nullification. When the Supreme Court ordered school desegregation "with all deliberate speed" in *Brown v. Board of Education II*, Arkansas enshrined segregation in its constitution and "instructed its state legislature to oppose 'in every Constitutional manner the Un-Constitutional desegregation decisions.'" Governor Orval Faubus deployed the Arkansas National Guard to obstruct nine black students from entering Little Rock Central High School. President Eisenhower deployed the Army to enforce the court order (Desai 2022).

Partisan federalism has increased the scope of governors using their authority to impede the federal government. A Republican governor, acting on the party's signature claim that without swift action, migration across the southern border would fatally damage the nation, took matters into his own hands. Building on his practice of busing unwanted migrants out of Texas to other states, Governor Greg Abbott in 2023 installed razor wire and floating barriers to deter migration along the border with Mexico. In August 2023 the federal government charged Texas with flouting federal laws that prohibited states from undertaking construction in rivers and from violating treaties—the Mexican government had formally protested the barriers on the Rio Grande multiple times. Abbott's border control initiatives, called Operation Lone Star, did not have appreciable success in deterring migration, but like Trump's family separation policy, the governor's policy was not vetted by immigration and border control experts and was oblivious to national and international law. Rather, it was a demonstration of cruel determination (Kriel et al. 2022). According to one whistleblower medic, the prison wire along the Rio Grande and other obstacles resulted in "drownings, maiming young children, snapped migrants' legs and entangled a pregnant woman who ultimately miscarried her baby" (O'Rourke 2023; Goodman 2023). In 2023 a federal judge ruled that Texas must remove the barrier buoys and razor wire: "Texas's conduct irreparably harms the public safety, navigation, and the operations of federal agency officials in and around the Rio Grande" (Richardson 2023b).

The idea that federal agencies can be undercut by actions at the state level is now routinely accepted. Governors have become ungovernors, too.

How Partisan Federalism Works

How has partisanship enflamed federalism to the point where states become agents of ungoverning? One factor enabling partisan federalism is that the national parties have become centralized, coherent, and polarized, and state parties have followed suit. Another is that partisan conflict in Washington has stymied policy goals and hamstrung legislation so that states became important sites for pursuing party agendas. Indeed, unified Republican government in 2017–18 did not produce policy apart from a massive tax cut; the action was in the states (Grumbach 2022, 68). A third factor is that the federal government depends increasingly on states to administer national programs; national and state governments are symbiotic. The United States did not create a centralized "welfare state" but transferred "many of the responsibilities—both financial and administrative—to state governments" (Kettl 2020, 110). Every one of the fifty states is an administrative state whose agencies and civil servants are needed to carry out national as well as state goals; indeed, "all of the real post-1960 growth in government employment has been at the state and local levels" (DiIulio 2012).

Several dynamics propel uniform national partisan politics across states. First, both red and blue states (i.e., trifecta states) are "staging ground[s] for organization and debate" for what is hoped will become uniform national policy. Same-sex marriage was first mandated in liberal states, for example (Gerken 2017). Or, states are staging grounds for obstructing national policy, as seen in the opposition in Republican states to the Affordable Care Act. Also, states implement regulatory or deregulatory practices in lieu of measures the party in D.C. is unable to enact for the country as a whole; robust greenhouse gas emission laws were passed in California, Hawaii, and New Jersey, for example (Bulman-Pozen 2014, 1101). Partisan federalism also works when blue states refuse to participate in federal programs passed by Republicans, in instructing officials not to collect Patriot Act surveillance information, for example, and encouraging other Democratic states to follow suit (Gerken 2017). These state efforts in affirming, obstructing, and initiating national party priorities are not spontaneous one-offs; Democratic and Republican Governors Associations often have a hand in orchestration.

A second dynamic propelling partisan federalism is the proliferation of political organizations dedicated to writing bills intended for adoption by the states. Coordinated, well-resourced groups scout out friendly territory, produce model laws, and lobby for them. As a result, very similar bills appear in a range of states—bills restricting the teaching of so-called critical race studies, for instance, or bills advancing disability insurance for workers. A team of investigative journalists studied over a million pieces of state legislation and discovered over ten thousand bills that were entirely copied from "model legislation" advanced by partisan advocacy groups, corporations, and think tanks. As the Center for Public Integrity said in 2019, "These copycat bills amount to the nation's largest, unreported special-interest campaign, driving agendas in every statehouse and touching nearly every area of public policy" (O'Dell and Penzenstadler 2019). The same passages in the same books are challenged in "campaigns orchestrated by a national clearinghouse with shadowy funding" (McCormick 2023). Networks of think tanks, interest groups, and friends and allies with money are part of the universe of legislation-writing that fuels and is fueled by partisan federalism.

Finally, powerful, well-funded associations orchestrate lawsuits on behalf of states in critical areas ranging from over-turning election results to challenging the authority of federal agencies. National partisan legal groups strategize litigation, identify sympathetic complainants and file cases in specific state and federal courts for hearings before judges likely to decide in their favor. Attorneys general in various states work together on strategies. One example is the suits joined by Republican officials from twenty-seven states to overturn the Affordable Care Act by challenging the national government's authority in this area, declaring the health care mandate a violation of state sovereignty. The sides were drawn not between constitutional advocates of national versus state authority, however, but on partisan grounds (Jost 2021).

The salience of partisan federalism can be measured by how common it has become for partisans in one state to support Republican or Democratic candidates and causes in states across the country, far from where they reside (Bulman-Pozen 2014, 1131–38). Increasingly aware citizens make contributions to state races at every level. An array of organizations exists to facilitate support for party candidates for Congress, governorships, and state legislatures. One impetus is to improve the chances of adding more seats for their party in Congress; this is called "surrogate representation" (Mansbridge 2003). Another is to bolster opposition or support for national proposals and, of course, to build structures of party solidarity.

Model legislation, orchestrated lawsuits, and citizen participation in the politics of states far away from their own are now entrenched features of the political landscape. Republican and Democratic Parties at the national and state levels employ them to advance their causes and to effectively defeat one another's political agendas. For decades, states had been viewed as backwaters of U.S. politics (Grumbach 2018). This is no longer the case.

Deconstructing Public Health Administration in the States

Two areas of state politics bring into focus how partisan federalism meets ungoverning: public health administration, especially during the Covid pandemic, and election administration.

The catastrophe of Covid provided a very public stage for ungoverning in the states. In the initial stages of the pandemic, states responded with different degrees of stay-at-home orders, business restrictions, masking, school closings, and more, but the differences did not correspond to partisan lines. That had changed by summer 2020, as partisan polarization became intense with rising radical anti-government rhetoric and policy (Wallace-Wells 2023). One cause of the shift was the presidential campaign, with Trump claiming that the pandemic was no big deal (Waldman 2020). In all fifty states, Republican legislators went on to file bills to curb public health authorities, banning mask mandates as "a burden on the public peace, health, and safety of the citizens of this state [Arkansas]" (Weber and Barry-Jester 2021). Local governments got into the act in Utah and Iowa, ordering that schools could not require masks. County commissioners with no public health expertise were authorized to veto county-wide public health orders. "It's time to take the power away from the so-called experts, whose ideas have been woefully inadequate" (Weber and Barry-Jester 2021). Although for the most part state public health officials remained in office and agencies were not eradicated, we saw hatchet-like acts of ungoverning, with expertise sidelined and institutions highjacked. Disdain for knowledgeable and experienced administration in a crisis situation was plain, and plainly inspired by Trump's repudiation of the recommendations of his own public health task force.

Imitating Trump, some Republican governors substituted their own dictates for a consultative and transparent process. Governor Kristi Noem of South Dakota, for instance, resisted medical experts' calls to shut down public activity, and early in the pandemic she refused entreaties by the state's largest medical association to implement stay-at-home orders (Beaumont and Groves 2020). By the end of 2020, South Dakota had the second-highest number of infections (adjusted for population) of any state in the country. One in nine South Dakotans had been infected, and one in six hundred had died of the virus (Bump 2021).

Vaccines were a fault line and a source of popular mobilization by the reactionary movement against public health. When Covid vaccines first became available, Governor DeSantis advocated vaccination of Florida's elderly population. But seeing an opportunity to indulge those who resented shutdowns and rejected vaccines, he soon reversed his position and opposed efforts by businesses to require vaccination (Caputo 2021). His surgeon general altered scientific data to claim that young men should not be vaccinated. And DeSantis flirted with conspiratorial allegations against vaccine manufacturers, suggesting that vaccine mandates were about profits not public health (Scott 2022). He directed the Florida Supreme Court to impanel a grand jury to hear charges against vaccine manufacturers. Against recommendations by medical experts, he banned mask mandates in schools (Hart 2021). He also formed a "public health integrity committee" to vet—and contradict—public health advice from the federal government. Undercutting national- and state-level public health experts and elevating his own dictates is what we would expect to see when ungoverning at the national level gets picked up by the states. A process of enlisting the advice of medical and scientific experts to deliberate about public health recommendations gave way to a governor who substituted his own will.

The idea is not that public health experts should have total control over the policies that states impose in response to a pandemic; they are not charged with that. But the wholesale rejection of expertise, even in its advisory capacity, and the substitution of a governor's will for a policymaking process is where we locate ungoverning.

Deconstructing Election Administration in the States

The attack on election administration starts, as many acts of ungoverning do, with conspiracism—outlandish charges that allege exactly the sort of disruption they aim to produce. Kaleidoscope image fragments and suggestive bits of misinformation substitute for evidence. Conspiracy charges move from the Wild West informality of X (formerly Twitter) to right-wing media and eventually to the courts. "Rigged!"—the charge was a campaign slogan repeated over and over in 2016, 2018, and of course 2020. It became a permanent incantation. It was taken up by the reactionary movement, by Republicans in Congress, and by officials in the states, and years later, it remains alive and resonant. It lives on as a core part of the Republican Party's identity—a new gloss on the old Lost Cause.

"Rigged!" accompanied Trump's entrance into national politics from the start. He leveled the charge during the Republican nomination contests in 2016, claiming that his loss to Senator Ted Cruz in the Iowa caucus was the result of fraud. "Ted Cruz didn't win Iowa, he stole it," Trump tweeted. He insisted that "either a new election should take place or Cruz results [should be] nullified" (Tennery 2016). In the lead-up to the general election against Hillary Clinton in 2016, Trump asserted that the election "is absolutely being rigged by the dishonest and distorted media pushing Crooked Hillary—but also at many polling places" (Smith 2020). After he won the election, Trump accepted the result, but continued to insist that he had lost the popular vote because of "serious voter fraud in Virginia, New Hampshire and California" (Homans 2022).

Two years later, he said that fraudulent voting by undocumented immigrants was responsible for the outcome of the 2018 midterm elections: "There were a lot of close elections that were—they seem to, every single one of them went Democrat. If it was close, they say the Democrat—there's something going on, fella." Undocumented immigrants "vote many times, not just twice, not just three times. . . . They vote—it's like a circle. They come back; they put a new hat on. They come back; they put [on] a new shirt. . . . You know what's going on. It's a rigged deal" (Rogers 2019b).

Having rehearsed the "Rigged!" conspiracy in 2016 and 2018, Trump brought the old charge to the 2020 election with renewed insistence. The list of "rampant fraud" claims included stealth voting by noncitizens, people voting multiple times or impersonating voters, and hundreds of thousands of votes being mysteriously dropped into the count, among many other accusations. Trump had primed his supporters to buy into the conspiracy, insisting that "the only way we're going to lose this election is if the election is rigged" (Chalfant 2020). On election night 2020, the results were too close to call. Nonetheless, Trump said, "This is a fraud on the American public. . . . We did win this election" (Trump 2020a). Two days later, while mail-in votes in many states were still being tabulated, he gave a speech from the White House, asserting, "If you count the legal votes, I easily win." Without evidence, he accused Democrats of trying to steal the election: "It's a corrupt system. . . . They want to find out how many votes they need, and then they seem to be able to find them. They wait and wait, and then they find them" (Trump 2020b). It would be four days—until the Saturday after the Tuesday election—before all the votes were counted and the major news networks could call the election for Biden. Trump refused to concede. He never did concede.

Twelve days later, the president's lawyers held a news conference to discuss the lawsuits they were filing that alleged fraud in close states. Trump's attorney Sidney Powell (who later in

2023 pled guilty to attempting to subvert the election outcome
in Georgia) alleged a communist plot to deprive him of his victory: "What we are really dealing with here and uncovering
more by the day is the massive influence of communist money
through Venezuela, Cuba, and likely China in the interference
with our elections here in the United States." She suggested
that software in U.S. voting machines had been used in Venezuela and had been rigged to benefit Hugo Chávez (who had
died almost a decade earlier). U.S. law enforcement agencies,
she suggested, had been responsible for the rigged software
(Blake 2020).

Venezuela? Cuba? China? Bad software written by the FBI
to serve (long-dead) anti-American foreign dictators? This is
not a narrative or explanation that tries to make sense of things.
It is what we called in *A Lot of People Are Saying* "conspiracy
without the theory": bare assertion intended to clear the path
to power by enveloping everyone in a fog of conspiratorial
confusion (Muirhead and Rosenblum 2019). Charges of rigged
elections were made credible not by evidence but by repetition,
in 2016, 2018, and 2020. They primed Trump's supporters to
expect the worst. And as they filled the air with one allegation
after another of fraud in Arizona, in Pennsylvania, in Georgia,
wherever Trump lost, they left some people enraged at being
robbed of their votes and left some people uncertain of what
to think.

Conspiracism works not only by creating true believers, but
by creating confusion. It substitutes nonsense, word clusters, for
evidence. Citizens who do their best to follow events nonetheless
find themselves uncertain and exhausted. It can be difficult to
see anything clearly through the blizzard of conspiracy charges.
"I don't know whether the election was stolen, but I do believe
there were irregularities," someone might say, as the various

charges of "Rigged!" pile up. Or, "I think there are issues with our elections." The process of collecting and tabulating ballots is not something citizens can watch, ballot by ballot, polling place by polling place, state by state. One can have confidence in election results only if one trusts that the administration of elections has integrity. That is what conspiracism erases and ungoverning exploits.

It bears mention that the ongoing aftereffects on election administration extend to local governments. In small, outer Cape Cod townships, clerks received requests for records about the 2020 election for years afterward. The requests represent a sort of "vigilante tactic" meant to disrupt and overwhelm the work of frontline town employees by asking for specific forms not readily available, like the "2020 General Election preliminary tally sheet, post-election tally, official results, election warrant," or detailed information about electronic voting machines. This is organized disruption—small-scale, local derangement of administration (Myers and Mann-Shafir 2022).

From Rigged! to Coup

Once followers were certain that the election had been stolen, and many others had lost confidence that anyone could really know the true election result, the president was in position to try to reverse the outcome. This was always Trump's plan in the weeks immediately following the November 2020 election. The "Rigged!" conspiracy gave way to "Stop the Steal!"

Challenging election results is one thing; actually *reversing* them is another. It requires an assault on institutions and procedures. Trump and his legal team filed sixty-two lawsuits contesting vote counts in state after state—in every case, without evidence. The intention was to give Republican judges an opportunity to exercise partisan power over the administration of elections. In the end, they lost every case. The president and his allies tested the integrity of officials ranging from the Department of Justice administrators to secretaries of state. They attempted to corrupt officials such as the Speaker of the Arizona House of Representatives. They harassed and intimidated public officials, even obscure and powerless poll workers. Between November 2020 and January 2021, they committed more than 150 specific acts aimed at overturning the election results, according to the Georgia indictment brought by Fulton County District Attorney Fani Willis.

At the core of the plan was the creation of alternative slates of electors to be sent to the Electoral College. The next step was getting the vice president to recognize these alternate slates at the joint session of Congress on January 6 (Feuer and Benner 2022). That would have created an indeterminate Electoral College result. Biden's inauguration would have been postponed or set aside, and the subsequent confusion would have opened any number of opportunities for Trump to seize control—including throwing the election to the House of Representatives, where the Republican majority might have installed him for another term. Doing all this involved a complicated series of actions. To destroy the credibility of the official slates of electors, Trump and his co-conspirators tried to corrupt the Department of Justice by pressuring officials to falsely endorse allegations of election fraud. They pressured state elected officials in Georgia and Arizona to certify fraudulent slates of electors (State of Georgia v. Donald John Trump, et al., Act 112 at 50 [2023]). They lied to committees of state legislatures, making up a variety of allegations about election fraud (*State of Georgia*, Act 78-80, at 103–105). Trump pressured Vice President Pence to violate the Electoral Count Act (*State of*

Georgia, Act 141 at 64), publicly expressing the hope that Pence would "act boldly" on January 6 and refuse to certify slates of Biden electors from states Trump had narrowly lost (Act 94). Every step in the regular, lawful process of election administration was assaulted.

The final step was to use violent MAGA followers to intimidate Congress and the vice president into doing Trump's bidding by refusing to certify legitimate slates of electors. Congress's *January 6 Report* detailed the president's speech to the crowd gathered, at his urging, before the attack on the Capitol. According to the report, his speech included five final attempts to pressure the vice president to refuse to certify the official results, including "So I hope Mike has the courage to do what he has to do." And "I hope he doesn't listen to the RINOs and the stupid people that he's listening to" (U.S. House Select Committee to Investigate the January 6th Attack on the United States Capitol 2022, 37). The report avers, "These statements to the assembled crowd at the Ellipse had Trump's intended effect" (37). The crowd at the Capitol chanted "Hang Mike Pence. Hang Mike Pence. Hang Mike Pence. Hang Mike Pence. Hang Mike Pence" (38). MAGA followers erected a gallows in front of the Capitol (Edmonson 2022). According to an aide to Chief of Staff Mark Meadows, when White House lawyer Pat Cipollone urged him to ask Trump to intervene, Meadows replied that Trump "thinks Mike [Pence] deserves it. He doesn't think they're doing anything wrong." Similarly, when Minority Leader Kevin McCarthy pleaded with Trump to send the National Guard to protect Congress from the assault, the president sided with the insurrectionists, remarking, "Well, Kevin, I guess these people are more upset about the election than you are" (111).

The insurrection was an attack not only on the *results* of elections but also on the *administration* of elections—on the offices, processes, and knowledgeable personnel without which voting and counting votes can be manipulated. To call it ungoverning draws attention to the actual apparatus and to the experience and discipline required to administer a national system of free and fair elections. The degradation of election administration cannot be reduced to other grievous phenomena that disfigure democratic elections—inadequate regulation of campaign finance, for example, and partisan gerrymandering. Election administration is at the core of ungoverning in the states.

Attack Thwarted

In *Federalist* no. 10, James Madison famously insisted that the survival of republican government could not depend on "enlightened statesmen" being "at the helm" (Madison 1787). It would require pitting ambition against ambition. One institutionalization of this is federalism.

In fact, the federal structure of U.S. government *was* essential in thwarting Trump's 2020 attempted coup. What stopped "Stop the Steal!" was not only judges who rejected baseless legal appeals but also, as we've seen, state officials who refused to go along with threats and entreaties to alter the election results. These officials were mainly in the six close states where Trump and his allies focused their pressure: Arizona, Nevada, Wisconsin, Michigan, Pennsylvania, and Georgia. Rusty Bowers, the Republican Speaker of the Arizona House of Representatives, resisted Trump's personal appeals and refused to call a special legislative session to nominate an alternate slate of electors. Bowers was backed up by Arizona's Republican governor, Doug Ducey, who certified the state's results and assured voters that they were accurate. In Georgia, Secretary of State Brad Raffensperger refused Trump's insistence that he "find" enough votes to flip the outcome and recorded the infamous phone call in which Trump made the appeal (*State of Georgia*, Act 112 at 50). He too was backed up by a Republican governor, Georgia's Governor Brian Kemp, who also certified the election results and who vowed to follow Georgia's legal procedures. When Trump phoned Kemp directly and asked him to call a special session of the Georgia General Assembly, he refused (Act 31 at 27). Trump's effort to reverse the election was stopped by key elected Republican resisters in state offices.

These officials very likely voted for Trump. As Republicans, they presumably hoped he would be reelected. But they were not willing to use every power at their disposal to ensure his victory. Their sense of responsibility attached to their office—to the oaths they took, to the laws that regulated procedures and outcomes. Their behavior was guided and constrained by a sense of the formality of governing; they understood that office was not simply a source of power but a responsibility to make public decisions in a certain kind of way, according to certain kinds of reasons and not others.

Arizona Speaker of the House Bowers refused to allow the partisan reasons that guided him in the voting booth to guide him as Speaker because he understood what was required of his office. The office of Speaker was not, for Bowers, a license to rule, but rather authority to govern. For his part, Bowers refused numerous personal entreaties by Trump's allies and Trump himself, who even called him at home on Christmas Day 2020. He was hounded and threatened by zealous Trump followers who convened in his neighborhood and directed their bullhorns toward his house. One supporter threatened Bowers's neighbor with a gun (Sanchez 2022; *State of Georgia*, Act 7 at 21, Act 20 at 24, Act 95 at 45).

In Michigan, the Republican leaders of the state house of representatives and state senate met with Trump but refused to cooperate, stating that they knew of no improprieties that could change the outcome of the election. Aaron Van Langevelde, a Republican on the Michigan Board of State Canvassers, refused efforts by Trump's allies to delay certification (Alberta 2020). Pennsylvania's Republican leadership also resisted pressure from Trump's legal team and refused to appoint a fraudulent slate of electors.

These officials had independent authority because of the state offices they occupied, and all of them used that authority to resist, or more modestly, to refuse to cooperate with Trump's coup. Trump was recruiting the forces of partisan federalism to assist his efforts. "If you want me elected, this is what you need to do," is essentially what he told state officials: express doubt about the results; hold special assemblies; appoint alternate slates of electors; find me the votes. When these officials refused, they asserted the independence of state authority in election administration. They stood up for the constraints of office and the formality and procedures that constitute governing.

In this respect, classic federalism worked as designed, but it is also fair to say that it just barely worked. The officials who resisted Trump were not honored or rewarded by their party or their constituents. In July 2022, Rusty Bowers was censured by the Arizona Republican Party for testifying before the January 6 Committee, and the state party announced that he was not in good standing. The party also censured the Republican governor, Doug Ducey. Bowers was defeated in his next race for the Arizona state senate. He lost to a Trump-endorsed election denier (Christie 2022).

Stories like those of Rusty Bowers in Arizona and Brad Raffensperger in Georgia are memorable because they were the exception. In some close states, Republicans colluded in Trump's effort to reverse the election. In Arizona, 81 percent of Republican state legislators took steps to "discredit or over-turn" the 2020 election, such as writing to Vice President Pence asking him to delay certification of the electors or supporting creating alternative slates of electors, "decertifying" the election results in their states, or holding partisan investigations of the election processes (misleadingly called "audits"). Over 70 percent of Republican state legislators took these steps in Wisconsin; 78 percent in Pennsylvania; and 48 percent in Michigan (Corasaniti, Yourish, and Collins 2022).

State officials who respect the bounds of their office in the federal system do not constitute a "bulwark" that cannot be breached. In fact, from start to finish, election administration is fraught with contingencies, and the resistance these Republican state officials marshaled was unpredictable. Overall, the margin of Biden's victory was just barely enough to make reversing the outcome difficult. The MAGA movement put enormous pressure on elected officials in six states and, it almost worked. If five or six such officials had placed loyalty or fear or submissiveness to Trump and his movement or personal political ambition above the responsibilities of their offices, the effort to reverse the election might have succeeded.

Attacking Election Administration—the Sequel

The lesson that Trump and his allies took from the failed coup of 2020 is that they needed to deconstruct election administration in a more permanent fashion. If they could replace independent state, county, and local officials with their own loyalists, if they could undo the processes by which ballots are counted and results certified, they would be able to impose the desired results on U.S. elections. The aim was to eradicate the states as independent entities that define and enforce standards of election integrity and to remake them as committed agents of the movement. With this, a whole new repertoire of ungoverning has been brought to the states.

The most prominent attack on election administration consisted of campaigns by election deniers for public office, especially for the position of secretary of state. The threat was all the more potent because these positions are relatively obscure; many voters have never paid attention to the office of secretary of state. Thirty-seven election deniers ran in the twenty-seven electoral contests for secretary of state nationwide in 2022, and thirteen proceeded to the general election (States United Action 2022).

In the face of this, Democrats organized to educate citizens about what the office of secretary of state is and to draw attention to down-ballot races, on which the essentials of election administration depend. The message of the Democratic Association of Secretaries of State focused on "just explaining . . . the role of a secretary of state in elections" (Paz 2022). This effort to explain what governing is about had effect. In elections for secretary of state, only three of the twenty-seven election deniers succeeded (States United Democracy Center 2022b). Of the seventeen election deniers running for secretary of state who were endorsed by the America First Secretary of State Coalition (an organization supporting election deniers), sixteen lost. And only six of twenty-two election deniers won races for governorships (States United Democracy Center 2022a).

And yet, election denial did not become a fringe phenomenon. By 2022, it was the dominant position taken by Republican officials and candidates. In the 2022 midterm elections, over 220 election deniers or election skeptics won races for the U.S. House, U.S. Senate, or governor in forty states. To be a viable Republican candidate in Republican states and districts, election denialism was, in practice, required (Dolores Huerta Research Center 2023).

Beyond running election deniers for office, other tactics to attack election administration have been chronicled by the Brennan Center for Justice. These include giving partisan majorities in the state legislature greater control over elections, for instance by assuming the power to appoint state and county election boards (Miller and Weiser 2023). In Texas, the Republican legislature and governor passed a law to "abolish the elections administrator's office in heavily Democratic Harris County," which includes Houston (Cassidy 2023). With every tactic, the goal is indirect but plain: to neuter the impartial administration of elections.

This goal also encompassed taking over state party organizations. After 2022, Trump loyalists and election deniers ran for state party chair positions in states from Idaho to Colorado, Arizona, Michigan, and Georgia (Riccardi and Cappelletti 2023). Kristine Karamo, who insisted that Donald Trump was the true victor of the 2020 election in Michigan, won the contest to lead the Michigan Republican Party in 2023. Before taking the helm of the state party, she lost a race for Michigan secretary of state by fourteen points—and never conceded. After she succeeded in her quest to become state party chair, Trump praised her as a "powerful and fearless Election Denier" (Forrest 2023). "Election denier" had become a laurel.

Some efforts to undo election administration occurred under the public radar. Take the case of Republican states abandoning "the most powerful tool available to combat voter fraud across state lines" (Greenblatt 2023). The Electronic Registration Information Center (ERIC), which collects data provided by the states about their voter rolls, once enjoyed bipartisan support. After 2020, however, Republican states withdrew their participation in the system; Texas was the largest Republican state to abandon it (Montellaro 2023). Trump exhorted "all Republican governors to sever their ties with the group" (Miller and Weiser 2023). The exit from ERIC underscores that it is not actual voter fraud but widespread opinion that voter fraud exists that really matters. If enough states participated, ERIC would make voter fraud impossible. But if voter fraud is impossible, then election denial becomes that much more unreasonable. The point is not to govern; it is to ungovern.

Going to Court: Doctrinal Attacks on Election Administration

One of the most comprehensive efforts to thoroughly subvert election administration involves an innovative legal strategy called the "independent state legislature doctrine" (ISL). The doctrine states that state legislative majorities alone are meant to control U.S. elections. It is a sweeping effort to eviscerate the ability of state courts to oversee partisan majorities in the legislature. The effort would strengthen the states as unrestrained instruments of partisanship. Election administration is an area where legal doctrine becomes an instrument of ungoverning.

The ISL doctrine did not come out of nowhere; it was part and parcel of the stolen election conspiracy. It was an attempt to legalize the fake elector scheme. ISL was a quickly concocted legal justification for unfettering state legislatures to endorse fraudulent or "alternative" slates of electors.

The ISL doctrine was advanced by Republican state legislators and was litigated in the case *Moore v. Harper* (2023). The doctrine is extreme. It says that neither state constitutions nor any other state authority can impose restrictions on the state legislature's regulation of federal elections. Not governors, not voters through ballot initiatives, not election administrators, not secretaries of state, and not even state-level courts have authority over state legislative acts concerning elections. The case advanced a novel reading of Article 1, Section 4 of the Constitution, which grants the states authority over the "times, places, and manner of holding elections." ISL claims that a plenary and exclusive authority lies with the legislature. If upheld, ISL would nullify a raft of state and federal laws, provisions in state constitutions, and court decisions concerning such things as voting rights and gerrymandering.

Moore was brought by South Carolina state legislators. The petitioners who filed amici briefs in support of ISL did not include the usual cast of experts—law professors, historians, and election administrators (Herenstein and Palmer 2022). Some conservative Republicans joined Democrats in opposing the ISL doctrine, understanding that it would allow partisan legislatures on *both* sides to overturn election results (White 2022). In the *Moore* decision, the majority of the Supreme Court rejected the most radical version of ISL. The Court upheld the authority of state courts to use state statutes and state constitutions to regulate election decisions made by partisan state legislators. Legislatures are "the mere creatures of the state constitutions and cannot be greater than their creators" (Moore v. Harper, 600 U.S. 1, 15 [2023], citing Max Farrand's records of the Constitutional Convention). The ruling avoids the worst part of the ISL doctrine—the total authority of state legislators—but it is troubling nonetheless. It creates the possibility that a partisan Supreme Court would intercede in state elections by reserving for itself the right to decide whether a state court had acted withing the "ordinary bounds of judicial review" (*Moore*, 600 U.S. at 3). The vague standard of "ordinary bounds" opens the door to voter confusion and waves of litigation challenging every election result (Hasen 2023; Pildes 2023). The decision puts federal courts "in a position to nudge elections towards the Justices' partisan preferences" (*Harvard Law Review* 2023, 298). Election administration in the states remains highly volatile.

Ungoverning in the states shows that there is more at stake than degrading federal agencies like the Department of Justice or the EPA. Beyond that, partisan federalism degrades other essential structures of administration, not least, elections. What does this disabling come to? What might it signal? How does ungoverning relate to the most fearsome forebodings for the United States—fascism, or authoritarianism, or destructive expressions of populism?

8

Forebodings

The Polish dissident Adam Michnik explained why he reflected over and over on the horrific twentieth-century enemies of liberal democracy: "Not so that the language of the reign of terror may never repeat itself, but because I'm convinced it will inevitably do so" (Cherniss 2021, 12). We are not believers in inevitability. Still, we share the forebodings of commentators and scholars, the warnings articulated by political officials, journalists, and witnessing professionals in fields from law to public health. Many flesh out their dread by looking back at the regimes that defined the terrors of the twentieth century. Is ungoverning an invitation to fascism? To some form of authoritarianism?

The forces of reaction in the United States today praise repressive regimes, including Putin's Russia, Orbán's Hungary, and even Nazi Germany. The affinity is declared. Hoped for. Even so, our judgment is that it is a mistake to suppose that ungoverning leads to fascism or straightforward authoritarianism, even if those concepts and examples offer illuminating points of comparison. None of the examples of anti-liberal, anti-democratic states should be dismissed; each adds something to our ability to assess the moment. But from what we see happening in the United States, the differences are compelling. Fascism and most forms of authoritarianism aim to capture the state and *use* it, not to destroy it. The one form of authoritarianism that points directly to where ungoverning goes is populist authoritarianism, where the anti-institutional thrust of populist leadership fuels an attack on governmental institutions. What we see is a virulent version, an authoritarian version, of indigenous American populism. We anticipate that if unchecked, ungoverning in the United States will lead to an incapacitated state, where the national government cannot offer a countervailing power to protect individuals and the nation itself from larger forces. Ungoverning leads to an even more fragmented country, where some state governments fill in for the diminished national state, while others continue the work of deconstruction.

Ungoverning introduces a form of populist authoritarianism made more dangerous by the fact that a large part of the country sees it as democratic. Looking abroad, we see examples of where ungoverning can go: to the kind of anarchy that exists in Venezuela or to electoral autocracy akin to what is unfolding in India. Yet, how things go in the United States will not precisely mirror other democracies, because the starting point with respect to the economy and institutional development, as well as the liberal tradition in the United States are so distinct. And because U.S. federalism provides unique resources for limiting the damage.

What is at stake in the fearsome forebodings is not only "democracy" but also its vital qualifier, "liberal."

Democracy's Liberalism

Liberalism puts limits on authority. It is not just an "idea," but a set of institutions and norms that cabin and restrain power: the rule of law, an independent judiciary, a free press, and mechanisms of political accountability. For the liberal, "what is to be feared is every extra-legal, secret, and unauthorized act by public agents or their deputies" (Shklar 1989, 30).

Yet, liberalism is not only about limits, about marking off what government may *not* do and the places it may *not* go. It also embraces political competition, party politics, and political opposition constrained by regulated rivalry. Winners do not use their power to lock up the opposition, and losers leave office peacefully.

Legitimate political opposition is only one manifestation of liberal democracy's acceptance and invitation to pluralism in its many forms. A liberal democracy embraces social movements. It is friendly to the voluntary associations of civil society that realize the freedom to form groups of all kinds, including political advocacy groups and associations based on race, religion, gender, ethnicity, and culture. It is home to all the other pluralities that make claims on government and on one another.

Finally, liberal democracy is not minimalist, but aspirational. Concerning individual freedom and self-development, "Every adult should be able to make as many effective decisions without fear or favor about as many aspects of her or his life as is compatible with the like freedom of every other adult" (Shklar 1989, 21). Liberalism aspires to justice. Both freedom and justice depend on a capacious state. Liberal democracy *requires* a government that protects rights, which in practice means an administrative state that endows government with the capacity to implement policies for the general welfare. Liberal democracy requires the machinery of government.

Viewed expansively, liberal governing goes beyond general principles and institutional design to encompasses an ethos. As Joshua Cherniss explains, this means a "stance" or "bearing," a pattern of disposition and commitment (Cherniss 2021, 6). In a similar spirit, Michael Walzer speaks of "liberalism as an adjective." Liberalism is not only a political ideology or set of institutions, then, but also a sensibility marked by tolerance and skepticism, by rejection of fanaticism and dogmatism. The adjective "liberal," Walzer explains, can't stand by itself; it qualifies a variety of nouns—not only "democracy" but also "nationalism," "socialism," and "conservatism" (Walzer 2023). It is no contradiction to speak of a liberal conservative or a liberal Republican Party.

In fact, officials from both parties and voters with sympathies for both parties fit this description. But the reactionary movement that has come to define the Republican Party is not liberal; it is not a defender of constitutional democracy or an independent judiciary or a free press or fairly administered elections. It is certainly not a friend of pluralism, which it sees as a series of alien impositions; "We the people" is exclusive, not inclusive. As we mentioned, leading Republican officials are comfortable with Viktor Orbán, the prime minister of Hungary, who pronounced his country an "illiberal democracy"; more, they look up to him, travel to visit him, and invite him to speak to their partisan groups (Tamkin 2023). We understand what the adjective "illiberal" rejects. Illiberal democracy is anti-pluralist. It sees opposition as the enemy and employs conspiracism and deconstruction as instruments of power. As the MAGA party and its leader demonstrate, illiberal democracy is ruthless.

Once liberal democracy is rejected by elected officials and a reactionary movement that openly despise and slough off the qualifier "liberal," fascism and authoritarianism no longer seem alien or distant.

Fascism

Trump's pronouncements in 2023 spiked the foreboding of fascism he had already introduced: "In honor of our great Veterans on Veteran's Day [*sic*] we pledge to you that we will root out the Communists, Marxists, Racists, and Radical Left Thugs that live like vermin within the confines of our Country." The language echoed Nazi dehumanization; commentators likened the former president to Hitler and Mussolini (LeVine 2023).

The fascist foreboding, which has a "unique place in our society's historical memory" (Greenberg 2021, 7), shadowed Trump. Secretary of State Madeleine Albright warned of incipient fascism, as did General Mark Milley and President Biden, who called Trump's so-called philosophy "semi-fascism" (Cadelago and Olander 2022). Historian Timothy Snyder raised the alarm in 2017: "When the men with guns who have always claimed to be against the system start wearing uniforms and marching with torches and pictures of the leader, the end is nigh" (Snyder 2017, 42; Greenberg 2021; Stanley 2020). No foreboding is as damning. The word "fascism," with nothing more, signals a five-alarm fire; it is a summons to all to come to a desperate rescue.

Right-wing extremism in Europe today has been called "legacy fascism" (Paxton 2004, 188). In France, Marine Le Pen's National Rally, for example, is a renamed version of her father's National Front, which had links to Nazis in the 1930s. The party expelled its founder, Jean-Marie Le Pen, in 2015 after he repeated his view that the Holocaust was "a detail of history" (BBC 2015). Nor were fascist tendencies unknown in the United States. European fascists learned a lot from racist policies here, and proto-fascism has been embraced by George Lincoln Rockwell's American Nazi Party; by Father Charles E. Coughlin's anti-communist, antisemitic Union Party; by public defenders of Hitler including Henry Ford; and by Charles Lindbergh's America First Committee (Bort 2019). Today, neo-Nazis appear at marches and rallies, and they were present among the January 6 violent insurrectionists who reminded General Milley of brownshirts.

The reactionary movement's chants and uniforms and slogans are, however, a noxious mash-up; alongside Nazi insignias and salutes are Christian crosses, Confederate flags, "Don't tread on me" signs, and the uniforms of anti-government militia. If the foreboding of fascism stands out, it is because insignias, slogans, threats, and racist policies (the Muslim ban, calling immigrants from Mexico "animals") recall the *mood* of the rise of fascism in the 1930s. As one historian described that mood, it "boiled with the readiness for violent action, anti-intellectualism, rejection of compromise, and contempt for established society." Another sobering description also applies: the accommodation of the rise of fascism by conservative elites in 1930s Germany who "felt a fastidious distaste for the crudities of fascist militants," but went along (Paxton 2004, 5, 13).

In assessing affinities between the present moment and the rise of fascism in 1930s Germany, two critical likenesses stand out. One is conspiracism and the "big lie." Another is the promise to restore national greatness after years of humiliating national weakness—a restoration that entails racial purification. The *Washington Post* kept count of Trump's everyday lies during his first term in office; there were 30,573 (Menand 2023, 59;

Washington Post 2021). Over time, lies large and small became an effective strike against what it means to know something, overwhelming common sense. They demonstrated Trump's intent to own reality and to impose his compromised sense of reality on the nation. Conspiracism is the most dangerous form lies take (Muirhead and Rosenblum 2019). It identifies enemies of the people, and it provokes action. Inuring people to tsunamis of lies, made effective in large part through little besides repetition, was preparation for the "big lie." Hannah Arendt's observation about lying in politics is to the point: "The policy of lying is hardly ever directed at the enemy"; it is for propaganda at home (Arendt 1972, 14).

Exploiting a concocted emergency is also common to both the historical rise of fascism and the reactionary movement in the United States. The Reichstag fire (charged to communists) and the "stolen election" of 2020 (rigged by Democrats) were crises invented to justify blatant deviations from lawful order. The threat was imminent: "Fight like hell or you're not going to have a country anymore" (Trump 2021). For those who warn of incipient fascism in the United States, the Reichstag fire and the "stolen election" of 2020 are paired.

Another source of fascist foreboding is the emotional trigger of casting the nation as humiliated, weakened, and deformed. The picture Trump conjured in his inaugural address of "American carnage" was a start. The enemies of America said to be responsible for decline and decay belong to the same cast of characters fingered by European fascists in the twentieth century: communists, socialists, liberals, foreigners, persons branded sexual "deviants," racial minorities, and Jews. We have become familiar with these themes: Christianity is debased, whiteness is diluted, sovereignty has been ceded. The United States, according to Trump, is a "Third World & Dying" country, a country held captive by "CRIMINALS & LEFTIST THUGS" (Roche 2023).

There is, too, the promise to restore national greatness—explicit in the MAGA slogan and essential to what the historian Robert Evans called the Nazis' "cultural revolution" (Evans 2003, 397). The appeal is to restoration: the *Third* Reich and Make America Great *Again*. Degeneration has reached a point of emergency, and restoring national greatness requires cleansing violence. As Trump said in anticipation of the 2024 presidential election, "In 2016, I declared: I am your voice. . . . Today, I add: I am your warrior. I am your justice. And for those who have been wronged and betrayed: I am your retribution" (Arnsdorf and Stein 2023). The promise of vengeance and restoration continued in apocalyptic terms: we are "engaged in an epic struggle to rescue our country from the people who hate it and want to absolutely destroy it. . . . We are going to finish what we started. We started something that was a miracle. We're going to complete the mission, we're going to see this battle through to ultimate victory. We're going to make America great again." After listing all the "villains and scoundrels" that he would "demolish," "drive out," "cast out," "throw off," "beat," "rout," and "evict," Trump continued, "We have no choice. This is the final battle" (Trump 2023a; Reed 2023).

In Nazi Germany, the phenomenon that encompassed the administrative state is called *Gleichschaltung*. This is the name given to the process by which the leader's will came to dominate the machinery of government as well as society. Many formal political and social institutions remained nominally in place during Hitler's regime, but their functions were obstructed and their purposes diverted to conform to the will of the leader. Staffing ministries with Nazi Party members to avoid having to contend with the entrenched civil service was central early on (Evans 2003, 397). As civil servants were replaced by party loyalists, settled procedures were replaced by orders from above. Officials strained to discern what the führer wanted and to implement it. Public officials learned to focus on his every word and to navigate his will with trepidation.

Ungoverning evokes *Gleichschaltung* insofar as what the leader wants becomes the only rationale for administrative action. A pointed example was the moment during the Covid pandemic when, instead of relying on federal agencies to distribute medical resources across the country efficiently, the president made determinations of allotments personally, and governors rightly feared that if they criticized him in any way, he would withhold vital medical supplies from their states (Cohen 2020).

All this said, the fascist foreboding can be misleading. In Germany, the bureaucratic apparatus was taken over and redirected. Ungoverning does not strengthen and redirect bureaucracy, it incapacitates the state. There is no *Mein Kampf* as a guide; leaders of the reactionary movement and the Republican Party have neither capacity nor inclination for totalist ideology. The aim is to destroy constraints; it is not to *do*, it is to undo.

Historian Udi Greenberg understood that those who raise the specter of fascism build on a long tradition of belief "in the use of history to mobilize" (Greenberg 2021, 7). Invoking fascism makes the worst imaginable. Yet, to the extent that fascism miscasts the threat, it is an ineffective alarm. Snyder's advice to keep a valid passport at hand and be ready to flee the country conjures escape from a totalitarian state that can act with effectiveness and without resistance (Snyder 2017, 97–98). Ungoverning disables those capacities. But for some, the word itself, "fascism," is the force required to mobilize for resistance now.

Populism with an Authoritarian Face

Like fascism, authoritarianism provides an initial shock of recognition. The willfulness that characterizes ungoverning, the persistent stabs at personal rule ("my generals"), are authoritarian at their core. Violations of the laws and norms of the office, amplified by wildly self-aggrandizing boasts and aggressive threats, are marks of longing for uncontested rule. The threat to "lock up" the opposition is a classic authoritarian move. It does not take "tanks in the street, machine guns in the hands of soldiers" to see authoritarianism at work (Issacharoff 2023, 3). Conspiracism is a necessary tool in converting opponents into "enemies of the people." The warning that "post-truth is pre-fascism" holds equally well for authoritarianism (Snyder 2017, 71).

The limitations of this analogy emerge when we consider again that ungoverning undermines the capacity of the state, which is not what authoritarian regimes want. Strong authoritarian governments like Russia, China, or, on a smaller scale, Singapore employ and depend on the size, scope, and reach of an elaborate administrative state. This is a necessity if authoritarians want to successfully wage war, control large populations, or manage an economy. Authoritarians employ experts, collect data, and measure outcomes, even if the data is sometimes manipulated and the measurements distorted, and the result is propaganda. There is tension, to be sure, between the authoritarian concentration of power and the independent standing of experts, which explains the tendency for a "climate of self-censorship to take over" (Blanchette 2022). That said, authoritarians stake their claim to power on governing, on shaping and implementing policy and delivering results (Gilson and Milhaupt 2011). The regimes that are touchstones of authoritarianism insist on anti-democratic, anti-liberal views of what government is for; they do not stand for the dismantling of administrative institutions. The classic contest between democratic and authoritarian regimes often centers there, on the capacity to govern. Franklin Roosevelt knew that part of winning World War II entailed giving the lie to the claim that authoritarian regimes govern better than liberal democracies.

Some analysts of the United States today view forebodings of fascism and authoritarianism as distractions from the real threat; on this view, those who raise either of the two specters "dodge the obligation to provide a responsible inquiry into American politics." "Abnormalizing Trump" by calling him a fascist or authoritarian "disguises that he is quintessentially American, the expression of enduring indigenous syndromes" (Moyn 2021). This seems right: an American version of populist authoritarianism speaks to the full array of present dangers. Deconstructing the administrative state is not the defining program of authoritarian regimes, unless they are populist (Peters and Pierre 2019, 1533).

Populist authoritarianism is at home in the United States because it arises out of democracy. Its leaders come to power through elections, confirming the sober claim that "most of the power of authoritarianism is freely given" (Snyder 2017, 17). The wave of populist electoral successes in Europe and the United States is vivid in Brexit (the United Kingdom's withdrawal from the European Union) and authoritarian populist successes of the Fidesz Party in Hungary and the Law and Justice Party in Poland.

Populism is a twisted version of democracy, however. One distortion is that the connection between the leader and the people is direct, personal, immediate, and emotional. It is shorn of institutions and offices (Galston 2018; Issacharoff

2023; Müller 2016; Urbinati 2019). In a populist regime, anything that comes between "the people" and the leader is intolerable. The leader's relation to followers requires his constant presence, with ceremonial occasions that stage the strongman signing orders or appearing with military officers, with frequent rallies, and with a never-ending stream of tweets. The people are constantly present to the leader, and, importantly, the leader is present to them. He understands and shares his followers' antipathies and their desire for action "right now." He cultivates a dynamic of constant, mutual recognition. Nadia Urbinati makes the point that "the populist leader needs to stay in permanent campaign mode because . . . the formality of elections has less value than the strength of the audience" (Urbinati 2019, 168). Ultimately, as we've seen, adherents to the reactionary movement were not content to be just an audience; they answered his calls to violence.

If one characteristic of populist authoritarianism is immediacy, an intense form of contact, the other side of populism is exclusion—that is, the designation of part of the citizenry as the true people ("real Americans") and the exclusion of others. Populism answers the elementary question of every democracy—who is "the people"?—with finality. The "people" is homogeneous, whether in religion, race, or ethno-nationalism, and in shared disgust with elites, political establishments, and ossified institutions. Here is Trump's pure version of exclusion: "The only important thing is the unification of the people—because the other people don't mean anything" (Müller 2017, 22).

The challenge populist authoritarianism poses to liberal democracy is daunting precisely because the leader is voted into office. There is no bright line between representative democracy and authoritarianism chosen by voters—when elections allow for rotation in office. We understand, then, why populism has been called "a new form of representative government" (Urbinati 2019, 1). It grows out of representative democracy, spurred by discontent with the parties and the "establishment" that have controlled the terms of political representation. Populism presents itself as a corrective.

Yet, though populism emerges from electoral democracy, it is poisonous to liberal democracy and friendly to authoritarianism, because it is radically opposed to pluralism. In the United States today, populists are revolted by a multiracial nation, a multireligious nation, a multicultural nation. And in its exclusiveness and anti-pluralism, populism derogates the formal liberal elements essential to democracy such as rights of speech and assembly, protection for minorities, a free press, rule of law. It is overtly illiberal and authoritarian. Recall the Hungarian leader Viktor Orbán's blunt 2014 declaration that "the new state that we are building is an illiberal state" (Linton 2019).

Forebodings invoke historical crises of democracy and alert us to the specificity of fascist and authoritarian threats. They caution against unanchored generalizations about democratic decline. They also help us identify and assess what is unusual, even unique about the present threat: the attack on state capacity and on the administrative state especially. Comparative political scientist Samuel Huntington insisted that "the most important political distinction among countries concerns not their form of government but their degree of government." He studied places "where political institutions have little power, less majesty, and no resiliency—where, in many cases, governments simply do not govern" (Huntington 1968, 2). That is the threat—not the specter of a fearsomely effective totalitarian state, but the threat to liberal democracy that comes from the willful degradation of a well-developed state.

Where Ungoverning Can Go

Ungoverning damages representative democracy in a particular kind of way. Although our focus in on the United States, this is not the only place we see it. It is an unusual phenomenon; as we have said, authoritarian rulers want to command a capacious state, not destroy the state they command. For the same reason, it is not the case that all authoritarian populists will incline to strategies of ungoverning. But some have pursued ungoverning as a mode of disabling any institution or group that might challenge their power. Two cases that stand out in the current political landscape are India and Venezuela.

Narendra Modi, India's prime minister since 2014, has transformed the largest democracy in the world into a form of "electoral authoritarianism" (Jaffrelot 2023, 310). He came to national prominence in 2002, when he exploited communal violence between Hindus and Muslims and assumed the role of defender of the Hindu majority. Over thirteen years as chief minister of Gujarat, he perfected modes of advancing himself by cultivating division and fear. In 2014 he brought these techniques to Indian national politics in his first campaign for prime minister. He was reelected in a landslide in 2019. Modi has presented himself as the defender against putative external threats from Pakistan and internal threats from Muslim terrorists.

As prime minister, Modi brought his own version of ungoverning to India, which Christophe Jaffrelot calls "deinstitutionalizing" (Jaffrelot 2023, 253–309). His aim was to incapacitate any institution that might challenge his power. This included the national ombudsman's office, the information commission, and the Central Vigilance Commission, charged with investigating offenses under the Prevention of Corruption Act. The techniques varied in familiar ways: sometimes vacancies were left unfilled; sometimes, when they were filled, loyalists got the appointments. The gutting of independent agencies was coupled with a concerted attack on the courts and on the press. Judicial openings were left unfilled, press outlets raided, journalists investigated and arrested. Finally, Modi brought the same treatment to his political opponents. They were investigated by the tax authorities, arrested, and barred from serving in Parliament (Gupta and Shih 2023). Modi also went after academics, pressuring university administrators to fire prominent critics (Chopra 2021). Independent officials and experts are disabled and replaced with loyalists, policing powers are politicized, and vigilantism is legitimated, all for the purpose of liberating the leader's will. Every institution and every person who can resist is attacked or corrupted.

Modi is a popular leader, and in the face of his appeals to Hindu nationalism, opposition parties have been unable to create a compelling alternative or to consolidate a viable majority coalition. India is a classic case of *democratic* backsliding, where electoral and majoritarian institutions are used to weaken the independence of the judiciary, the press, and the university, as well as to erode protections for opponents and critics (Tudor 2023). While a form of majoritarianism is preserved, governing is sacrificed. In India, populist authoritarianism and ungoverning go together.

The Indian state has long been capable in some respects and profoundly incapable in others (D. Kapur 2020). India is famous for its political corruption. At the same time, the state's capacity to recruit, retain, and empower experts in areas like macroeconomic management has helped underwrite widespread prosperity. And notwithstanding Modi's authoritarianism, India's standing in the international world has not suffered, even as democracy-rating organizations like Varieties of

Democracy categorize the country as an "electoral autocracy," downgrading it completely out of the "democracy" category (V-Dem Institute 2023, 39). Whether ungoverning becomes self-defeating—whether it incapacitates not only Modi's critics but also Modi himself, by disabling the state he commands—remains to be seen.

Comprehensive disabling defines the result of decades of ungoverning in Venezuela. Hugo Chávez, who ruled Venezuela from his election in 1999 until his death in 2013, came to power as a populist hero of the poor. At first, he aspired to govern, undertaking serious land reform and initiating public health programs that brought doctors and medical care to the rural peasantry. But he could not tolerate experts limiting his will, or institutions mediating his command, and his interest in governing soon gave way to his more abiding interest in personal rule. He altered the constitution to remove term limits on the presidency and to compress the bicameral legislature into a single assembly he could dominate. His opponents were branded enemies of the state, and he hounded the independent press nearly out of existence.

Chávez's moods substituted for policy. His cabinet of incompetent loyalists tracked his decrees as they changed hour to hour. Chávez went through 180 cabinet ministers in a decade. As one reporter chronicled, "The disciples invested everything in submission. All categories had to show loyalty—it was the first condition of ascent—but the disciples went further by making instant, complete obedience their specialty. They brought no ideas or special talents, controlled no constituencies" (Carroll 2013, 119–20, 134; Neuman 2022, 269). Because Chávez's favorite color was red, his ministers wore red baseball caps, red shirts, red skirts. One day, Chávez appeared on his palace balcony wearing yellow and pronounced there was too much red. Panic ensued, as ministers quickly adjusted their wardrobes. Several weeks later, red was back.

Eventually, having dismissed anyone with expertise and the integrity to speak truth to power, Chávez destroyed the economy of what had once been one of the richest nations on earth. Impoverishment was comprehensive: the country lacked food, doctors, and medicine. Political repression and economic collapse have created a Venezuelan diaspora; more than 7.7 million people, over 20 percent of the country, have left since 2015 (Salas-Wright et al. 2022; United Nations High Commission on Refugees 2023). In his work on populism, legal scholar Samuel Issacharoff uses the history of fragile democracies as a warning to mature ones (Issacharoff 2023, 97). But Venezuela's anarchy is not the danger that ungoverning poses in the United States, for no political leader, not even a populist authoritarian bent on deconstruction, has the capacity to disintegrate working government at every level. Deconstruction of departments and programs at the national level meets the constraints of fifty states and partisan federalism. As we have shown, states are some insurance against degradation of government everywhere and all the way down by an authoritarian president, a party committed to ungoverning, and an armed and animated reactionary movement. Deconstruction can go anywhere and all the way down, but it cannot go everywhere.

How to characterize the result of abdication of governing in the United States? One way of looking at it is that ungoverning bears a family resemblance to what social scientists have called neo-feudalism, evoking the era before the creation of the nation-state, when feudal lords "maintained their own military forces, and operated feudal courts to resolve disputes" (Stone and Kuttner 2020). Neo-feudalism means citizens cannot rely on the national government to protect them against the ravages of concentrated capital. This insecurity is amplified by the way ungoverning at the national level causes citizens to rely more and more on state governments. Under conditions of partisan polarization, the protections that state governments offer are highly variable and often unpredictable, underlining the day-to-day experience of uncertainty and vulnerability.

Neo-feudalism

The term "neo-feudalism" refers to the state stepping back from acting as a "counterweight to the concentrated power that flowed to concentrated wealth in a capitalist economy" (Stone and Kuttner 2020). The objective of a diminished state is not efficiency, as privatization or deregulation would aim for. Neither privatization nor deregulation evokes, as neo-feudalism does, the full scope of devolution of responsibility for governing.

One example of neo-feudalism is corporate escape from the purview of regulatory agencies that protect workers' and consumers' rights and the replacement of this public system with confidentiality agreements and compulsory arbitration. These remove consumer and employment disputes from the courts and assign them to private systems of adjudication. The crux of neo-feudalism is reversion of "entire realms of public law, public property, due process, and citizen rights" to unaccountable control by private business" (Stone and Kuttner 2020).

Consider another, more familiar development: the expansion of private residential communities across the nation that take over and override many of the functions of local government. Homeowner associations make and enforce their own laws and provide their own services. Elected boards of directors (with votes distributed by ownership shares) regulate myriad aspects of property and daily life among neighbors. Homeowners are subject to legal covenants that run with property in perpetuity. These associations are not just a matter of the "secession of the successful"; they are communities of choice for the middle class as well (Rosenblum 1998, 146).

We can see ungoverning as the counterpart of neo-feudalism. Both represent a retreat from whole areas of public responsibility once judged essential and thought to be secure. But there is a key difference. Neo-feudalism describes a steady devolution of public authority to private entities. It is cousin to ungoverning in its result: government effectively abdicates state functions. But neo-feudalism focuses on the private seizure of what were regulatory state functions. It serves specific material interests. And nothing in neo-feudalism requires popular support, much less enflames a movement. In sum, ungoverning is not only the transfer of authority to private entities. It is incapacitating government simpliciter, with no concern for alternative public or private institutions. Nor is ungoverning principally the work of economic elites; it is directly, avowedly the partisan aim of mobilized forces of reaction and authoritarian will.

We've emphasized throughout this book the ambition to "bring it all crashing down," and the apocalyptic aura of restoration that characterizes ungoverning. We've also emphasized institutional sites of resistance to the willful exercise of presidential power that drives ungoverning. Another aspect of ungoverning is that it necessarily proceeds erratically and indiscriminately, creating both unpredictability and insecurity.

Insecurity of Expectation

Federalism in the United States has always meant a great deal of variation in the policies of the states. Ungoverning's attack on state capacity at the national level renders citizens more and more dependent on their states for many of the protections they expect from government. Given partisan polarization, policy regimes in the states vary enormously, depending on whether the state is "blue" (reliably run by Democrats) or "red" (reliably controlled by Republicans). And in swing states that neither party reliably controls, the policies on which people depend are even more uncertain. The patchwork nation produces variation and unpredictability.

When it comes to women's access to reproductive health care, citizens correctly identify some states as dangerous places and others as safe havens. As Republican states pass draconian laws criminalizing abortion—as in the Texas bounty law that encourages ordinary citizens to report and bring civil suits against doctors and anyone else who facilitates an abortion after six weeks—Democratic states strengthen access (Texas Heartbeat Act, TX S.B. 8 [2021]). They also work to protect citizens in Republican states by providing to those states' residents health care they cannot receive at home. Governor Jay Inslee and other Democratic officials declared Washington state a "sanctuary" of this kind (Demkovich 2022). Even those in "safe states" are aware of their own vulnerability.

A report by the Human Rights Campaign describes insecurity of expectation and fear. Five hundred and twenty-five anti-LGBTQ+ bills were introduced in 2023 legislative sessions, including more than 220 targeting transgender men, women, and children. LGBTQ+ Americans could become "a new class of political refugees" (Blow 2023). The term "refugee" underscores the radical insecurity, emotional toll, and actual physical danger of either staying put or leaving. Movement of citizens from state to state is commonplace in the United States; people move for work or to be near family or to settle in communities that seem congruent with their values. But they are not fleeing.

There is more: anxiety and even fear are experienced widely, even by those who are not members of vulnerable, despised groups and are not specific targets of reactionary animus. Ungoverning produces fear of violence even in situations other than those we have discussed such as election work or Covid masking. The near absence of federal regulation of weapons has left regulation of guns to the states. But no one can feel entirely safe from violence; weapons (and their owners) cross state borders. Assault weapons, open-carry policies, and men and women driven by a fantasy of government tyranny travel. Permission for intimidation travels. People who shoot up supermarkets and drag shows travel. The map of the United States as red and blue illustrates the patchwork and, what is unstated, the comparative vulnerability from state to state.

Uncertainty and anxiety also infuse citizens' encounters with the administrative state where "the state meets the street" (Zacka 2017). What federal or state programs will be steadily available? What might be defunded and degraded tomorrow? True, uncertainty often accompanies interaction with government bureaucracies and is heightened by even regular changes in federal or state policy. The complex institutional mechanics of getting food stamps (or not) has immediate consequences. The difference now is that uncertainty and fear of loss are heightened by ungoverning's rapid, chaotic changes. For men and women personally and individually, expectations with regard to benefits and services and the protections of regulation on which day-to-day lives depend are unsettled. Insecurity holds not only for the recipients of benefits or targets of regulation but also for workers in federal and state agencies and in non-profits who are dependent on national government programs for their livelihoods. Ungoverning at the national level radically accentuates the importance of variation among the states for the expectations on which day-to-day lives rely.

With all this, insecurity is not restricted to the consequences of specific acts of ungoverning. It is atmospheric. We can speak without exaggeration of an undercurrent of moral anxiety. Ungoverning upsets expectations, and insecurity of expectation has been rightly understood as a painful condition.

The consequences of ungoverning are continuously disruptive, *and are meant to be*. For the many people directly affected and others who witness and fear for themselves, vulnerability can be infantilizing. It can be paralyzing. Fear taxes personal and collective agency. In this way, ungoverning degrades the vital moral underpinnings of liberal democracy.

9

Courts and Constitutional Attacks

We have named ungoverning and shown how it works. We have identified its political purposes. We have looked at its effects. And we have discussed the actions taken by an ungoverning president, party, and movement. This political effort to dismantle the administrative state is mirrored by an allied judicial effort to rein in administrative authority. It is not too much to say that there is, as one recent law review title puts it, a "judicial assault on the administrative state" (Seligman 2023).

These judicial arguments against administrative authority function politically to normalize ungoverning; they are the tip of the spear of the attack on the administrative state. The doctrines used to attack administrative institutions are highly technical and are little known and little understood outside of law schools. But the most unqualified versions of these legal doctrines are potentially as destructive as the political project of ungoverning.

When it was developed in earnest in the Progressive Era and during the New Deal, the legal standing of the administrative state was controversial. These initial attacks abated with the rise of the bipartisan Administrative Procedure Act, which we discussed in chapter 2. But in recent decades, those attacks have been revived. The rise of a conservative Supreme Court has led some legal scholars to suggest we are seeing the "1930s redux"—a new contest over the authority of the administrative state and even the very existence of independent agencies that harkens back to foundational arguments that first arose during the New Deal (Metzger 2017b).

The most comprehensive objections to the administrative state see it as not merely running afoul of an arcane corner of law, but as violating the very heart of the Constitution. In this view, the Constitution establishes the fundamental legislative power (Article I), executive power (Article II), and judicial power (Article III), and vests these powers in the two houses of Congress, the presidency, and the courts, respectively. The administrative state, the argument goes, usurps all three fundamental government powers (Sunstein and Vermeule 2020, 1–3).

Administrative agencies are said to violate Article I because administrators appropriate the rulemaking power that is properly legislative. The posture that Congress cannot give away its legislative authority to another entity is referred to as the "nondelegation doctrine." The charge is that Congress does this when it sets out general programmatic goals and assigns agencies the authority to design policy and to write rules to implement those goals. In fact, since the New Deal era, Congress's delegation to agencies has been seen as necessary and permitted "if it provided 'intelligible principles' to cabin agency discretion and 'suitable procedural safeguards'" (Kovacs 2021). That long-standing view is now aggressively disputed.

In this comprehensive attack, the problem with Article II is that the independence of key agencies removes them from the president's constitutional authority over the executive branch. This contradicts the standing view that the president cannot remove and replace all the officials on the Federal Trade Commission, the Securities and Exchange Commission, or the Federal Reserve. To advocates of the "unitary executive thesis," which we will expand on shortly, the Constitution vests appointment power over executive officials in the "president alone" (Humphrey's Executor v. United States, 295 U.S. 602 [1935]; Kovacs 2021, 119; Freeman and Jacobs 2021, 633). The "alone" matters. As unitary executive advocates see it, Article II's wording places *all power* in a single person: "The executive Power shall be vested in a President of the United States of America" (Brettschneider 2018, 53–70). Having independent agencies led by commissioners with staggered terms, who cannot be removed except for cause, violates the president's constitutional authority.

Finally, the administrative state is said to conflict with Article III's judicial power because departments issue binding interpretations of statutes and executive orders, enforce those rules, and then adjudicate appeals that result from their own rules. Even if it were conceded that agencies can issue rules (a quasi-legislative function) and enforce them (an executive function), the courts have the right to oversee and overrule agency determinations.

Justice Roberts alluded to this comprehensive constitutional attack on the administrative state approvingly in his dissent in *City of Arlington v. Federal Communications Commission* (569 U.S. 290 [2013]), where he noted that according to the *Federalist*, "the accumulation of all powers, legislative, executive, and judiciary, . . . may justly be pronounced the very definition of tyranny." The administrative state, he wrote, blends exactly these powers:

> Although modern administrative agencies fit most comfortably within the Executive Branch, as a practical matter they exercise legislative power, by promulgating regulations with the force of law; executive power, by policing compliance with those regulations; and judicial power, by adjudicating enforcement actions and imposing sanctions on those found to have violated their rules. The accumulation of these powers in the same hands is not an occasional or isolated exception to the constitutional plan; it is a central feature of modern American government. (*Arlington*, 569 U.S. at 312)

Even so, in this case, Roberts concluded, "It would be a bit much to describe the result as 'the very definition of tyranny' but the danger posed by the growing power of the administrative state cannot be dismissed" (*Arlington*, 569 U.S. at 315).

For other constitutional critics, however, the administrative state *is* the definition of tyranny. Philip Hamburger put it strongly: the administrative state represents the infusion of alien Germanic ideas of administration onto the Anglo-American legal tradition, ideas that are monarchic and absolutist. "The danger from administrative law," he says, "can be understood as the risk of introducing Prussian-style rule" (Hamburger 2014, 505). The rejection of the administrative state *tout court* as an unconstitutional legacy of the New Deal has created a legal rhetoric of "anti-administrativism" that "forms a notable link between the contemporary political and judicial attacks on national administrative government" (Metzger 2017b, 4). If the administrative state violates the first three articles of the Constitution and the separation of powers, then either the Constitution has to be reinterpreted or revised, or the administrative state has to be completely refashioned, its scope diminished and its work curtailed. As one unyielding critic argues, "The post–New Deal administrative state is unconstitutional, and its validation by the legal system amounts to nothing less than a bloodless constitutional revolution" (Lawson 1994, 1231).

This is not a fringe view. Justices Clarence Thomas, John Roberts, Samuel Alito, and Neil Gorsuch have all suggested that central features of the administrative state may be unconstitutional (Metzger 2017b, 3). One of Clarence Thomas's first mentors, the political scientist John Marini, argues that the twentieth century replaced the sovereignty of the people with "the sovereignty of government, understood in terms of the modern concept of the rational or administrative state" (Marini 2019, 13).

To be sure, there are two faces to the legal criticism of the administrative state. The first, as we just saw, sees the entire edifice as unconstitutional. The second is more restrained. It takes seriously the charge that there is a "deeply rooted tension between core tenets of American constitutionalism and the rise of the modern administrative state" but does not seek to dismantle the administrative state in toto (Postell 2017). "I have never met anyone who is opposed to 'the administrative project,'" says one scholar (Nielson 2017, 4). As they see it, redefining the purview of regulatory agencies is simply an effort to restrict agency authority on the margins. That is not, however, the aim of those who advocate the radical doctrine of the "unitary executive."

The Unitary Executive

The unitary executive doctrine dates to the 1970s and 1980s (Crouch, Rozell, and Sollenberger 2020). Taken literally, the doctrine is correct; the Constitution did create a unitary executive by vesting executive power in *one* person rather than a council (Sunstein and Vermeule 2021, 83). But as it is wielded by critics of the administrative state, it means much more: it invests the president with complete power of oversight and control over the administrative state.

The upshot of such a doctrine would be most damaging to the "independent agencies" like the Securities and Exchange Commission (SEC), the Federal Election Commission (FEC), and the Federal Trade Commission (FTC). As we noted in chapter 2, such agencies are often led by boards or commissions whose members cannot be removed by either Congress or the president. Appointments are often staggered so that no one president can fully control them, and commissioners can be removed only for cause, meaning that they have been found responsible for wrongdoing or other actions that call into question their integrity or fitness.

Yet, according to the extreme unitary executive doctrine, presidents should be able to remove such appointments anytime they please and replace them with new people of their choosing. This means, in effect, that a president could charge the SEC with investigating companies run by his political opponents and fire commissioners if they refused. Presidents could remove FCC commissioners because they refuse to pull licenses from broadcasting networks that are insufficiently obsequious in their reporting. They could fire commissioners at the FEC who refuse to investigate candidates from the opposition party. The unitary executive doctrine portends a president who can remove any agency official at any time.

This is how seemingly small and precise judicial decisions about presidential removal power are far more threatening than their legalistic tone would suggest. One example is the majority decision in the Supreme Court case *Seila Law v. Consumer Financial Protection Bureau* (2020). Consonant with the unitary executive doctrine, the decision affirmed the president's power to remove and replace the head of the bureau. Using the same reasoning, the president would have the power "not only to remove officials but to tell them how to do the jobs Congress assigned to them." The president could "tell the EPA head . . . exactly at what level to set national air quality standards" (Heinzerling 2022, 10). The doctrine would also free the president to remove "Schedule F" civil service protection for tens of thousands of workers in the federal government. It would liberate the president from any procedural constraint imposed by the legislature (Lessig and Sunstein 1994). This is how an innovative legal doctrine aligns with the ambitions of an ungoverning president.

This points to one significant caveat. Increasing the president's constitutional authority over the administrative state in the already imperial presidency does not dictate that this authority will always be used to weaken or deconstruct the machinery of government. The unitary executive thesis would redound to the *office* of the president. In theory, it would be institutionalized and passed on to presidents of any party from one election to the next. The authority of a unitary executive could be used by a progressive president to strengthen and expand the machinery of government in the service of advancing social and economic equality.

For this reason, progressives friendly to administration have embraced presidential control over the administrative state, as Elena Kagan did in her 1994 argument in favor of presidential administration. Kagan defended the expansion of presidential control of administration under Reagan and its expansion under Clinton, who used it to "showcase and to advance presidential policies" (Kagan 2001, 2248). In her telling, presidential control was used by Presidents Reagan and George H. W. Bush for deregulatory purposes but "operated during the Clinton presidency as a mechanism to achieve progressive goals" (Kagan 2001, 2249). Again, the powers Kagan defends adhere to the office, not the person.

The medieval metaphor of the "king's two bodies" distinguished the Crown from the person of the monarch. The "Crown" would be greatly empowered under the unitary executive doctrine. If it were to guide interpretation of presidential power, it would apply to every occupant of the office, whether centrist or extremist or nihilist. At the same time, a willful president intent on personal rule and not on reconfiguring the authority of the office would exploit unitary executive authority. He or she would push the bounds of appointments and firings, procedures, and expertise and would be loosed to degrade agency capacity. As one pointed observation put it, "Effective political leaders will have no need for the theory of the unitary executive, and the theory will not compensate for what leadership alone can provide" (Skowronek, Dearborn, and King 2021, 126).

But the maximal versions of unitary executive theory ultimately collapse the division between office and person. To hold that the president may change rules as he pleases, fire personnel for reasons of personal animus regardless of civil service protections, and scuttle legislatively stipulated processes for making and implementing policy is to liberate the president from law. It also removes the norms and professionalization, the expertise and process, the statutes and protections built up to insulate administration from arrant politicization. Congressman Adam Schiff, the manager of the first Trump impeachment team, put it well: "If the President can obstruct his own investigation, if he can effectively nullify a power the Constitution gives solely to Congress . . . to prevent Presidential misconduct, then the President places himself beyond accountability and above the law. Cannot be indicted, cannot be impeached. It makes him a monarch, the very evil against which our Constitution and the balance of powers it carefully laid out, was designed to guard against" (166 *Cong. Rec.* S378, 2020).

For Trump, the doctrine confirmed his instinct that the presidency invested him with the power of personal rule. He was pleased to pronounce, "I have an Article II, where I have the right to do whatever I want as president" (Brice-Saddler 2019). If Trump put the unitary executive doctrine crudely, that seems to be the political thrust for advocates of the theory: it is not institutional reform, but license to act out fundamental hostility to government itself and to degrade institutions in favor of personal will.

Unitary executive theory cannot be reduced to a highbrow legal version of brash "deconstruction of the administrative state" pursued by Steve Bannon and the former president. And yet, it has the effect of enabling even more expansive executive action vis-à-vis agencies and departments without express limitations. Those who want to liberate presidential will and equip the president to destroy the administrative state grasp onto the doctrine. Paired with a president and party at war against a "deep state," unitary executive theory predicts deconstruction.

Judicial Oversight: Pragmatic Solution or Assault?

Unitary executive is one among several constitutional interpretations advanced in legal academies, taken up by advocacy groups, and tapped by judges that can provide justification for ungoverning. Unitary executive theory is still just a theory. A more potent addition to the arsenal of ungoverning is actually being worked out in courts today—the attack on so-called *Chevron* deference. The Supreme Court's 1984 ruling in *Chevron USA v. Natural Resources Defense Council* set out what became the long-standing doctrine of judicial deference to administrative departments. It "has a strong claim to being the most important case in all of administrative law" (Sunstein 2019, 1615).

In *Chevron*, the Court famously held that when congressional statutes are ambiguous and when an agency's interpretation is reasonable, judges should defer to agency rulings. According to this decision, courts should assume that Congress meant to confer discretion about how to achieve a result to experts in the agencies. The governing assumption in *Chevron* is that the Court cannot impose its own interpretation of statutes. *Chevron* affirmed that agencies could interpret laws as they saw fit unless the interpretation is "plainly erroneous or inconsistent with the regulation" (Metzger 2017b, 25). The decision assigns primacy to the legislature over courts in setting the parameters of delegation to the administrative state; this is what is meant by "*Chevron* deference."

At the same time, by leaving interpretation of Congress's purposes to agencies, *Chevron* gave presidents more power over agencies through their political appointments. This was acceptable to conservatives when Reagan was president, and Republicans initially supported *Chevron* deference in order to protect the ability of appointees to change agency direction (Scalia 1989a)—as Reagan did when he appointed anti-environmentalist Anne Gorsuch head of the EPA.

But what seemed acceptable to conservatives during the Reagan administration ceased to be acceptable when the administrative state fell under the control of Presidents Clinton and Obama. In fact, Obama turned to the administrative state to achieve his policy goals in response to a Republican Congress bent on obstruction. That was the political impetus for conservatives to set out to reverse deference to the agencies established in *Chevron*. Put simply, "The political value of administrative independence has flipped" (Sunstein 2019, 1664). It flipped from a tool conservatives could use in service of their policy agenda to a tool in the hands of those promoting a progressive agenda. The view that *Chevron* was not only wrong but unconstitutional would be put to work.

This swerve came at the same time as increasing politicization of judicial appointments—lifelong appointments, in the case of the Supreme Court—that redounded to the benefit of conservatives (Strauss 2021, 28). While they could not count on controlling the presidency, they had confidence that they would control the Supreme Court and thus could argue against the *Chevron* decision. The aim was to give friendly, unelected federal judges authority over interpreting the bounds of administrative independence.

And with this, the language of court decisions lost its sober judiciousness and became fierce in its disregard of precedent: *Chevron* is "nothing more than a judicially orchestrated shift of power from Congress to the Executive Branch," Justice Kavanaugh asserted (Sunstein 2019, 1616). The politicization of judicial appointments gave the legal assault on the independence of agency judgments life. Under Trump, nominees for the Supreme Court were not just vetted but proposed by the Federalist Society for their commitment to shrink the federal government. In the early years of his presidency, Trump made strategic alliances with the conservative establishment he largely excoriated and spurned, and this was one of those instances: "We're going to have great judges, conservative, all picked by the Federalist Society" (Milhiser 2016).

In *West Virginia v. Environmental Protection Agency* (2022), the conservative majority on the Supreme Court showed what it meant to reject Justice Scalia's earlier affirmation of *Chevron* and to constrict administrators' latitude. A majority ruled that a critical public policy—regulating greenhouse gas emissions from fossil fuel–fired power plants—was an unconstitutional seizure of power by the EPA. The Court rejected the argument that Congress had given the agency authority to respond to the climate crisis when it tasked the EPA to come up with the best system for controlling power plant emissions. The Court found it "'highly unlikely' that Congress would leave to 'agency discretion' the decision of how much coal-based generation there should be over the coming decades" (West Virginia v. EPA, 142 S. Ct. 2587, 2612 [2022], quoting the Court's 1994 decision in MCI v. AT&T). The ruling was emphatic: Congress alone can specify, by statute, the mechanisms of regulation, and on "major questions," broad delegation to authorize agency action should be treated with "skepticism" (*West Virginia*, 142 S. Ct. at 2590, 2593).

With this, the majority invented a new canon, the major questions doctrine, without providing guidance as to what counts as a "major question." The Court went further and designated *itself* the arbiter of whether administrative actions address "major questions" (*West Virginia*, 142 S. Ct. at 2591). Just about any issue of economic and political significance could fit that designation, from immigration to gender discrimination. The major questions doctrine is an invitation to "constant litigation" (Coffee 2022). The Supreme Court opened the door wide to claims that Congress has granted unconstitutional authority to administrators, and through it marched claimants and judges who would weaken the federal government. Justice Kagan wrote in her dissent that *West Virginia v. EPA* amounts to outright political obstruction of the Clean Power Plan, the issue in the case. The Court's ideological posture (and sense of *political* urgency) is revealed by the fact that the case itself was irregular. It was not brought in response to an actual controversy; the plan under review had never gone into effect, and by the time it was reviewed, President Trump had repealed it.

West Virginia is the product of partisan shift. Although it appears to invite Congress to step in and pass new legislation to clarify its intent, in reality, it requires Congress to do what in practice it cannot, for two reasons. For one, Congress has relied on administrative expertise and processes for fifty years, and had to; the challenges of bringing a 435-person body into coherent agreement on the technicalities of exactly how to achieve the goals of environmental protection Congress endorses are insuperable. In addition, when ferocious partisan division besets Congress—and where one party is anti-government—it is very difficult for the political branch to authorize any specific course of action.

Nor does *West Virginia* vest authority in the executive. Again, the power actually redounds to the federal courts—in particular, to the Supreme Court—which now can, by itself, overrule agency interpretations and incapacitate agencies when they are acting on (undefined) "major questions." It has constricted the authority of "the most knowledgeable branch" and claimed more authority for itself, the least knowledgeable branch (Sunstein 2016). In creating this doctrine, the Court proffered in effect a wide-open invitation to organized interests to litigate agency decisions and to conservative courts to constrain or hamstring or circumvent the administrative state.

At issue here is nothing less than the state's capacity to address critical needs as they develop. Justice Kagan underscored the point: faulty and politically biased doctrinal analysis disregards the uncertain and therefore chaotic consequences of the decision. The majority certainly intended to upend the EPA's capacity, and it turned a blind eye to what would come next. As Kagan wrote, "Let's say the obvious: The stakes here are high. Yet the Court today prevents congressionally authorized agency action to curb power plants' carbon dioxide emissions. The Court appoints itself—instead of Congress or the expert agency—the decision-maker on climate policy. I cannot think of many things more frightening" (*West Virginia*, 142 S. Ct. at 2620).

West Virginia was the first big bite at the *Chevron* doctrine of deferring to agency interpretation of ambiguous laws. How far will the courts go? Scholars range in their predictions from "trimming doctrine around the edges" (Adler 2021) to overturning *Chevron* entirely. Overturning it would mean "an entirely new start with respect to judicial review of agency interpretations of law and would introduce a high degree of uncertainty." It would mean "upheaval," "a large shock to the legal system" (Sunstein 2019, 1620, 1670). It would be a shock not just to the legal system, but to governing. It would provide a constitutional foothold for wholesale attacks on the administrative state.

Cases working their way through the legal system amount to a potent route for ungoverning. Conservative judges in federal courts are doing the work, step by step, of enabling the attack on administrative agencies. They are chipping away at state capacity. "If Congress cannot delegate to agencies, it cannot govern" (Rosenblum 2023).

Judges in federal courts are taking one basic function of constitutional law to the extreme. The common notion is that constitutionalism bars the excesses of government. It is protective of spheres of liberty, and so it should be. But constitutionalism also aims at creating structures of state capacity, the ability of government to govern. The "challenges involved in at once creating and limiting state power" are being acted out today by parties and judges determined to limit or erase the capacity to govern when and where it is most needed (Khosla and Tushnet 2022, 95). The most comprehensive legal critiques of administration function as the tip of the spear that provides a sharp weapon for the political forces of ungoverning.

Revaluing Administration

Some legal analysts lay out calibrated defenses of administrative necessity and constitutional authority, and these defenders of administrative institutions do not align completely with partisanship. Some are conservatives and some, as we would expect, are progressives (Vermeule 2016; Metzger 2017b). *Law and Leviathan: Redeeming the Administrative State* is the work of a collaboration between a progressive and a conservative scholar of administrative law (Sunstein and Vermeule 2020). Many developed their positions before the era of arrant deconstruction; others address it directly, as do the authors in Mark Tushnet's edited collection of essays in a special issue of *Daedalus*, "The Administrative State in the Twenty-First Century: Deconstruction and/or Reconstruction" (Tushnet 2021). Gillian Metzger makes the overarching argument that the administrative state is "constitutionally obligatory"; the president has a constitutional duty to "take Care that the Laws be faithfully executed," and in order to fulfill that duty, government must have "sufficient bureaucratic apparatus and supervisory mechanisms" to implement the laws passed by Congress (Metzger 2017b, 87, 89). Other legal scholars emphasize that the administrative state is fundamentally democratic because it is brought into being by Congress as an essential instrument for solving problems (Beermann 2018). Arguing that the administrative state is a foundation of the modern constitution, Jon D. Michaels defends it against privatization on one side and unconstrained executive authority on the other. He argues for a combination of political appointees, expert civil service, and popular participation within the administrative state to replicate the constitutional separation of executive, legislative, and judicial authority (Michaels 2017, 59, 75).

Ultimately, however, the contest over the authority of the administrative state will need to reach beyond the domain of legal analysis. What is needed are not only constitutional arguments but political reforms that resonate broadly. In the end, the administrative state depends not only on the opinions of law professors and judges, but also on citizens who regard it as necessary and as having meaning, value, and authority. Yet, attention to the administrative state has been almost wholly the property of the legal profession. For decades, political science had all but abandoned its once-central study of public administration. And with rare exceptions, administration has never been a concern of democratic theory.

That is changing. From political science and political theory come defenses of the value, necessity, and authority of government bureaucracy, including accounts of the administrative state's history and necessity, such as Francis Fukuyama's *Political Order and Political Decay* (2014) or Stephen Skowronek, John A. Dearborn, and Desmond King's account of the tension between administrative independence and executive control in *Phantoms of a Beleaguered Republic: The Deep State and the Unitary Executive* (2021). Other accounts too, such as *Bring Back the Bureaucrats* (DiIulio 2014); *Valuing Bureaucracy: The Case for Professional Government* (Verkuil 2017); and *In Praise of Bureaucracy; Weber, Organization, Ethics* (Du Gay 2000) offer imaginative, sometimes radical proposals for reform. Three prescriptions stand out: *simplification*, *democratization*, and *relegitimation*. There is much to grapple with in these assessments and proposals for reform. Most were written before the advent of ungoverning. Our question is whether these analyses and prescriptions are powerful enough to answer the forces of ungoverning.

The spirit of simplification defines John J. DiIulio Jr.'s *Bring Back the Bureaucrats* (2014). In the United States, governing is parceled out among the federal government, state and local governments, private for-profit contractors, and nonprofit grantees. What DiIulio calls "Leviathan by proxy" is the problem. Privatizing and sharing administrative functions is "superficially anti-statist," but in fact, it simply camouflages the size, cost, and inefficiency of state programs (4). The large, complex programs that actually work effectively to serve national needs are administered from the center, directly, DiIulio argues. The administrative costs of Social Security and Medicare, for example, amount to about a quarter of the federal budget, yet the programs are well managed by fewer employees than work for Princeton University. As things stand, public administration reflects "not the slightest real regard for what it takes to translate the policies, programs, or regulations into time and cost-effective administrative action" (47).

DiIulio intends his argument for simplification to be nonpartisan. "If every post-1960 federal policy, program, rule, or regulation had to be administered directly and exclusively by full-time federal bureaucrats," he predicts that the result would be agreeable to both progressives and conservatives. Progressives would get effective programs; conservatives would get cost-effective programs. Perhaps. But the partisan contest that defined U.S. politics when he wrote in 2014 has given way to something more ferocious—and to ungoverning. DiIulio wants an "administrative presidency" where presidents are not just agenda-setters or communicators but chief administrators. This reflects the expectation that presidents would take responsibility for the success of the administrative state (DiIulio 2014, 95). Ungoverning reveals that this expectation is unwarranted. "Bring back the bureaucrats" speaks strongly, even sensibly, to disorder, costly duplication, and fragmented oversight, but it does not speak to this moment when the Republican Party and a reactionary movement define themselves by their wholesale opposition to the administrative state—the "deep state."

A second line of defense of the administrative state is coupled with a different critical analysis: the democratic deficit in making regulatory policy. This requires that reforms take a different orientation (Rahman 2017). Progressive Era attempts to check corporations and financial markets focused on managerial, technocratic government that insulated expert regulators from political conflict, political theorist K. Sabeel Rahman argues. But expertise presumably insulated from politics has not worked as a defense against agency capture and the persistent, disproportionate influence of financial interests. That deficiency becomes more and more problematic as "regulatory agencies play an increasingly large role as quasi-legislatures" (144).

Rahman's "structuralist" strategy is to address domination by incorporating the countervailing power of civic participation into the regulatory apparatus. Acknowledged or not, he writes, agencies are "inevitably sites in which democratic struggles take place," and this reality mandates participation, which would include, he points out, "pressure from social movements" (Rahman 2017, 146). "Empowered democracy" is not a resort to the mob, he writes reassuringly. Indeed, it offers a response to the dangers of "more pathological and exclusionary forms of mass mobilization or populism" (177). This proposal would be anathema to political forces who are opposed to democratic inclusion and social equality and who see the administrative state as essential to those goals. Rahman would tether the regulatory function of the administrative state to popular opinion; his position rests on the democratic legitimacy of public administration (Rahman 2018).

The French political philosopher Pierre Rosanvallon's analysis and corrective go beyond simplification and democratization of public administration. His goal is *relegitimation* of democracy altogether, and he assigns administration a central place (Rosanvallon 2011). Since the 1980s, he argues, democracy has rested on two sources of legitimation—elections with universal suffrage representing the general will, and the civil service representing objective generality. Both have been eroded. Elections have become "desacralized" and public administration has been damaged by misplaced confidence in the self-regulating market.

What is needed is "a radical pluralization of legitimacy" (Rosanvallon 2011, 3–4, 8). That means a closer connection between electoral institutions that are episodic and partisan on one side and governing institutions (permanent oversight bodies, regulatory agencies, and constitutional courts) that attend to the general interest on the other (12, 221). But how can these dissonant forms be brought together to relegitimate democracy? Rosanvallon advocates a "public commission" in the form of citizen juries or issue-based conventions. Experts would "inventory needs and demands, supply clear analyses, organize debates, and propose an array of choices." Citizens would deliberate and decide. The aim is "an effective social reappropriation of power" and with it, the relegitimation of democracy (216, 221). At the theoretical level, Rosanvallon is onto the core problem that afflicts government—legitimacy. The question is how to operationalize the "radical pluralization" of legitimacy he recommends.

Each of these proposals for simplification, democratization, and relegitimation bring something essential to the subject of administrative reform. They are not addressing the comprehensive attack we call ungoverning, but still, without these critical analyses, those who resist the forces of ungoverning may find themselves defending the administrative state without qualification.

Many proposed reforms aim to enhance the connection between citizens and the administrative state. Democratic theorist Jane Mansbridge offers a modest proposal that speaks to our account of the vulnerability of the administrative state, a vulnerability rooted in its illegibility and in everyday experiences of bureaucracy that elicit frustration and rage. The difficulty the public has understanding the justification of public policy is endemic, Mansbridge writes. Departments regularly consult the organized social and economic interests that comprise their major "stakeholders," but at both the policy level and at the street level, when ordinary citizens speak up, they speak "into the void" (Mansbridge 2022, 215). Her prescription is "recursivity": regular, scheduled processes by which administrators themselves explain the reasons for their actions, listen to citizens' disagreement, respond, pose their own questions, and follow up. She calls this interactive system "Citizens' Initiative for Administrative Accountability" (215).

We prescribe something akin to this in our conclusion; explanation "from the horse's mouth" can have some impact on some people, and opportunities to respond, protest, or come around are crucial. Recursivity is necessary and practicable. Mansbridge's understated observation that "administrative law-making . . . could easily use more normative and perceived legitimacy" (Mansbridge 2022, 214) is certainly correct.

As we've said, the administrative state suffers from endemic vulnerabilities. It is illegible; the colossus is hard to grasp, hard to navigate, confusing yet coercive. It is the creature of the legislature and executive and subject to the judgment of courts, and its business is a tangle of making, enforcing, and adjudicating policy. Not least, close encounters with the bureaucracy do little to create appreciation of its effectiveness or legitimacy—the judgments citizens make all the time.

Yet, the work of the administrative state is necessary. Necessity is patent in times of emergency—in a deadly pandemic, for example, when we expect that the state will underwrite vaccine research and production, somehow, and then deliver hundreds of millions of vaccines to every willing citizen's arm, fast and free. We expect the state to respond in the hours after a hurricane. Even those governors who oppose disaster aid when the storm hits somewhere else will reverse themselves when the wind and water hit their state and their citizens stand homeless. When his deputies faltered after Hurricane Katrina hit New Orleans in 2003, President George W. Bush didn't invoke Reagan and say, "Folks, don't look to D.C. for help—government is not the solution to your problems, government is the problem." He acknowledged what everyone knows: in a crisis too large for every other institution to address—including the myriad civil society groups that quickly arrive at the scene—government *is* the solution.

Necessity should be easier for people to grasp than legitimacy. But it is not always, and not now. The damage to government capacity wreaked by the forces of ungoverning is amplified by its surround of conspiracism and broad assaults on expert knowledge and regular process. Where even a catastrophe is not recognized for what it is—the Covid-19 pandemic, for example, or climate change—appeals to necessity will be cast as lies (Lifton 2023). Where a party and a movement deny common ground, even the ground beneath our feet, the basic requirements of governing are vulnerable.

Repairing the administrative state demands efforts on two fronts, then: rehabilitating institutions, to be sure, but also instilling appreciation of its necessity.

10

A Government That Governs

Ungoverning—the intentional destruction of state capacity—is rare. Until recently, the very thought of a political ambition of this kind in the United States was unfathomable. While elements of it can be traced back to Reagan's invitation to see government as more an attack on freedom than a solution to national problems, ungoverning defined the Trump administration between 2016 and 2020 and came to define both the Republican Party and the reactionary movement fused with it. Not only Trump but also other Republican officials share the stated aim, for instance, to starve and thereby incapacitate the Internal Revenue Service (IRS)—and with it, government programs of all kinds (Kiel and Eisinger 2018). The aim is not to rewrite the tax code or methods of tax collection, but to strangle government. What is true of the attack on the IRS is also true of the panoply of attacks on the institutions of the administrative state, including the State Department, the Justice Department, the Postal Service, the FBI, and even the Department of Defense. The goal, again, is not reform, but incapacitation—disabling, hijacking, circumventing, and derailing the agencies that shape, implement, and enforce public policy.

This is not to say that ungoverning is without purpose. The overarching goal is to concentrate power in the *person* of the president. It is a tool of populist authoritarianism. The promise is that rooting out the nefarious "deep state" and deconstructing its foothold in agencies and departments are the route to restoration of some lost period of "greatness." A time when whites dominated U.S. politics, society, and the economy, or more broadly, a time in the past when reactionary movement followers felt recognized and at home. Ordinary governing—policies and programs shaped and implemented by administrators—cannot bring about restoration; the path runs through disabling and undoing.

Trump doubled down on ungoverning after his historic indictment by Special Counsel Jack Smith for his role in the January 6 attack on the Capitol and for stealing confidential government documents when he was finally compelled to leave office. The twice-impeached, four times–indicted former president in pursuit of a return to power denounced the conspiracy against him, and his followers threatened and intimidated judges and prosecutors. "His trials are his presidential campaign" (Danner 2023). He promised to pardon violent, rogue followers who were jailed for participation in the January 6 insurrection; to gut the FBI; to obliterate the independence of the Justice Department and take personal control of prosecutions. First, of course, he would put an end to his own long list of criminal indictments. He also promised to control the outcome of future elections: "If I happen to be president, and I see somebody who's doing well and beating me very badly, I say, 'Go down and indict them.' . . . They'd be out of business" (Samuels 2023).

These steps go hand in hand with the overt and increasingly specific plan to incapacitate the administrative state, to eliminate its expertise and regular processes and the ethos of public service by purging tens of thousands of civil servants and installing loyalists at will, diminishing or eradicating the civil service protections afforded many career federal employees. Beyond Trump, other Republican candidates for the presidential nomination followed suit, blasting the "fake narrative that an insurrection had occurred on January 6" and promising to "clean house" (Draper 2023a). One 2024 primary election candidate, Vivek Ramaswamy, promised to issue mass layoffs of the federal workforce and to shut down the FBI, the Department of Education, the Bureau of Alcohol, Tobacco, Firearms, and Explosives, the Nuclear Regulatory Commission, and "many more" (Smith 2023). Nikki Haley, the so-called moderate in the Republican primary field, promised to put a term limit on federal civil servants and to fire everyone after they had served for five years (Rampell 2023). Elected Republicans in Congress, too, vowed to defund and purge federal agencies. Ungoverning has been accepted and weirdly normalized by officials and party leadership whose remit is to govern. And within itself, the ungoverning party has become ungovernable. In September 2023, Kevin McCarthy, then the newly elected Republican Speaker of the House and a Trump supporter who placated the far-right wing of his caucus, was ousted from the speakership by his own party. Having tasted his own medicine, he fumed that his party wanted to "burn the place down" (Wilson et al. 2023).

Political commentator Mark Danner is more sanguine about the aims of anti-government forces. He predicted in 2023 that the Heritage Foundation and other, newer think tanks "will seek not to destroy the government but rather to neuter it a bit and then wield it as a weapon" (Danner 2023, 83). But as we have shown, neutering and wielding agencies as weapons *is* the destruction of the administrative state. And using government as a weapon, as an instrument of the leader's personal will, is the aim of populist authoritarianism.

Is the Solution a Reformed Republican Party?

For conservatives who have long opposed government's power to regulate and redistribute, ungoverning may seem like a welcome development. Businesses will have a freer hand to do as they will, and the wealthy will not fear being audited by the Internal Revenue Service. Conservatives who have long opposed the New Deal state may accede to ungoverning as a way to dismantle the offices and departments in the administrative establishment whose mission, as they see it, is to advance progressive policies. For those who see the administrative state as equivalent to the progressive state, and both as equivalent to big government and unfreedom, deconstruction may look like the solution. Ungoverning takes the strain of contemporary conservatism that says the government is the problem and draws it to a conclusion: eradicate the problem.

The anti-government face of conservatism has not been its only face, though. Conservatism means to conserve, not destroy. It values prudence and says *go slow*. In chapter 5 we outlined the ambivalent legacy of Ronald Reagan, who combined a qualified aim to correct what he saw as the excesses of big government with a more radical opposition to government itself. As we noted, both Bush presidents tried to resolve that ambivalence in favor of a philosophy of governing that emphasized caution and compassion. But neither succeeded, and in the wake of their failures, only extreme hostility to government remained.

The idea that we could do without an administrative state has its allure: no regulations, no bureaucrats, no standard operating procedures and "red tape." Utopians on the left as well as on the right have imagined a politics in which somehow, the state might wither away. For Friedrich Engels, under socialism the state would eventually join the "Museum of Antiquities, by the side of the spinning wheel and the bronze axe" (Engels [1884] 1978, 755). If it weren't so damaging, it would be an amusing irony that Republicans today are carrying this feature of Marxist ideology into U.S. politics, with the difference that the state's withering away would be replaced by its imminent, intentional destruction.

What we see is the retreat of authentically conservative approaches to governing. An essential antidote to ungoverning would be a rehabilitation of conservatism and a reform of the Republican Party as a party committed to governing. To state the obvious, even conservative goals require policies that are formulated and applied by administration (Galston 2022). A prominent school of libertarians, for instance, has embraced building state capacity; the individualism they celebrate requires it (Cowen 2020; Murphy and O'Reilly 2020). That said, although a conservatism that values governing is promoted by some Republican leaders and commentators, it is not a force in national political life. The party today is inseparable from the reactionary movement and from the goal of deconstructing the administrative state.

Seventy-five years after Lionel Trilling wrote that the conservative impulse is expressed only in "irritable mental gestures which seek to resemble ideas," former Texas governor Rick Perry, in an inimitable moment during his campaign for the presidency in 2011, illustrated that the destructive gesture had displaced any genuine philosophy of governing (Trilling 1951, xv).

He forgot the names of the three agencies he pledged to abolish if he were elected president: "It's three agencies of government when I get there that are gone: Commerce, Education . . . the, uh. What's the third one there, let's see. . . . I can't. The third one I can't. Sorry. Oops" (Franke-Ruta 2011). This is where "conservatism" has landed.

Speaking to the Public

In this moment of democratic backsliding, attention has focused on the institutional weaknesses that made populist authoritarianism and its destructive impact possible. In the United States, many proposed solutions demand constitutional change, including amending countermajoritarian elements like the Electoral College, the malapportionment of the Senate, and lifetime appointments to the Supreme Court. Sensible proposals for institutional reform abound—reforming partisan gerrymandering, for example (Levitsky and Ziblatt 2023). Few, however, address how essential a functioning administrative state is to democracy, or how vital it is to rehabilitate it in the minds of citizens. Rehabilitation of the machinery of government does not require constitutional amendment, which in any case is practically impossible under current circumstances, or massive structural reforms. But in a way, it is just as difficult, because the ultimate challenge is to make the administrative state legible, its functions appreciated, and beyond that, the scope and bounds of its authority broadly accepted.

The task is to touch what Lincoln called "the public mind" (Lincoln 1858)—or "minds," in the plural, really, so that citizens not only recognize the need for government to grapple with some of the greatest problems ever faced, but also have a durable understanding of the necessary role of the administrative state in this. That is the challenge: to ensure that the practical importance of the work of administration is appreciated. There is another challenge, too: to ensure public understanding of where its authority lies, of its legitimacy as well as its necessity.

The project of appreciation is vital and will remain so, even if the forces of ungoverning are defeated. For from the point of view of a government that governs, understanding offers protection against regression. More, an ignorant and disaffected public is itself a kind of civic damage. The health of the administrative state will therefore require more than officials who want to govern. It will require public understanding and appreciation of what the administrative state is and what it does, and why it matters.

This begins with underscoring what government does that no private entity can do alone—not in a general sense, but in particulars in terms of, for example, food safety, Medicare, educating disabled children, defending civil rights, and national security. That includes illuminating the invisible work of the administrative state in stopping catastrophes before they occur, in preventing and not just responding to crises, and in anticipating risks, as Michael Lewis emphasizes (Lewis 2018). One official in the Department of Agriculture put the problem simply: "We don't teach people what governing actually does" (119).

Reaching public minds does not mean countering the illegibility of the administrative state by constructing flowcharts or rewriting the *Sourcebook of United States Executive Agencies*. Understanding is not tested by adding questions about the Department of Agriculture to high school exams in civics. It means basic understanding of how policy is made and implemented and why the institutions of administration are at the heart of this work. It means correcting the misleading lessons schoolchildren learn about how laws are made and adding accounts about how these laws are actually put into effect. Not least, it means elaborating on the various talents of the civil servants who do this work and thus the public careers open to young people. For the lesson, too, is that the civil service is not the domain of subversives or elites, but is a location of careers open to talent. In 2023, in anticipation of the Fourth of July, journalist David Corn saluted "some of the greatest patriots in the land: government bureaucrats." He wrote, "Smart and talented people . . . have spent much, if not all, of their adult lives employed at the EPA, the Labor Department, the Justice Department, the National Institutes of Health, the State Department, and other agencies . . . developing or implementing policies that will improve the lives of thousands (or millions) of Americans and others around the planet" (Corn 2023b).

One indispensable method of reaching public minds is storytelling, with concrete, real-life narratives told by administrators from every level of government, including local civil servants who bring that old saw of a "human face" to life. Veteran civil servants are the educators who describe what they do and why, but also how they do it and why. Stories that show why programs require data, knowledge, regular process. Stories that illuminate the professional ethos, that identify government employees as civil *servants*. Storytelling is an informal way of instituting Mansbridge's more formal notion of back and forth, or recursivity, between citizens and public officials.

Reaching the public mind demands something more: personal stories from civil servants recounting their experiences of having their agency hijacked or circumvented. Stories of what it means personally, and to the work of government, when they are intimidated, fired, silenced, or face the wrath of the forces of ungoverning. This means speaking out as a witness to the cost of ungoverning, as election workers, among others, have done.

The administrative state depends on citizens valuing the work it does. We've seen citizen activists rise up to resist attacks on specific programs like Obamacare, but they don't speak on behalf of the institutions that shape the policy and bring health care to them. "Democracy" is a rallying cry today, and so is fidelity to the Constitution. We don't expect rallying around the Department of Commerce or marches and chants to "bring back middle-level bureaucrats!" But we can expect the practical necessity of administration to have purchase. Former House Speaker John Boehner acknowledged this in his memoir: "Some sort of bureaucracy is needed to run a country of hundreds of millions of people. And when people in that bureaucracy have been there a long time and have institutional knowledge, they usually make things work better rather than worse" (Boehner 2021, 191).

Events play a part here. Events call out the lie of deconstruction. Republican governors, even while demonstrating antipathy to administrative process and expertise, still have to govern, and in critical situations they will be judged for their effectiveness. After hurricanes hit Florida in 2022 and 2023, Governor DeSantis—who as a member of Congress had opposed federal disaster relief after Hurricane Sandy hit New York in 2013—requested disaster relief from President Biden. Biden delivered, and DeSantis proudly announced to his constituents that he had gotten tens of millions in relief funds for Floridians (Flegenheimer 2022; Office of the Governor of Florida 2023a). DeSantis's anti-government opposition to federal programs and swift turnaround is not just cynical; it points to a sinister consequence of ungoverning if it is unchecked. For if the Republican Party succeeds in degrading one part of the machinery of government after another, there is no assurance that the federal government will be able to respond to emergencies, no matter how urgently governors require assistance. Can Republican governors, who admit the need for disaster relief, convey the importance of administration to Republicans in Congress? Without vivid illustrations of what administration does, we have no assurance that Republicans in Congress will staff or sustain the Federal Emergency Management Agency or, for that matter, the National Weather Service.

Just as citizens assume that the U.S. government will include a Congress, courts, and the presidency, they need to appreciate that government must include an administrative state. The "fourth branch" is also a necessity.

Beyond appreciating its necessity, there remains the more difficult matter of its legitimacy. In chapter 2 we sketched a normative theory of the administrative state's legitimacy centered on the values of knowledge and process. The ground of its legitimacy is both epistemic and legal. Yet, whereas the terms of the U.S. government's overall legitimacy—"democracy" and the "Constitution"—are exalted, the terms we invoked— "expertise" and "regular process"—are arid. They are unexciting terms, even forbidding.

What is ultimately needed is not only a normative theory of legitimacy, but broad public endorsement of the meaning, value, and authority of the administrative state. The administrative state is essential to democracy because it is essential to implementing policies that address the needs and wants of the people as the elected branches see them. But when those policies are highly contested, when they are viewed as existential contests between warring tribes, then the administrative state, the entity charged with bringing them into the world, loses its value and authority. And this is of course the contemporary condition of U.S. politics. Where the parties are so deeply divided on so many deeply divisive matters, the departments and agencies that bring policy to life will rarely have broad public support. Their very existence will be challenged. They will be the targets of those who want to "bring it all crashing down."

Even if political legitimacy—the full public endorsement of the administrative state's meaning, value and authority—is out of reach, appreciating its necessity is not. Appreciating the administrative state's irreplaceable part in making democratic government work is a reasonable expectation. In this moment, to expose and resist ungoverning and to reclaim and rehabilitate state capacity, this may be enough.

We have defined and diagnosed ungoverning and the purposes of those who would destroy the administrative state. The future of ungoverning does not depend on the fate of one leader and his effort to entrench personal rule. Ungoverning is now a defining purpose of the Republican Party. It also defines a reactionary movement that has given up on ordinary politics and instead intimidates "enemies" and threatens violence. Justices of the Supreme Court are intent for their own reasons on weakening the capacity of the administrative state. There is a constituency for ungoverning. The shadow ungoverning casts over American political life will remain until citizens appreciate and assert the necessity for institutions that give government the capacity to govern.

ACKNOWLEDGMENTS

We acknowledge first the historians, legal scholars, and fellow political theorists who have been "startled into thought" and work to illuminate the grave, unanticipated assaults on American democracy that have marked the past decade. *Ungoverning* is our addition to this groundswell of engagement with political peril.

Once again, Rob Tempio, our editor at Princeton University Press, peppered us with ideas and guided us over the hurdles necessary to bring this work to life. Anonymous readers for the press commented on the original book proposal and on the finished manuscript, offering sharp suggestions for clarifying the concept of ungoverning and elucidating the political history of these novel attacks on governing.

Generous and demanding friends and colleagues read the work and offered encouragement and criticism: Corey Brettschneider, William Galston, Steve Macedo, Shep Melnick, Herschel Nachlis, Samuel Popkin, Kirun Sankaran, Dennis Thompson, and Jeffrey Tulis.

Nancy thanks Robert Jay Lifton, her partner in daily conversations about what he named "malignant normality." Our back-and-forth was illuminating, comforting, and oddly hopeful.

Russell thanks Toni Barry for her love and support.

REFERENCES

ABC News. 2023. "Giuliani Trial: Jury Awards Election Workers Nearly $150 Million in Damages." December 15, 2023. https://abc7chicago.com/rudy-giuliani-election -fraud-lawsuit-shaye-moss/14189218/.

Achen, Christopher H., and Larry M. Bartels. 2017. *Democracy for Realists: Why Elections Do Not Produce Responsive Government.* Rev. ed. Princeton, NJ: Princeton University Press.

Adler, Jonathan H. 2021. "A Rearguard Defense of the Administrative State." *Regulation* 44, no. 2 (Summer): 65–67. https://www.cato.org/regulation/summer-2021 /rearguard-defense-administrative-state.

Agassi, Denny. 2023. "Florida Is Set to Arrest People in Restrooms Regardless of Legal Gender Status in Sweeping Bill." *Reckon*, May 18, 2023. https://www.al.com /reckon/2023/05/florida-is-set-to-arrest-people-in-restrooms-regardless-of-legal -gender-status-in-sweeping-bill.html.

Alberta, Tim. 2020. "The Michigan Republican Who Stopped Trump." *Politico*, November 24, 2020. https://www.politico.com/newsletters/politico-nightly /2020/11/24/the-michigan-republican-who-stopped-trump-490984.

Altman, Howard, Davis Winkie, Sarah Sicard, Meghann Myers, and Leo Shane III. 2020. "Calls for Martial Law and US Military Oversight of New Presidential Election Draws Criticism." *Military Times*, December 2, 2020. https://www .militarytimes.com/news/your-military/2020/12/02/calls-for-martial-law-and-us -military-oversight-of-new-presidential-elections-draws-criticism/.

Alvey, Rebekah. 2024. "Conservatives Want Trump 2.0 to Bury Climate Science." *Politico*, February 2, 2024. https://www.politico.com/newsletters/power-switch /2024/02/02/conservatives-want-trump-2-0-to-bury-climate-science-00139283.

Anti-Defamation League. 2023. "Murder and Extremism in the U.S. in 2022." February 22, 2023. https://www.adl.org/resources/report/murder-and-extremism -united-states-2022.

Arendt, Hannah. 1958. *The Human Condition.* Chicago: University of Chicago Press.

Arendt, Hannah. (1963) 1994. *Eichmann in Jerusalem: A Report on the Banality of Evil.* Rev. and enlarged edition. New York: Penguin.

Arendt, Hannah. 1972. *Crises of the Republic.* New York: Harcourt Brace Jovanovich.

Aristotle. (350 B.C.E.) 2013. *Politics.* Translated with introduction and notes by Carnes Lord. 2nd ed. Chicago: University of Chicago Press.

Arnold, R. Douglas. 1992. *The Logic of Congressional Action*. New Haven, CT: Yale University Press.

Arnsdorf, Isaac, and Jeff Stein. 2023. "Trump Touts Authoritarian Vision for Second Term: I Am Your Justice." *Washington Post*, April 21, 2023. https://www.washingtonpost.com/elections/2023/04/21/trump-agenda-policies-2024/.

Bade, Rachel. 2016. "Final Benghazi Report Details Administration Failures." *Politico*, June 8, 2016. https://www.politico.com/story/2016/06/benghazi-report-obama-clinton-224854.

Bagley, Nicholas. 2019. "The Procedure Fetish." *Michigan Law Review* 118 (3): 345–402.

Ballotpedia. 2023. "State Government Trifectas." Updated February 7, 2024. https://ballotpedia.org/State_government_trifectas#cite_note-3.

Banerjee, Neela. 2020. "How Trump's 'Secret Science' Rule Would Put Patients' Privacy at Risk." *Inside Climate News*, January 20, 2020. https://insideclimatenews.org/news/20012020/epa-secret-science-rule-patient-privacy-risk-study/.

Barr, William. 2018, June 8. "Memorandum to Deputy Attorney General Rod Rosenstein and Assistant Attorney General Steve Engel Re. Mueller's 'Obstruction' Theory." *New York Times*, June 8, 2018. https://int.nyt.com/data/documenthelper/549-june-2018-barr-memo-to-doj-mue/b4c05e39318dd2d136b3/optimized/full.pdf.

Bartels, Larry M. 1991. "Constituency Opinion ad Congressional Policy Making: The Reagan Defense Buildup." *American Political Science Review* 85, no. 2 (June): 457–74.

Bash, Kaustuv. 2022. "Drug Price Law to Spur Creative Claims as Industry Readies Fight." *Bloomberg News*, September 29, 2022. https://news.bloomberglaw.com/health-law-and-business/drug-price-law-to-spur-creative-claims-as-industry-readies-fight.

Basu, Jonathan, and Zachary Swan. 2021. "Off the Rails: Episode 9, Trump's War with His Generals." *Axios*, March 16, 2021. https://www.axios.com/2021/05/16/off-the-rails-trump-military-withdraw-afghanistan.

BBC. 2015. "French National Front Expels Founder Jean-Marie Le Pen." August 20, 2015. https://www.bbc.com/news/world-europe-34009901.

BBC. 2020. "Coronavirus: Outcry after Trump Suggests Injecting Disinfectant as Treatment." April 24, 2020. https://www.bbc.com/news/world-us-canada-52407177.

Beaumont, Thomas, and Stephen Groves. 2020. "A *f* for Future Office: Virus Tests a GOP Governor." *AP News*, May 5, 2020. https://apnews.com/article/5fd996989 95959a4ac3fe88625732367.

Beer, Samuel H. 1966. "Liberalism and the National Idea." *Public Interest* 5 (Fall): 70–82.

Beermann, Jack M. 2018. "The Never-Ending Assault on the Administrative State." *Notre Dame Law Review* 93 (4): 1599–652.

Benen, Steve. 2017. "Trump Launches Infrastructure Initiative with Fake Signing Ceremony." *MSNBC*, June 6, 2017. https://www.msnbc.com/rachel-maddow-show/trump-launches-infrastructure-initiative-fake-signing-ceremony-msna994011.

Benen, Steve. 2023. "Romney: GOP Members Feared Far-Right Violence Ahead of key Votes." *MSNBC*, September 15, 2023. https://www.msnbc.com/rachel-maddow

-show/maddowblog/romney-gop-members-feared-far-right-violence-ahead-key
-votes-rcna105272.

Ben Sasson-Gordis, Avishay. 2022. "Citizenship, Enmity, and the Normative Theory of Domestic Military Use." *Armed Forces and Society*. Published online September 6, 2022. https://doi.org/10.1177/0095327X221120048.

Ben Sasson-Gordis, Avishay. 2023. "Democratic Backsliding, and the Limits of the Right to Be Wrong about Politics." Unpublished paper on file with authors.

Bermeo, Nancy. 2016. "On Democratic Backsliding." *Journal of Democracy* 27, no. 1 (January): 1–19.

Bhargava, Deepak, Shahrzad Shams, and Harry Hanbury. 2023. "The Death of 'Deliverism.'" *Democracy Journal*, June 22, 2023. https://democracyjournal.org/arguments -the-death-of-deliverism/.

Blake, Aaron. 2020. "Trump's Legal Team Lights a Fuse Beneath Its Credibility." *Washington Post*, November 19, 2020. https://www.washingtonpost.com/politics/2020 /11/19/trumps-legal-team-lights-fuse-beneath-its-remaining-credibility/.

Blanchette, Jude. 2022. "Xi Jinping's Faltering Foreign Policy." *Foreign Affairs*, March 16, 2022. https://www.foreignaffairs.com/articles/china/2022-03-16/xi -jinpings-faltering-foreign-policy.

Blow, Charles M. 2023. "L.G.B.T.Q. Americans Could Become a 'New Class of Political Refugees.'" *New York Times*, June 6, 2023. https://www.nytimes.com/2023/06/14 /opinion/transgender-florida.html.

Blum, Rachel M., and Christopher Sebastian Parker. 2021. "Panel Study of the MAGA Movement—Group Affinities." https://sites.uw.edu/magastudy/demographics -group-affinities/.

Boehner, John. 2021. *On the House: A Washington Memoir*. New York: St. Martin's Press.

Bort, Ryan. 2019. "When Nazis Took Over Madison Square Garden." *Rolling Stone*, February 19, 2019. https://www.mnhs.org/lindbergh/learn/controversies.

Bradner, Eric, and Kate Sullivan. 2023. "Trump Baselessly Rails against 'Prosecutorial Misconduct' at Waco Rally as Investigations Loom." *CNN*, March 26, 2023. https://www.cnn.com/2023/03/25/politics/texas-trump-2024-rally/index.html.

Brettschneider, Corey. 2018. *The Oath and the Office: A Guide to the Constitution for Future Presidents*. New York: W. W. Norton.

Brice-Saddler, Michael. 2019 "While Bemoaning Mueller Probe, Trump Falsely Says the Court Gives Him the 'Right to Do Whatever I Want.'" *Washington Post*, July 23, 2019. https://www.washingtonpost.com/politics/2019/07/23/trump-falsely-tells -auditorium-full-teens-constitution-gives-him-right-do-whatever-i-want/.

Bridges, Lord. 1950. *Portrait of a Profession: The Civil Service Tradition*. University Press.

Bright Line Watch. 2021. "Tempered Expectations and Hardened Divisions a Year into the Biden Presidency." November 21, 2021. https://brightlinewatch.org/tempered -expectations-and-hardened-divisions-a-year-into-the-biden-presidency/.

Broadway, Luke, and Catie Edmondson. 2023. "Divided House Approves GOP Inquiry into Weaponization of Government." *New York Times*, January 10, 2023.

https://www.nytimes.com/2023/01/10/us/politics/house-republican-committee-weaponization-government.html/.

Brooks, Rosa. 2016. "The Military Wouldn't Save Us from Trump's Illegal Orders." *Washington Post*, March 4, 2016. https://www.washingtonpost.com/opinions/the-military-wouldnt-save-us-from-president-trumps-illegal-orders/2016/03/04/9ef8fd44-e0ea-11e5-846c-10191d1fc4ec_story.html.

Brown, Alex. 2014, "Let Me Google That for You—Now a Congressional Bill." *The Atlantic*, July 23, 2014. https://www.theatlantic.com/politics/archive/2014/07/let-me-google-that-for-younow-a-congressional-bill/441264/.

Buchanan, Maggy Jo, Phillip Wolgin, and Claudia Flores. 2021. "The Trump Administration's Family Separation Policy Is Over." *American Prospect*, April 12, 2021. https://www.americanprogress.org/article/trump-administrations-family-separation-policy/.

Bulman-Pozen, Jessica. 2014. "Partisan Federalism." *Harvard Law Review* 127, no. 4 (February): 1077–146.

Bump, Philip. 2021. "The Governor of the State Second Hardest Hit by the Corona Virus Probably Shouldn't Be Bragging about It." *Washington Post*, February 3, 2021. https://www.washingtonpost.com/politics/2021/02/03/governor-state-second-hardest-hit-by-coronavirus-probably-shouldnt-be-bragging-about-it/.

Burns, Robert, and Jill Colvin. 2018. "Trump Sends Troops to Border, an Issue That Fires Up Base." *AP News*, October 25, 2018. https://apnews.com/article/immigration-north-america-donald-trump-ap-top-news-latin-america-e7ffd2d5764244cdb1d1474bd895a863.

Burns, Walter J. 2019. "The Lost Art of American Diplomacy: Can the State Department Be Saved?" *Foreign Affairs* 98, no. 3 (May/June): 98–107.

Burns, William J. 2020. "The Damage at the State Department Is Worse Than You Can Imagine." *The Atlantic*, March 12, 2020. https://www.theatlantic.com/ideas/archive/2020/03/how-rebuild-state-department/607837/.

Cadelago, Christopher, and Olivia Olander. 2022. "Biden Calls Trump's Philosophy 'Semi-Fascism.'" *Politico*. https://www.politico.com/news/2022/08/25/biden-trump-philosophy-semi-fascism-00053831.

Campbell, John L. 2023. *Institutions Under Siege: Donald Trump's Attack on the Deep State*. Cambridge: Cambridge University Press.

Caputo, Marc. 2021. "White House Seizes an Opportunity to Whack DeSantis." *Politico*, August 11, 2021. https://www.politico.com/news/2021/08/11/biden-desantis-florida-covid-surge-504064.

Carroll, Rory. 2013. *Comandante: Hugo Chavez's Venezuela*. New York: Penguin.

Carter, Ashton, Dick Cheney, William Cohen, Mark Esper, Robert Gates, Chuck Hagel, James Mattis, Leon Panetta, William Perry, and Donald Rumsfeld. 2021. "All 10 Living Former Defense Secretaries: Involving the Military in Election Disputes Would Cross into Dangerous Territory." *Washington Post*, January 3, 2021. https://www.washingtonpost.com/opinions/10-former-defense-secretaries-military-peaceful-transfer-of-power/2021/01/03/2a23d52e-4c4d-11eb-a9f4-0e668b9772ba_story.html.

Cassidy, Christina A. 2023. "GOP State Legislatures Seek Greater Control over State and Local Election Offices." *AP News*, June 25, 2023. https://apnews.com/article/republicans-election-offices-control-democrats-power-grab-d62c69dd4f695b241f84ef2dc331ee8c.

Chabria, Anita. 2021. "Two Californians Charged with Plot to Blow Up Democratic Headquarters in Sacramento." *Los Angeles Times*, July 16, 2021. https://www.latimes.com/california/story/2021-07-16/two-californians-charged-in-plot-to-blow-up-democratic-headquarters.

Chalfant, Morgan. 2020. "Trump: The Only Way We Are Going to Lose This Election Is if the Election Is Rigged." *The Hill*, August 17, 2022. https://thehill.com/homenews/administration/512424-trump-the-only-way-we-are-going-to-lose-this-election-is-if-the/.

Chappell, Bill. 2017. "I'm the Only One That Matters, Trump Says of State Dept. Job Vacancies." *NPR*, November 3, 2017. https://www.npr.org/sections/thetwo-way/2017/11/03/561797675/im-the-only-one-that-matters-trump-says-of-state-dept-job-vacancies.

Cherniss, Joshua L. 2021. *Liberalism in Dark Times: The Liberal Ethos in the Twentieth Century*. Princeton, NJ: Princeton University Press.

Chopra, Ritika. 2021. "Pratap Bhanu Mehta's Exit 'Direct Consequence of his Role as Critic of Govt': Ashoka University Faculty Writes to V-C, Board Trustees." *Indian Express*, March 18, 2021. https://indianexpress.com/article/india/pratap-bhanu-mehta-exit-ashoka-university-critic-govt-faculty-v-c-board-trustees-7234380/.

Christie, Bob. 2022. "Arizona House Speaker Rusty Bowers Loses State Senate Bid." *AP News*, August 2, 2022. https://apnews.com/article/2022-midterm-elections-arizona-donald-trump-censures-phoenix-62fa69d8c6c08c29c1452eeca5e025fa.

Cillizza, Chris. 2018. "The Governing Wing of the Republican Party Is Nearing Extinction." *The Point with Chris Cillizza, CNN Politics*, January 29, 2018. https://www.cnn.com/2018/01/29/politics/frelinghuysen-retirement-house-analysis/index.html.

Cillizza, Chris. 2019. "The Awful Reality That Donald Trump's Repeated Attacks on John McCain Prove." *CNN*, March 19, 2019. https://www.cnn.com/2019/03/19/politics/donald-trump-john-mccain-dead/index.html.

Clark, Dartunorro. 2020. "Twitter Fact Checks Trump's Tweets for the First Time, Calls Mail-in Voting Claim 'Misleading.'" *NBC News*, May 26, 2020. https://www.nbcnews.com/politics/donald-trump/twitter-fact-checks-trump-s-misleading-tweet-mail-voting-n1215151.

Coffee, John C., Jr. 2022. "The Two-Front War on the Administrative State: How Far Will the Supreme Court Go?" Columbia Law School's Blog on Corporations and the Capitol Markets, July 5, 2022. https://clsbluesky.law.columbia.edu/2022/07/05/the-two-front-war-on-the-administrative-state-how-far-will-the-supreme-court-go/.

Cohen, Lizbeth. 2020. "States Are in Crisis. Why Won't Trump Help?" *New York Times*, April 29, 2020. https://www.nytimes.com/2020/04/29/opinion/states-coronavirus-federalism.html.

Cohen, Michael A. 2021. "Give It a Rest Mark Milley." *Truth and Consequences* (blog), July 15, 2021. https://truthandcons.substack.com/p/give-it-a-rest-mark-milley.

Collier, Roger. 2017. "Why Trumpcare Failed." *Canadian Medical Association Journal* 189, no. 17 (May 1): E645–46. https://doi.org/10.1503/cmaj.1095414.

Congressional Research Service. 2022. *Federal Workforce Statistics Sources: OPM and OMB*. CRS Report R43590. June 28, 2022. https://crsreports.congress.gov /product/pdf/R/R43590/20.

Corasaniti, Nick, Karen Yourish, and Keith Collins. 2022. "How Trump's 2022 Election Lies Have Gripped State Legislatures." *New York Times*, May 22, 2022. https:// www.nytimes.com/interactive/2022/05/22/us/politics/state-legislators-election -denial.html.

Corn, David. 2022. *American Psychosis: A Historical Investigation of How the Republican Party Went Crazy*. New York: Hachette.

Corn, David. 2023a. "Mike Johnson Urged a Religious Test for Politicians." *Mother Jones*, October 31, 2023. https://www.motherjones.com/politics/2023/10/mike -johnson-urged-a-religious-test-for-politicians/.

Corn, David. 2023b. "The Patriotism of Government Bureaucrats." *Our Land* (newsletter), July 1, 2023. https://link.motherjones.com/public/31958698.

Cottle, Michelle. 2023. "What Trump's Debate Stunt Says to Republican Voters." *New York Times*, August 18, 2023. https://www.nytimes.com/2023/08/18/opinion /editorials/trump-not-doing-debates.html.

Cowen, Tyler. 2020. "What Libertarianism Has Become and Will Become—State Capacity Libertarianism." *Marginal Revolution*, January 1, 2020. https://www .marginalrevolution.com.

Crews, Clyde Wayne, Jr. 2016. "Donald Trump Promises to Eliminate Two Regulations for Every One Enacted." *Forbes*, November 22, 2016. https://www.forbes .com/sites/waynecrews/2016/11/22/donald-trump-promises-to-eliminate-two -regulations-for-every-one-enacted/?sh=ff346fe45864.

Crouch, Jeffrey, Mark J. Rozell, and Mitchel A. Sollenberger. 2020. *The Unitary Executive Theory: A Danger to Constitutional Government*. Lawrence: University Press of Kansas.

C-SPAN. 2019. "Impeachment Inquiry, House Hearings: Lt. Col. Vindman and Jennifer Williams." November 19, 2019. https://www.c-span.org/video/?466376-1 /impeachment-hearing-lieutenant-colonel-vindman-jennifer-williams.

CTV News. 2024. "Trump Demands Release of January 6 Hostages." YouTube video, 0:24. January 8, 2024. https://youtu.be/t60sp41dzUg?si=3ffUP7P3xeer_jJl.

Cunningham, Noble E. 1978. *The Process of Government under Jefferson*. Princeton, NJ: Princeton University Press.

Dale, Daniel, and Brandon Miller. 2019. "Anatomy of a Fiasco: A Detailed Timeline of Trump's Alabama Map Meltdown." *CNN*, September 6, 2019. https://www.cnn .com/2019/09/06/politics/fact-check-timeline-of-trumps-alabama-dorian-map -fiasco/index.html.

Danner, Mark. 2023. "The Grievance Artist." *New York Review of Books*, November 2, 2023, 82–85. https://www.nybooks.com/articles/2023/11/02/the-grievance -artist-trump-mark-danner/.

Davis, Susan, and Montanaro Domenico. 2017. "McCain Votes No, Dealing Death Blow to Republican Healthcare Efforts." *NPR*, June 27, 2017. https://www.npr.org/2017/07/27/539907467/senate-careens-toward-high-drama-midnight-health-care-vote.

DeBonis, Mike, and Jacqueline Alemany. 2022. "Trump Sought to Lead Armed Mob to Capitol on Jan. 6, Aide Says." *Washington Post*, June 28, 2022. https://www.washingtonpost.com/national-security/2022/06/28/trump-sought-lead-armed-mob-capitol-jan-6-aide-says/.

Demkovich, Laurel. 2022. "'They will be welcome': Inslee, Washington Democrats Commit to 'Sanctuary' for Those Needing Abortions in Other States." *Spokesman-Review* (Spokane, WA), May 3, 2022. https://www.spokesman.com/stories/2022/may/03/they-will-be-welcome-inslee-washington-democrats-o/.

Derchin, Michael. 2022. "Fly the Friendly Skies of Steven Breyer." *Wall Street Journal*, February 10, 2022. https://www.wsj.com/articles/fly-the-friendly-skies-of-stephen-breyer-deregulation-airlines-supreme-court-retirement-summer-11644533187.

Desai, Samarth. 2022. "Looking Back: Nullification in American History." *Constitution Daily* (blog), National Constitution Center, February 4, 2022. https://constitutioncenter.org/blog/looking-back-nullification-in-american-history.

Diamond, Jeremy. 2016. "Donald Trump to Protestor: 'I'd Like to Punch Him in the Face.'" *CNN*, February 23, 2016. https://www.cnn.com/2016/02/23/politics/donald-trump-nevada-rally-punch/index.html.

Dias, Elizabeth. 2020. "Christianity Will Have Power." *New York Times*, August 8, 2020. https://www.nytimes.com/2020/08/09/us/evangelicals-trump-christianity.html.

Diaz, Jaclyn. 2021. "Justice Department Rescinds Trump's 'Zero Tolerance' Immigration Policy." *NPR*, January 27, 2021. https://www.npr.org/2021/01/27/961048895/justice-department-rescinds-trumps-zero-tolerance-immigration-policy.

Dickens, Charles. (1857) 2021. *Little Dorrit*. San Tan Valley, AZ: Pure Snow.

Dickerson, Caitlin. 2022. "The Secret History of the U.S. Government's Family-Separation Policy." *The Atlantic*, August 7, 2022, 37–76. https://www.theatlantic.com/magazine/archive/2022/09/trump-administration-family-separation-policy-immigration/670604/.

DiIulio, John, Jr. 2012. "Facing Up to Big Government." *National Affairs*, Spring 2012. https://www.nationalaffairs.com/publications/detail/facing-up-to-big-government.

DiIulio, John, Jr. 2014. *Bring Back the Bureaucrats*. West Conshohocken, PA: Templeton Press.

Dionne, E. J., Jr. 2021. "Say It Loud, Democrats: Economic Issues Are 'Values' Issues Too." *Washington Post*, December 5, 2021. https://www.washingtonpost.com/opinions/2021/12/05/say-it-loud-democrats-economic-issues-are-values-issues-too/.

District Attorney, New York County. 2023. "District Attorney Bragg Announces 34-Count Felony Indictment of Former President Donald J. Trump." Press release,

April 4, 2023. https://manhattanda.org/district-attorney-bragg-announces-34 -count-felony-indictment-of-former-president-donald-j-trump/.

Dixon, Matt. 2023. "Trump Delivers Fiery Post-Indictment Speech: 'They're coming after you.'" *NBC News*, June 10, 2023. https://www.nbcnews.com/politics/donald -trump/trump-deliver-fiery-posFt-indictment-speech-georgia-rcna88561.

Dolores Huerta Research Center for the Americas at UC Santa Cruz and the Promise Institute for Human Rights, UCLA School of Law. 2023. *Summary List of Election Deniers and Skeptics Elected to Office during the 2022 US Midterms*. Santa Cruz and Los Angeles: Author. https://promiseinstitute.law.ucla.edu/wp-content /uploads/2023/04/Summar-List-of-Election-Deniers-and-Skeptics-Elected-to -Office-During-the-2022-U.S.-Midterms.pdf.

Donovan, Chris, and Adam Kelly. 2017. "Fact Checking Trump's 'Repeal and Replace' Obamacare Timeline." *ABC News*, March 25, 2017. https://abcnews.go.com /Politics/fact-checking-trumps-repeal-replace-obamacare-timeline/story?id =46360908.

Dorf, Michael C. 2023. "The Misguided Unitary Executive Theory Gains Ground." *Verdict*, June 19, 2023. https://verdict.justia.com/2023/06/19/the-misguided-unitary -executive-theory-gains-ground.

Douglas, R. Douglas. 1990. *The Logic of Congressional Action*. New Haven, CT: Yale University Press.

Draper, Robert. 2023a. "Far Right Pushes a Through the Looking Glass Narrative on January 6." *New York Times*, June 23, 2023. https://www.nytimes.com/2023/06 /23/us/politics/jan-6-trump.html.

Draper, Robert. 2023b. "From Gingrich to McCarthy, the Roots of Governance by Chaos." *New York Times*, January 7, 2023. https://www.nytimes.com/2023/01/07 /us/politics/speaker-mccarthy-gingrich-trump.html.

Duara, Nigel. 2022. "Foes of Guns and Abortion Resurrect an Old Idea." *Cal Matters*, August 9, 2022. https://calmatters.org/justice/2022/08/bounty-hunting-abortion -guns/.

Dudley, Susan E. 2021. "Milestones in the Evolution of the Administrative State." In "The Administrative State in the Twenty-First Century: Deconstruction and/or Reconstruction," ed. Mark Tushnet. Special issue, *Daedalus* 150, no. 3 (Summer): 34–48.

Du Gay, Paul. 2000. *In Praise of Bureaucracy: Weber, Organization, Ethics*. Thousand Oaks, CA: Sage.

Duster, Chandelis. 2022. "Greene again Downplays Capitol Riot and Says It Would Have Been Armed If She Led It." *CNN*, December 12, 2022. https://www.cnn .com/2022/12/12/politics/marjorie-taylor-greene-armed-insurrection-comments /index.html.

Edelman, Adam. 2022. "Mother-Daughter Election Workers Threatened by Trump Say There's 'Nowhere' They Feel Safe." *NBC News*, June 11, 2022. https://www .nbcnews.com/politics/congress/election-workers-targeted-trump-ruby-freeman -shaye-moss-say-s-nowhere-rcna34640.

Edlin, Ruby, and Lawrence Norden. 2023. "Poll of Election Officials Shows High Turn-over amid Safety Threats and Political Interference." Brennan Center for Justice, April 23, 2023. https://www.brennancenter.org/our-work/analysis-opinion/poll-election-officials-shows-high-turnover-amid-safety-threats-and.

Edling, Max M. 2003. *A Revolution in Favor of Government: Origins of the US Constitution and the Making of the American State*. New York: Oxford University Press.

Edmondson, Catie. 2022. "'So the Traitors Know the Stakes': The Meaning of the Jan. 6 Gallows." *New York Times*, January 20, 2022. https://www.nytimes.com/2022/06/16/us/politics/jan-6-gallows.html.

Edsall, Thomas B. 2020. "What Is Trump Playing At?" *New York Times*, November 11, 2020. https://www.nytimes.com/2020/11/11/opinion/trump-concession-transition.html.

Edsall, Thomas B. 2023. "Why the Ranks of Populism Are Filled with Nasty Characters." *New York Times*, January 18, 2023. https://www.nytimes.com/2023/01/18/opinion/rpublicans-populism-political-psychology.html.

Eizenstat, Stuart. 2018. "Lessons in Bipartisan Deregulation from 30,000 Feet." *The Hill*, November 6, 2018. https://thehill.com/opinion/finance/415001-lessons-in-bipartisan-deregulation-from-30000-feet/.

Elmendorf, Christopher S. 2024. "Don't San Francisco-ize Clean Energy." *The Atlantic,* January 28, 2024. https://www.theatlantic.com/ideas/archive/2024/01/clean-energy-san-francisco-environmentalism/677276/.

Engels, Friedrich. (1884) 1978. "The Origin of the Family, Private Property, and the State." In *The Marx-Engels Reader*. 2nd ed., edited by Robert C. Tucker, 734–59. New York: W. W. Norton.

Environmental Protection Agency. 2021. "EPA Finalizes Rule Strengthening Transparency." Press release. January 5, 2021. https://www.epa.gov/newsreleases/epa-finalizes-rule-strengthening-transparency-pivotal-science-underlying-significant.

Equality Florida Action. 2023. "Equality Florida Issues Advisory Warning for Florida." April 11, 2033. https://eqfl.org/florida-travel-advisory.

Estlund, David M. 2008. *Democratic Authority: A Philosophic Framework*. Princeton, NJ: Princeton University Press.

Evans, Richard. 2003. *The Coming of the Third Reich*. New York: Penguin.

Eymeri-Douzans, Jean-Michel. 2022. "France: Under the Rule of a Contested Politico-Administrative Elite Whose Legitimacy Erodes." In *Handbook on the Politics of Public Administration*, edited by Andreas Ladner and Fritz Sager, 289–302. Northampton, MA: Edward Elgar.

Fabiola, Cineas. 2021. "Donald Trump Is the Accelerant: A Comprehensive Timeline of Trump Encouraging Hate Groups and Political Violence." *Vox*, January 9, 2021. https://www.vox.com/21506029/trump-violence-tweets-racist-hate-speech.

Feuer, Alan, and Katie Benner. 2022. "The Fake Electors Scheme, Explained." *New York Times*, August 3, 2022. https://www.nytimes.com/2022/07/27/us/politics/fake-electors-explained-trump-jan-6.html.

Finkelstein, Claire O., and Richard Painter. 2020. "Invoking Martial Law to Reverse the 2020 Election Could Be Criminal." *Just Security*, December 22, 2020. https://www.justsecurity.org/73986/invoking-martial-law-to-reverse-the-2020-election-could-be-criminal-sedition/.

Fiorina, Morris P. 1981. *Retrospective Voting in American National Elections*. New Haven, CT: Yale University Press.

Flavelle, Christopher, Lisa Friedman, and Carol Davenport. 2020. "Trump Administration Removes Scientist in Charge of Climate Change." *New York Times*, November 9, 2020. https://www.nytimes.com/2020/11/09/climate/michael-kuperberg-climate-assessment.html.

Flegenheimer, Matt. 2022. "DeSantis, Once a 'No' on Storm Aid, Petitions a President He's Bashed." *New York Times*, September 9, 2022. https://www.nytimes.com/2022/09/29/us/politics/desantis-biden-hurricane-ian-aid.html.

Flores, Andrew R., Rebecca L. Stotzer, Ilan H. Meyer, and Lynn L. Langton. 2022. "Hate Crimes against LGBT People: National Crime Victimization Survey, 2017–2019." *PLoS One* 17, no. 12 (December 21): e0279363. https://doi.org/10.1371/journal.pone.0279363.

Forrest, Jack. 2023. "Michigan Election Denier Who Has Yet to Concede Her 2022 Loss Will Chair State GOP." *CNN*, February 20, 2023. https://www.cnn.com/2023/02/20/politics/kristina-karamo-michigan-gop-chair/index.html.

Franke-Ruta, Garance. 2011. "'Oops.' Rick Perry's Incredible Brain-Freeze Moment." *The Atlantic*, November 9, 2011. https://www.theatlantic.com/politics/archive/2011/11/oops-rick-perrys-incredible-brain-freeze-moment-video/248221/.

Frank, Richard G., Leslie Dach, and Nicole Lurie. "It Was the Government That Produced COVID-19 Vaccine Success." *Health Affairs*, May 14, 2021. https://www.healthaffairs.org/content/forefront/government-produced-covid-19-vaccine-success.

Freeman, Jody, and Sharon Jacobs. 2021. "Structural Deregulation." *Harvard Law Review* 135, no. 2 (December): 535–665.

French, David. 2023. "The Rage and Joy of MAGA America." *New York Times*, July 6, 2023. https://www.nytimes.com/2023/07/06/opinion/maga-america-trump.html.

Fried, Amy, and Douglas B. Harris. 2021. *At War with the Government: How Conservatives Weaponized Distrust from Goldwater to Trump*. New York: Columbia University Press.

Fukuyama, Francis. 2014. *Political Order and Political Decay: From the Industrial Revolution to the Globalization of Democracy*. New York: Farrar, Strauss, and Giroux.

Galston, William A. 2018. *Anti-Pluralism: The Populist Threat to Liberal Democracy*. New Haven, CT: Yale University Press.

Galston, William A. 2022. "What Is National Conservatism?" *Persuasion*, September 12, 2022. https://www.persuasion.community/p/what-is-national-conservatism.

Gardener, Amy, and Paulina Firozi. 2021. "Here's the Full Transcript of the Audio of the Call between Trump and Raffensperger." *Washington Post*, January 5, 2021.

Gerken, Heather. 2017. "We're About to See States' Rights Used Defensively against Trump." *Vox*, January 20, 2017. https://www.vox.com/the-big-idea/2016/12/12/13915990/federalism-trump-progressive-uncooperative.

Gibson, Ginger. 2023. "Trump Says Immigrants Are Poisoning the Blood of Our Country; Biden Campaign Likens Comments to Hitler." *NBC News*, December 17, 2023. https://www.nbcnews.com/politics/2024-election/trump-says-immigrants-are-poisoning-blood-country-biden-campaign-liken-rcna130141.

Gilens, Martin, and Benjamin I. Page. 2014. "Testing Theories of American Politics: Elites, Interest Groups, and Average Citizens." *Perspectives on Politics* 12, no. 3 (September): 564–81.

Giles, Christopher. 2021. "Trump's Wall: How Much Has Been Built during His Term." *BBC*, January 12, 2021. https://www.bbc.com/news/world-us-canada-46748492.

Gilson, Ronal, and Curtis J. Milhaupt. 2011. "Economically Benevolent Dictatorships: Lessons for Developing Democracies." *Journal of Comparative Law* 59, no. 1 (Winter): 227–88.

Gingrich, Newt. 1994. "A Contract with America." Legislative agenda. September 22, 1994. https://legalectric.org/f/2016/11/Gingrich-CONTRACT.pdf.

Goldberg, Michelle. 2022. "The Midterm Race That Has It All." *New York Times*, September 24, 2022. https://www.nytimes.com/2022/09/24/opinion/house-republican-elections.html.

Goldberg, Michelle. 2023. "DeSantis Allies Plot the Hostile Takeover of a Liberal College." *New York Times*, January 9, 2023. https://www.nytimes.com/2023/01/09/opinion/chris-rufo-florida-ron-desantis.html.

Goldmacher, Shane, Jonathan Swan, Maggie Haberman, and Stephanie Lai. 2023. "Trump's Second-Term Goal: Shattering the Norms He Didn't Already Break." *New York Times*, May 11, 2023. https://www.nytimes.com/2023/05/11/us/politics/trump-2024-cnn-town-hall-html.

Goodman, J. David. 2023. "Gov. Abbott's Policing of Texas Border Pushes Limits of State Power." *New York Times*, July 26, 2023. https://nytimes.com/2023/07/26/us/texas-greg-abbott-border-migrants.html.

Goodman, J. David, and Nicholas Nehamas. 2023. "DeSantis Calls for 'Deadly Force' against Suspected Drug Traffickers." *New York Times*, June 26, 2023. https://www.nytimes.com/2023/06/26/us/politics/ron-desantis-border-drug-traffickers.html.

Greenberg, Udi. 2021. "What Was the Fascism Debate?" *Dissent*, Summer 2021. https://www.dissentmagazine.org/article/what-was-the-fascism-debate.

Greenblatt, Alan. 2023. "How Election Deniers Are Making Voter Fraud Easier." *Governing*, March 27, 2023. https://www.governing.com/now/how-election-deniers-are-making-voter-fraud-easier.

Gregorian, Dareh. 2022. "GOP Senate Candidate Releases 'RINO Hunting' Ad Aimed at Fellow Republicans." *NBC News*, June 20, 2022. https://www.nbcnews.com

/politics/2022-election/gop-senate-candidate-releases-rino-hunting-ad-aimed-fellow-republicans-rcna34388.

Grenoble, Ryan. 2022. "Miami Dade County Hires Three Proud Boys as Poll Workers." *Huffington Post*, November 2, 2022. https://www.huffpost.com/entry/miami-dade-proud-boys-poll-watchers_n_636281f8e4b045895a988178.

Grumbach, Jacob. 2018. "From Backwaters to Major Policymakers: Policy Polarization in the States, 1970–2014." *Perspectives on Politics* 16 (2): 416–35. https://doi.org/10.1017/S153759271700425X.

Grumbach, Jacob. 2022. *Laboratories against Democracy: How National Parties Transformed State Politics*. New York: Polity.

Gupta, Anant, and Gerry Shih. 2023. "India's Top Opposition Leader Gandhi Expelled from Parliament after Conviction." *Washington Post*, March 24, 2023. https://www.washingtonpost.com/world/2023/03/24/rahul-gandhi-expelled-parliament-bjp/.

Gurley, Gabrielle. 2021. "Romanticizing Secession." *American Prospect*, January 6, 2021. https://prospect.org/power/02-23-2023-republican-secession.

Gutmann, Amy. 1994. *Multiculturalism*. Princeton, NJ: Princeton University Press.

Haelle, Tara. 2021. "As Kids Head Back to School, Battles over Masks Are Pitting Parents against Governors." *National Geographic*, August 26, 2021. https://www.nationalgeographic.com/science/article/as-kids-head-back-to-school-battles-over-masks-are-pitting-parents-against-governors.

Hagstrom, Andrew. 2022. "Trump to Hannity: Presidents Can Declassify Documents 'by Thinking about It.'" *Fox News*, September 9, 2022. https://www.foxnews.com/politics/trump-hannity-presidents-can-declassify-documents-thinking-about-it.

Hamburger, Philip. 2014. *Is Administrative Law Unlawful?* Chicago: University of Chicago Press.

Hamel, Gary, and Michele Zanini. 2023. "America Should Be More Like Operation Warp Speed." *The Atlantic*, December 28, 2023. https://www.theatlantic.com/ideas/archive/2023/12/operation-warp-speed-trump-lessons/676913/.

Hamilton, Alexander. 1787. *Federalist* no. 27. December 27, 1787. Founders Online, National Archives. https://founders.archives.gov/documents/Hamilton/01-04-02-0184.

Hamilton, Alexander. 1791. *Report on the Subject of Manufactures* (Final Version). December 5, 1791. Founders Online, National Archives. https://founders.archives.gov/documents/Hamilton/01-10-02-0001-0007.

Harper, Karen Brooks. 2021. "Verbal and Physical Attacks on Health Workers Surge as Emotions Boil during Latest COVID-19 Wave." *Texas Tribune* (Austin), September 1, 2021. https://www.texastribune.org/2021/09/01/coronavirus-texas-hospital-attacks-health-workers/.

Hart, Benjamin. 2021. "Ron DeSantis Takes Hatred of Masks to a New Level." *New York Magazine*, August 10, 2021. https://nymag.com/intelligencer/2021/08/ron-desantis-takes-hatred-of-mask-mandates-to-a-new-level.html.

Hartocollis, Anemona, and Eliza Fawcett. 2023. "The College Board Strips Down Its A.P. Curriculum for African American Studies." *New York Times*, February 1,

2023. https://www.nytimes.com/2023/02/01/us/college-board-advanced -placement-african-american-studies.html.

Harvard Law Review. 2023. "Leading Case: *Moore v. Harvard.*" *Harvard Law Review* 137, no. 1 (November): 290–99. https://harvardlawreview.org/priint/volume 137 /moore-v-harper/.

Hasen, Rick. 2023. "Supreme Court Rejects Novel Legislative Theory but Leaves the Door Open for 2024 Election Challenges." *Election Law Blog,* June 28, 2023. https://electionlawblog.org/?p=137154.

Havel, Václav. (1963) 1992. "*The Garden Party.*" In *The Garden Party and Other Plays,* 3–51. New York: Grove Press.

Heath, Joseph. 2020. *The Machinery of Government: Public Administration in the Liberal State.* New York: Oxford University Press.

Hegel, Georg Wilhelm Friedrich. (1821) 1967. *The Philosophy of Right.* Translated with notes by T. M. Knox. New York: Oxford University Press.

Heinzerling, Lisa. 2022. "How Government Ends." *Boston Review,* September 28, 2022. https://www.bostonreview.net/articles/how-government-ends/.

Henry, Melissa. 2023. "Club Q Shooting Suspect Reportedly Visited Gay Club 6 Times before Mass Shooting in Colorado Springs." KKTV News, February 22, 2023. https://www.kktv.com/2023/02/22/club-q-shooting-suspect-reportedly-visited -gay-club-more-than-6-times-before-mass-shooting-colorado-springs.

Herenstein, Ethan, and Brian Palmer. 2022. "Fraudulent Document Cited in Supreme Court Bid to Torch Election Law." *Politico,* September 15, 2022. https://www .politico.com/news/magazine/2022/09/15/fraudulent-document-supreme-court -bid-election-law-00056810.

Hirschman, Albert O. 1970. *Exit, Voice, and Loyalty: Responses to Decline in Firms, Organizations, and States.* Cambridge, MA: Harvard University Press.

Hochschild, Arlie R. 2016. *Strangers in Their Own Land.* New York: New Press.

Hochschild, Arlie. 2018. "Is Trump a Bully or a Protector? That Depends on Whom You Ask." *The Guardian,* October 11, 2018. https://www.theguardian.com/commentisfree /2020/oct/11/is-donald-trump-a-bully-or-bold-protector-that-depends-on-whom -you-ask.

Holan, Angie Drobnic. 2019. "In Context: Donald Trump's 'Very Fine People on both Sides' Remarks" (transcript). *Politifact,* April 26, 2019. https://www.politifact .com/article/2019/apr/26/context-trumps-very-fine-people-both-sides-remarks/.

Holley, Peter. 2022. "Are Texas Republicans Serious about Secession?" *Texas Monthly* (Austin), November 2022, https://www.texasmonthly.com/news-politics/are -texas-republicans-serious-about-secession/.

Holmes, Stephen. 2012. "Fragments of a Defunct State." *London Review of Books* 34, no. 1–5 (January). https://www.lrb.co.uk/the-paper/v34/n01/stephen-holmes /fragments-of-a-defunct-state.

Homans, Charles. 2022. "How 'Stop the Steal' Captured the American Right." *New York Times,* July 19, 2022. https://www.nytimes.com/2022/07/19/magazine/stop -the-steal.html.

Homans, Charles. 2023. "A Trump Rally, a Right-Wing Cause, and the Enduring Legacy of Waco." *New York Times*, March 24, 2023. https://www.nytimes.com/2023/03 /24/us/politics/donald-trump-waco-branch-davidians.html.

Hopkins, Daniel J. 2018. *The Increasing United States*. Chicago: University of Chicago Press.

Howie, Craig. 2022. "White House to Trump: You Cannot Only Love American When You Win." *Politico*, December 3, 2022. https://www.politico.com/news/2022/12 /03/white-house-trump-constitution-america-00072069.

"H.R. 6747: Clean Electricity and Transmission Acceleration Act of 2023." 2023. GovTrack.us, December 13. https://www.govtrack.us/congress/bills/118 /hr6747.

Human Rights Watch. 2018. "Q&A: Trump Administration's 'Zero Tolerance' Policy." August 16, 2018. https://www.hrw.org/news/2018/08/16/qa-trump-administrations -zero-tolerance-immigration-policy.

Huntington, Samuel P. (1957) 1981. *The Soldier and the State: The Theory and Politics of Civil-Military Relations*. Cambridge, MA: Harvard University Press.

Huntington, Samuel P. 1968. *Political Order in Changing Societies*. New Haven, CT: Yale University Press.

Inglehart, Ronald. 2016. *The Silent Revolution: Changing Values and Political Styles among Western Publics*. Princeton, NJ: Princeton University Press.

Institute for Research and Education in Human Rights. 2022. *Breaching the Mainstream: A National Survey of Far-Right Membership in State Legislatures*. Kansas City, MO: Author. https://www.irehr.org/reports/breaching-the-mainstream/.

Isidore, Chris. 2008. "Bailout Plan Rejected—Supporters Scramble." *CNN Money*, September 29, 2008. https://money.cnn.com/2008/09/29/news/economy/bailout/.

Issacharoff, Samuel. 2023. *Democracy Unmoored: Populism and the Corruption of Popular Sovereignty*. New York: Oxford University Press.

Jackson, David. 2016. "Trump Accepts GOP Nomination, Says 'I Alone Can Fix' System." *USA Today*, July 21, 2016. https://www.usatoday.com/story/news/politics /elections/2016/07/21/donald-trump-republican-convention-acceptance-speech /87385658/.

Jacobs, Nicholas F., and Sidney M. Milkis. 2022. *What Happened to the Vital Center? Presidentialism, Populist Revolt, and the Fracturing of America*. Oxford: Oxford University Press.

Jaffrelot, Christophe. 2023. *Modi's India: Hindu Nationalism and the Rise of Ethnic Democracy*. Princeton, NJ: Princeton University Press.

Janda, Kenneth. 2022. *The Republican Evolution: From Governing Party to Antigoverning Party, 1860–2020*. New York: Columbia University Press.

Jefferson, Thomas. (1776) 1975. "The Declaration of Independence." In *The Portable Thomas Jefferson*, edited by Merrill D. Peterson. New York: Viking.

Jossey, Paul H. 2016. "How We Killed the Tea Party." *Politico Magazine*, August 14, 2016. https://www.politico.com/magazine/story/2016/08/tea-party-pacs-ideas -death-214164/.

Jost, Timothy. 2021. "The Supreme Court Throws Out the ACA Lawsuit Not the ACA." *Commonwealth Fund* (blog), June 21, 2021. https://www.commonwealthfund.org/blog/2021/supreme-court-throws-out-aca-lawsuit-not-aca.

Jouvenal, Justin. 2023. "An Election Chief Says the 'Big Lie' Ended Her Career. She's Fighting Back." *Washington Post*, November 2, 2023. https://www.washingtonpost.com/dc-md-va/2023/11/02/lynchburg-elections-registrar-lawsuit/.

Judis, John B. 2016. *The Populist Explosion: How the Great Recession Transformed American and European Politics.* New York: Global Economic Reports.

Kabaservice, Geoffrey. 2012. *Rule and Ruin: The Downfall of Moderation and the Destruction of the Republican Party, from Eisenhower to the Tea Party.* Oxford: Oxford University Press.

Kagan, Elena. 2001. "Presidential Administration." *Harvard Law Review* 114, no. 8 (June): 2245–385.

Kalmoe, Nathan P., and Lilliana Mason. 2022. *Radical American Partisanship: Mapping Violent Hostility, Its Causes, and the Consequences for Democracy.* Chicago: University of Chicago Press.

Kapur, Devesh. 2020. "Why Does the Indian State Both Fail and Succeed?" *Journal of Economic Perspectives* 34, no. 1 (Winter): 1–24.

Kapur, Sahil. 2020. "Trump Says Obamacare Must Die. Biden Says He'll Make It into 'Bidencare.'" *NBC News*, October 22, 2020. https://www.nbcnews.com/politics/2020-election/trump-says-obamacare-must-die-biden-says-he-ll-make-n1244454.

Karni, Annie. 2023. "McCarthy Wins Speakership after Hard Right Vote." *New York Times*, January 6, 2023. https://www.nytimes.com/2023/01/06/us/politics/house-speaker-vote-mccarthy.html.

Katz, Bruce. 2014. "Nixon's New Federalism 45 Years Later." Brookings, August 11, 2014. https://www.brookings.edu/articles/nixons-new-federalism-45-years-later/.

Katz, Eric. 2023. "DeSantis Pledges to Eliminate Agencies and Slash Federal Workforce, Following a Long Line of GOP Candidates." *Government Executive*, June 30, 2023. https://www.govexec.com/workforce/2023/06/desantis-pledges-eliminate-agencies-and-slash-federal-workforce-following-long-line-recent-gop-candidates/388108/.

Kaufman, Ellie, Marshall Cohen, Jason Hoffman, and Nicky Robertson. 2020. "Trump Says He Opposes USPS Because of Mail-in Voting." *CNN*, August 13, 2020. https://www.cnn.com/2020/08/13/politics/trump-usps-funding-comments-2020-election/index.html.

Kelleher, Jennifer Sinco, Terry Tang, and Olga R. Rodriguez. 2021. "Mask, Vaccine Conflicts Descend into Violence and Harassment." *AP News*, August 21, 2021. https://apnews.com/article/health-coronavirus-pandemic-2eba81ebe3bd54b3bcde890b8cf11c70.

Kelley, Robin D. G. 2016. "Black Study, Black Struggle." *Boston Review*, March 1, 2016. https://www.bostonreview.net/forum/robin-kelley-black-struggle-campus-protest/.

Kelly, Michael. 1995. "The Road to Paranoia." *New Yorker*, June 11, 1995. https://www
.newyorker.com/magazine/1995/06/19/the-road-to-paranoia.

Kessler, Jeremy, and Charles Sabel. 2021. "The Uncertain Future of Administrative
Law." In "The Administrative State in the Twenty-First Century: Deconstruc-
tion and/or Reconstruction," ed. Mark Tushnet. Special issue, *Daedalus* 150, no. 3
(Summer): 188–207.

Kettl, Donald F. 2020. *The Divided States of America: Why Federalism Doesn't Work*.
Princeton, NJ: Princeton University Press.

Khosla, Madhav, and Mark Tushnet. 2022. "Courts, Constitutionalism, and State
Capacity: A Preliminary Inquiry." *American Journal of Comparative Law* 70, no. 1
(March): 95–138. https://doi.org/10.1093/ajcl/avac009.

Kiel, Paul, and Jesse Eisinger. 2018. "How the IRS Was Gutted." *Pro Publica*, December 11, 2018. https://www.propublica.org/article/how-the-irs-was-gutted.

Klein, Ezra. 2023a. "Three Reasons the Republican Party Keeps Coming Apart at the
Seams." *New York Times*, January 15, 2023. https://www.nytimes.com/2023/01
/15/opinion/mccarthy-republicans-coming-apart.html.

Klein, Ezra. 2023b. "The Problem with Everything-Bagel Liberalism." *New York
Times*, April 2, 2023. https://www.nytimes.com/2023/04/02/opinion/democrats
-liberalism.html.

Knight, Heather. 2024. "San Francisco Tried to Build a $1.7 Million Toilet. It's Still Not
Done." *New York Times*, January 24, 2024. https://www.nytimes.com/2024/01/24
/us/san-francisco-toilet.html.

Koh, B. C. 1991. *Japan's Administrative Elite*. Berkeley: University of California Press.

Konczal, Mike. 2015. "Hail to the Pencil Pusher: American Bureaucracy's Long and
Useful History." *Boston Review*, September 21, 2015. https://www.bostonreview
.net/articles/mike-konczal-government-bureaucracy/.

Korte, Gregory, and Alan Gomez. 2018. "Trump Ramps Up Rhetoric on Undocumented
Immigrants: 'These aren't people. These are animals.'" *USA Today*, May 16, 2018.
https://www.usatoday.com/story/news/politics/2018/05/16/trump-immigrants
-animals-mexico-democrats-sanctuary-cities/617252002/.

Kovacs, Kathryn E. 2021. "From Presidential Administration to Bureaucratic Dictator-
ship." *Harvard Law Review* 135, no. 2 (December): 104–32.

Kriel, Lomi, Perla Trevizo, Andrew Rodriguez Calderon, and Keri Blakinger.
2022. "Gov. Greg Abbott Brags about His Border Initiative. The Evidence
Doesn't Back Him Up." *Texas Tribune* (Austin), March 22, 2022. https://www
.texastribune.org/2022/03/21/operation-lone-star-lacks-clear-metrics-measure
-accomplishments/.

Krugman, Paul. 2021. "How Saboteurs Took Over the GOP." *New York Times*,
December 2, 2021. https://www.nytimes.com/2021/12/02/opinion/republicans
-government-shutdown.html.

Kunzru, Hari. 2021. "As American as Family Separation." *New York Review of Books*,
July 1, 2021. https://www.nybooks.com/articles/2021/07/01/as-american-as
-family-separation/.

Kurtz, David. 2023. "America Is in the Grip of a Reign of White Supremacist Terror." *Talking Points Memo*, August 28, 2023. https://talkingpointsmemo.com/morning -memo/america-is-in-the-grip-of-reign-of-white-supremacist-terror.

Kuttner, Robert. 2023. "Can States Plug Gaps in Federal Policy?" *American Prospect*, October 9, 2023. https://prospect.org/blogs-and-newsletters/tap/2023-10-09-can -states-plug-gaps-in-federal-policy/.

Laclau, Ernesto. 2007. *On Populist Reason*. New York: Verso.

Landemore, Hélène. 2017. *Democratic Reason: Politics, Collective Intelligence, and Rule of the Many*. Princeton, NJ: Princeton University Press.

Landis, John L. 1938. *The Administrative Process*. New Haven, CT: Yale University Press.

Landler, Mark. 2018. "Trump Abandons Nuclear Deal He Long Scorned." *New York Times*, May 8, 2018. https://www.nytimes.com/2018/05/08/world/middleeast /trump-iran-nuclear-deal.html.

Landy, Marc K., Marc J. Roberts, and Stephen R. Thomas. 1990. *The Environmental Protection Agency: Asking the Wrong Questions*. Oxford: Oxford University Press.

Lane, Melissa. 2023. *Of Rule and Office: Plato's Ideas of the Political*. Princeton, NJ: Princeton University Press.

Lavelle, Marianne. 2020. "Trump EPA's 'Secret Science' Rule Would Dismiss Studies that Could Hold Clues to Covid-19." *Inside Climate News*, August 4, 2020. https:// insideclimatenews.org/news/08042020/epa-secret-science-coronavirus-covid/.

Lawson, Gary. 1994. "The Rise and Rise of the Administrative State." *Harvard Law Review* 107, no. 6 (April): 1231–54.

Layne, Nathan. 2021. "'Truth Matters,' Says Georgia Official in Resisting Trump's Pressure." *Reuters*, January 3, 2021. https://www.reuters.com/article/uk-usa-election -georgia-raffensperger-idUKKBN2980QZ.

Lemann, Nicholas. 2003. "The Controller." *New Yorker*, May 4, 2003. https://www .newyorker.com/magazine/2003/05/12/the-controller.

Lemkin Institute for Genocide Prevention. 2022. "Statement on the Genocidal Nature of the Gender Critical Movement's Ideology and Practice." November 29, 2022. https://www.lemkininstitute.com/statements-new-page/statement-on-the -genocidal-nature-of-the-gender-critical-movement%E2%80%99s-ideology-and -practice.

Lennard, Natasha. 2023. "Texas Republicans Just Proposed a Bounty on Drag Shows." *The Intercept*, March 24, 2023. https://theintercept.com/2023/03/24/texas -bounty-hunter-drag-bill/.

Leonhardt, David. 2022. "Perils of Invisible Government." *New York Times*, April 21, 2022. https://www.nytimes.com/2022/04/21/briefing/bidin-invisible-govern ment.

Lessig, Lawrence, and Cass R. Sunstein. 1994. "The President and the Administration." *Columbia Law Review* 94 (1): 1–123.

Levi, Margaret. 2022. "Trustworthy Government: The Obligations of Government and the Responsibilities of the Governed." *Daedalus* 151, no. 4 (Fall): 215–33.

LeVine, Marianne. 2023., "Trump Calls Political Enemies 'Vermin,' Echoing Dictators Hitler, Mussolini." *Washington Post*, November 12, 2023. https://www.washingtonpost.com/politics/2023/11/12/trump-rally-vermin-political-opponents/.

Levitsky, Steven, and Daniel Ziblatt. 2018. *How Democracies Die*. New York: Crown.

Levitsky, Steven, and Daniel Ziblatt. 2023. *Tyranny of the Minority: Why American Democracy Reached the Breaking Point*. New York: Crown.

Lewis, David E. 2021. "Is the Failed Pandemic Response a Symptom of a Diseased Administrative State?" In "The Administrative State in the Twenty-First Century: Deconstruction and/or Reconstruction," ed. Mark Tushnet. Special issue, *Daedalus* 150, no. 3 (Summer): 68–88.

Lewis, Michael. 2018. *The Fifth Risk*. New York: W. W. Norton.

Lifton, Robert Jay. 2019. *Losing Reality: On Cults, Cultism, and the Mindset of Religious and Political Zealotry*. New York: New Press.

Lifton, Robert Jay. 2023. *Surviving Our Catastrophe: Resistance and Renewal from Hiroshima to the Covid-19 Pandemic*. New York: New Press.

Lin, Summer, Richard Winton, Rebecca Ellis, Jeong Park, Libor Jany, Rong-Gong Lin II, Julia Wick, Hayley Smith, Debbie Truong, Grace Toohey, and Laura Newberry. 2023. "Authorities Identify 72-Year-Old Man as Suspected Gunman in Lunar New Year Mass Shooting." *Los Angeles Times*, January 22, 2023. https://www.latimes.com/california/story/2023-01-22/la-me-monterey-park-mass-shooting.

Lincoln, Abraham. 1858. "House Divided Speech." June 16, 1858, Springfield, Illinois. https://www.abrahamlincolnonline.org/lincoln/speeches/house.html.

Lincoln, Abraham. 1861. "First Inaugural Address." March 4, 1861. https://avalon.law.yale.edu/19th_century/lincoln1.asp.

Linton, Besser. 2019. "Hungary's Viktor Orbán Has Attempted to Dissolve Europe's Values—but Brussels Is Fighting Back." *ABC News*, May 27. https://www.abc.net.au/news/2019-05-27/inside-the-illiberal-hungary-of-viktor-orban/11151500.

Lizza, Ryan, Rachael Bade, and Eugene Daniels. 2022. "Politico Playbook: Michael Bennet on 2022, the Worst Years of His Life and Magic Mushrooms." *Politico*, December 2, 2022. https://www.politico.com/newsletters/playbook/2022/12/02/michael-bennet-on-2022-the-worst-years-of-his-life-and-magic-mushrooms-00071869.

LoBianco, Tom. 2015. "Donald Trump on Terrorists: 'Take Out Their Families.'" *CNN*, December 3, 2015. https://www.cnn.com/2015/12/02/politics/donald-trump-terrorists-families/index.html.

Lobosco, Katie. 2023. "House GOP Keeps Up Attacks on IRS with Bill to Abolish the Agency." *CNN*, January 23, 2023. https://www.cnn.com/2023/01/23/politics/irs-fair-tax-republicans-abolish/index.html.

Locke, John. (1690) 1961. *Two Treatises of Government*. Edited by Peter Laslett. New York: Cambridge University Press.

Lowi, Theodore J. 1969. *The End of Liberalism: Ideology, Politics, and the Crisis of Public Authority*. New York: W. W. Norton.

Madison, James. 1787. "The Same Subject Continued: The Union as a Safeguard against Domestic Faction and Insurrection" (*Federalist* no. 10). November 23, 1787. https://guides.loc.gov/federalist-papers/text-1-10#s-lg-box-wrapper-25493273.

Magner, Mike. 2023. "Republicans Take Aim at Climate Change in Spending Bills." *Roll Call*, July 11, 2023. https://rollcall.com/2023/07/11/republicans-take-aim-at -climate-funds-in-spending-bills.

Mann, Thomas E., and Norman J. Ornstein. 2012. *It's Even Worse Than It Looks: How the American Constitutional System Collided with the New Politics of Extremism*. New York: Basic Books.

Mann, Thomas E., and Norman J. Ornstein. 2017. "How Republicans Broke Congress." *New York Times*, December 2, 2017. https://www.nytimes.com/2017/12 /02/opinion/sunday/republicans-broke-congress-politics.html.

Manning, John F., and Matthew C. Stephenson. 2013. *Legislation and Regulation*. St. Paul, MN: Thomson Reuters.

Mansbridge, Jane. 2003. "Rethinking Representation." *American Political Science Review* 97, no. 4 (November): 515–28.

Mansbridge, Jane. 2022. "Recursive Representation: The Basic Idea." In *Constitutionalism and a Right to Effective Government*, edited by Vicki C. Jackson and Yasmin Dawood, 206–20. Cambridge, MA: Cambridge University Press.

Mansfield, Harvey C. 1989. *Taming the Prince: The Ambivalence of Modern Executive Power*. New York: Free Press.

Marini, John. 2019. *Unmasking the Administrative State: The Crisis of American Politics in the Twenty-First Century*. Edited by Ken Masugi. New York: Encounter Books.

Markel, Patchen. 2006. "The Rule of the People: Arendt, Arche, and Democracy." *American Political Science Review* 100, no. 1 (February): 1–14.

Martosco, David. 2014. "Ted Cruz: 'Abolish the IRS' and Station All 110,000 Agents 'on the Southern Border.'" *Daily Mail* (London), July 20, 2014. https://www .dailymail.co.uk/news/article-2698810/Ted-Cruz-Abolish-IRS-station-110-000 -agents-southern-border.html.

Mashaw, Jerry L. 2012. *Creating the Administrative Constitution: The Lost One Hundred Years of American Administrative Law*. New Haven, CT: Yale University Press.

Mass, Julia Harumi, and Michael German. 2013. "The Government Is Spying on You: ACLU Releases New Evidence of Overly Broad Surveillance of Everyday Activities." ACLU, September 13, 2013. https://www.aclu.org/news/national-security /government-spying-you-aclu-releases-new-evidence.

Mayer, Jane. 2022. "State Legislatures Are Torching Democracy." *New Yorker*, August 6, 2022. https://www.newyorker.com/magazine/2022/08/15/state-legislatures-are -torching-democracy.

Mazzetti, Mark, and Maggie Haberman. 2022. "A Jan. 6 Mystery: Why Did It Take So Long to Deploy the National Guard?" *New York Times*, July 21, 2022. https:// www.nytimes.com/2022/07/21/us/politics/national-guard-january-6-riot.html.

McCarthy, Justin. 2021. "Record High 70% in U.S. Support Same Sex Marriage." Gallup, June 8, 2021. https://news.gallup.com/poll/350486/record-high-support-same -sex-marriage.aspx.

McCaskill, Nolan D., and Matthew Nussbaum. 2017. "Trump Signs Executive Order Saying That for Every One New Regulation, Two Must Be Revoked." *Politico*, January 30, 2017. https://www.politico.com/story/2017/01/trump-signs-executive

-order-requiring-that-for-every-one-new-regulation-two-must-be-revoked
-234365.

McCormick, Patricia. 2023. "Kids Know Books about Abuse Are Not Pornography. 'Moms' Should, Too." *New York Times,* May 7, 2023. https://www.nytimes.com /2023/05/07/opinion/sexual-assualt-book-ban.html.

McHarris, Philip V., and Thenjiwe McHarris. 2020. "No More Money for the Police." *New York Times,* May 30, 2020. https://www.nytimes.com/2020/05/30/opinion /george-floyd-police-funding.html?referringSource=articleShare.

McKibben, Bill. 2020. "Trump's Attack on the Postal Service Is a Threat to Democracy— and to Rural America." *New Yorker,* August 11, 2020. https://www.newyorker .com/news/daily-comment/trumps-attack-on-the-postal-service-is-a-threat-to -democracy-and-to-rural-america.

Medina, Jennifer. 2023. "G.O.P. Contenders Feed Voter Distrust in Courts, Schools, and the Military." *New York Times,* August 7, 2023. https://www.nytimes.com /2023/08/07/us/politics/trumo-republican-primary-cadidate-trust-html.

Mejdrich, Kellie. 2017. "GOP Leaps on Congressional Review Act to Kill Obama Rules." *Roll Call,* February 23, 2017. https://rollcall.com/2017/02/23/gop-leaps -on-congressional-review-act-to-kill-obama-rules/.

Mello, Michelle M., Jeremy A. Greene, and Joshua M. Sharfstein. 2020. "Attacks on Public Health Officials During COVID-19." *JAMA—The Journal of the American Medical Association* 324 (8): 741–42. https://jamanetwork.com/journals/jama /fullarticle/2769291.

Menand, Louis. 2023. "Making the News." *New Yorker,* February 6, 2023, 59–65.

Mettler, Suzanne. 2011. *The Submerged State: How Invisible Government Policies Undermine American Democracy.* Chicago: University of Chicago Press.

Metzger, Gillian E. 2017a. *The Administrative Procedure Act: An Introduction.* Washington, DC: Poverty & Race Research Action Council. https://policycommons.net /artifacts/1584889/the-administrative-procedure-act/2274658/.

Metzger, Gillian E. 2017b. "Foreword: 1930s Redux: The Administrative State under Siege." *Harvard Law Review* 131, no. 1 (November): 1–95.

Michaels, Jon D. 2017. *Constitutional Coup: Privatization's Threat to the American Republic.* Cambridge, MA: Harvard University Press.

Milhiser, Ian. 2016. "Trump Says He Will Delegate Judicial Selection to the Conservative Federalist Society." *Think Progress,* June 15, 2016. https://archive.thinkprogress .org/trump-says-he-will-delegate-judicial-selection-to-the-conservative-federalist -society-26f622b10c49/.

Milibank, Dana. 2022. *The Destructionists: The Twenty-Five Year Crack-Up of the Republican Party.* New York: Doubleday.

Milkis, Sidney, and Daniel J. Tichenor. 2019. *Presidents, Social Movements, and the Transformation of American Politics.* Chicago: University of Chicago Press.

Miller, Lauren, and Wendy R. Weiser. 2023. "Election Denier's Playbook for 2024." Brennan Center for Justice, May 3, 2023. https://www.brennancenter.org/our -work/research-reports/election-deniers-playbook-2024.

Milley, Mark A. 2020. "Message to the Joint Force." Memorandum. June 2, 2020. https://pbs.twimg.com/media/EZpyCwzWsAAaIrN?format=jpg&name=large.

Mintz, Joel A. 1995. *Enforcement at the EPA: High Stakes and Hard Choices*. Austin: University of Texas Press.

Miroff, Nick. 2018. "A Family Was Separated at the Border and This Distraught Father Took His Own Life." *Washington Post*, June 9, 2018. https://www.texastribune.org /2018/06/09/father-suicide-family-separated-texas-border/.

Montellaro, Zach. 2023. "Texas Jettisons Bipartisan Voter List Program ERIC." *Politico*, July 20, 2023. https://www.politico.com/news/2023/07/20/texas-leaves-eric -voting-00107466.

Moore, Jack. 2017. "Steve Bannon, Trump's Closest Adviser, Just Wants to See the World Burn." *GQ*, January 30, 2017. https://www.gq.com/story/steve-bannon -shadow-president.

Morello, Carol, and Anne Gearan. 2017. "In First Month of Trump Presidency, State Department Has Been Sidelined." *Washington Post*, February 22, 2017. https:// www.washingtonpost.com/world/national-security/in-first-month-of-trump -presidency-state-department-has-been-sidelined/2017/02/22/ccl70cd2-f924 -11e6-be05-1a3817ac21a5_story.html.

Morris, David Z. 2017. "Steve Bannon Says Trump's Cabinet Picks Are Intended to 'Deconstruct' Regulation and Agencies." *Fortune*, February 25, 2017. https:// fortune.com/2017/02/25/bannon-trump-cabinet-cpac/.

Morris, Frank. 2021. "USDA Research Agencies 'Decimated' by Forced Move— Undoing the Damage Won't Be Easy." *NPR*, February 2, 2021. https://www.npr .org/2021/02/02/963207129/usda-research-agencies-decimated-by-forced-move -undoing-the-damage-wont-be-easy.

Moyn, Samuel. 2021. "Allegations of Fascism Distract from the Real Danger." *The Nation*, January 18, 2021. https://www.thenation.com/article/society/trump-fascism/.

Muirhead, Russell, and Nancy Rosenblum. 2019. *A Lot of People Are Saying: The New Conspiracism and the Assault on Democracy*. Princeton, NJ University Press.

Müller, Jan-Werner. 2016. *What Is Populism?* Philadelphia: University of Pennsylvania Press.

Müller, Jan-Werner. 2017. "Donald Trump's Use of the Term 'the People' Is a Warning Sign." *The Guardian*, January 24. 2017. https://www.theguardian.com/commentisfree /2017/jan/24/donald-trumps-warning-sign-populism-athoritarianism-inauguration.

Muravchik, Stephanie, and Jon A. Shields. 2023. "Republicans in Wyoming See Clearly What's Happening." *New York Times*, September 7, 2023. https://www.nytimes .com/2023/09/07/opinion/nationalization-politics-wyoming.html.

Murphy, Ryan, and Colin O'Reilly. 2020. "Assessing State Capacity Libertarianism." *Cato Journal*, Fall 2020. https://www.cato.org/cato-journal/fall-2020/assessing -state-capacity-libertarianism.

Myers, K. C., and Sophie Mann-Shafir. 2022. "Officials Are Buried in Records Requests from Out of State." *Provincetown (MA) Independent* 4, no. 162 (November 3): A1, A14.

Naidoo, Kamban. 2016. "The Origins of Hate-Crime Laws." *Fundamina* 22 (1): 53–66. https://dx.doi.org/10.17159/2411-7870/2016/v22n1a4.

Neuman, William. 2022. *Things Are Never So Bad That They Can't Get Worse: Inside the Collapse of Venezuela*. New York: St. Martin's Press.

New York Times. 2017. "Full Transcript and Video of Trump's News Conference in New York." August 15, 2017. https://www.nytimes.com/2017/08/15/us/politics/trump -press-conference-transcript.html.

Nguyen, Tina. 2017. "'Idiots,' 'Anarchists' and 'Assholes': John Boehner Unloads on Republicans in Post Retirement Interview." *Vanity Fair*, October 30, 2017. https:// www.vanityfair.com/news/2017/10/john-boehner-on-republican-party.

Nielson, Aaron L. 2017. "Confessions of an 'Anti-Administrativist.'" *Harvard Law Review* 131 (1): 1–12.

Nielson, Aaron L. 2021. "Deconstruction (Not Destruction)." In "The Administrative State in the Twenty-First Century: Deconstruction and/or Reconstruction," ed. Mark Tushnet. Special issue, *Daedalus* 150, no. 3 (Summer): 143–55.

Noel, Brandon. 2023. "What the Rapid Repair of I-95 in Philadelphia Says about America's Infrastructure." *For Construction Pros*, June 26, 2023. https://www .forconstructionpros.com/infrastructure/article/22865801/what-the-rapid-repair -of-i95-in-philadelphia-says-about-americas-infrastructure.

Norris, Pippa, and Ronald Inglehart. 2019. *Cultural Backlash: Trump, Brexit, and Authoritarian Populism*. New York: Cambridge University Press.

NPR. 2019. "President Trump Tells Asylum-Seekers That 'Our Country Is Full.' Is It?" *NPR Morning Edition*, April 15, 2019. https://www.npr.org/2019/04/15/713387924 /trump-tells-asylum-seekers-that-our-country-is-full-is-it.

O'Dell, Rob, and Nick Penzenstadler. 2019. "You Elected Them to Write New Laws. They're Letting Corporations Do It Instead." Center for Public Integrity, April 4, 2019. https://publicintegrity.org/politics/state-politics/copy-paste-legislate/you -elected-them-to-write-new-laws-theyre-letting-corporations-do-it-instead/.

Office of the Director of National Intelligence. 2023. *Annual Threat Assessment of the U.S. Intelligence Community*. https://www.dni.gov/files/ODNI/documents /assessments/ATA-2023-Unclassified-Report.pdf.

Office of the Federal Register, National Archives and Records Service. 2022. *The United States Government Manual*. Washington, DC: Author. https://www.govinfo.gov /content/pkg/GOVMAN-2022-12-31/pdf/GOVMAN-2022-12-31.pdf.

Office of the Governor of Florida. 2023a. "Governor Ron DeSantis Announces $50 Million Available for Local Governments Impacted by Hurricanes Ian and Nicole." Press release. March 3, 2023. https://www.flgov.com/2023/03/03 /governor-ron-desantis-announces-50-million-available-for-local-governments -impacted-by-hurricanes-ian-and-nicole/.

Office of the Governor of Florida. 2023b. "Governor Ron DeSantis Signs Sweeping Legislation to Protect the Innocence of Florida's Children." Press release. May 17, 2023. https://www.flgov.com/2023/05/17/governor-ron-desantis-signs-sweeping -legislation-to-protect-the-innocence-of-floridas-children/.

O'Keefe, Ed. 2014. "The House Has Voted 54 Times in Four Years on Obamacare: Here's the Full List." *Washington Post*, March 21, 2014. https://www.washingtonpost.com/news/the-fix/wp/2014/03/21/the-house-has-voted-54-times-in-four-years-on-obamacare-heres-the-full-list/.

Oreskes, Naomi, and Erik M. Conway. 2023. *The Big Myth: How American Business Taught Us to Loathe Government and Love the Free Market*. New York: Bloomsbury.

O'Rourke, Beto. 2023. "One Person Can End Cruelty at the Border." *New York Times*, July 25, 2023. https://www.nytimes.com/2023/07/25/opinion/beto-orourke-abbott-lonestar-texas.html.

Orren, Karen, and Stephen Skowronek. 2017. *The Policy State: An American Predicament*. Cambridge, MA: Harvard University Press.

Pahlka, Jennifer. 2023. *ReCoding America: Why Government Is Failing in the Digital Age and Howe We Can Do Better*. New York: Metropolitan Books.

Parrillo, Nicholas R. 2013. *Against the Profit Motive: The Salary Revolution in American Government*. New Haven, CT: Yale University Press.

Partnership for Public Service. 2023. "Political Appointee Tracker." July 31, 2023. https://ourpublicservice.org/performance-measures/political-appointee-tracker/.

Paulson, Henry M., Jr. 2010. *On the Brink: The Race to Stop the Collapse of the Global Financial System*. New York: Business Plus.

Paxton, Robert O. 2004. *The Anatomy of Fascism*. New York: Vintage.

Paz, Christian. 2022. "Democrats' Quietly Effective Strategy for Defeating Election Deniers." *Vox*, November 19, 2022. https://www.vox.com/policy-and-politics/23465033/democrats-secretary-of-state-strategy-election-deniers.

Pepper, David. 2022. *Laboratories against Democracy: How National Parties Transformed State Politics*. New York: Polity.

Perls, Hannah. 2021. "The Downfall of the 'Secret Science' Rule, and What It Means for Biden's Environmental Agenda." Harvard Law School Environmental Energy and Law Program, March 5, 2021. https://eelp.law.harvard.edu/2021/03/final-secret-science-rule/.

Pestritto, Ronald J. 2007. "The Progressive Origins of the Administrative State: Wilson, Goodnow, and Landis." *Social Philosophy and Politics* 24 (1): 16–54.

Peters, B. Guy, and Jon Pierre. 2019. "Populism and Public Administration: Confronting the Administrative State." *Administration and Society* 51 (10): 1521–45. https://doi.org/10.1177/0095399719874749.

Peters, Jeremy. 2018a. "How Trump-Fed Conspiracy Theories about Migrant Caravan Intersect with Deadly Hatred." *New York Times*, October 29, 2018. https://www.nytimes.com/2018/10/29/us/politics/caravan-trump-shooting-elections.html.

Peters, Jeremy W. 2018b. "Trump's New Judicial Litmus Test: Shrinking 'the Administrative State.'" *New York Times*, March 26, 2018. https://www.nytimes.com/2018/03/26/us/politics/trump-judges-courts-administrative-state.html.

Peters, Jeremy W. 2022. *Insurgency: How Republicans Lost Their Party and Got Everything They Ever Wanted*. New York: Crown.

Pettypiece, Shannon. 2023. "Marjorie Taylor Greene Calls for National Divorce between Liberal and Conservative States." *NBC News*, February 20, 2023. https://www.nbcnews.com/politics/congress/marjorie-taylor-greene-calls-national-divorce-liberal-conservative-sta-rcna71464.

Phelps, Jordyn. 2015. "Donald Trump Says He Would Bring Back Waterboarding." *ABC News*, November 22, 2015. https://abcnews.go.com/Politics/donald-trump-bring-back-waterboarding/story?id=35354443.

Phillips, Kevin. 1969. *The Emerging Republican Majority*. New York: Arlington House.

Pildes, Richard H. 2023. "The Supreme Court Rejected a Dangerous Elections Theory. But It's Not All Good News." *New York Times*, June 28, 2023. https://www.nytimes.com/2023/06/28/opinion/supreme-court-independent-state-legislature-theory.html.

Plumer, Brad. 2017. "Trump Wants to Kill Two Regulations for Every New One Issued. Sort of." *Vox*, January 30, 2017. https://www.vox.com/science-and-health/2017/1/30/14441430/trump-executive-order-regulations.

Polantz, Katelyn. 2023. "Trump Does Not Have the Right to Say and Do Exactly What He Pleases." *CNN*, October 16, 2023. https://www.cnn.com/2023/10/16/politics-trump-gag-order-chutkan-hearing/index/htm.

Polarization Research Lab. 2024. "The Path to the 2024 Presidential Election: Partisan Violence." February 5, 2024. https://prlpublic.s3.amazonaws.com/reports/January2024.html#executive-summary.

Popkin, Samuel L. 2021. *Crackup: The Republican Implosion and the Future of Presidential Politics*. New York: Oxford University Press.

Postell, Joseph. 2017. *Bureaucracy in America: The Administrative State's Challenge to Constitutional Government*. Columbia: University of Missouri Press.

Puzzanghera, Jim. 2022. "In the Wake of Trump's Lies, a Brain Drain of Local Election Experience in Georgia." *Boston Globe*, October 24, 2022. https://apps.bostonglobe.com/nation/politics/2022/10/democracy-under-siege/trumps-lies-brain-drain-local-election-experience-georgia/.

Ragland, Will, Ryan Koronowski, Danielle Dietz, and Alexandra Mork. 2022. "Guns and Political Violence Play a Role in MAGA Republican Campaign Ads." Center for American Progress, July 13, 2022. https://www.americanprogressaction.org/article/guns-and-political-violence-play-central-role-in-maga-republican-campaign-ads/.

Rahman, K. Sabeel. 2017. *Democracy against Domination*. Oxford: Oxford University Press.

Rahman, K. Sabeel. 2018. "Reconstructing the Administrative State in an Era of Economic and Democratic Crisis." Review of *Constitutional Coup: Privatization's Threat to the American Republic*, by Jon D. Michaels. *Harvard Law Review* 131, no. 6 (April): 1671–712

Rai, Sarakshi. 2021. "Ted Cruz Wants Texas to Secede if 'Things Become Hopeless' in the US." *The Hill*, November 8, 2021. https://thehill.com/homenews/state-watch/580613-ted-cruz-wants-texas-to-secede-if-things-become-hopeless-in-the-us/.

Ramaswamy, Vivek (@VivekGRamaswamy). 2023. "I will shut down the fourth branch of government, the administrative state. You cannot tame that beast. You must end it." Twitter, June 2, 2023, https://twitter.com/VivekGRamaswamy/status/1668284303141109763.

Rampell, Catherine. 2023. "Supposed 'Moderates' Like Nikki Haley Would Blow Up Government Too." *Washington Post*, December 1, 2023. https://www.washingtonpost.com/opinions/2023/12/01/nikki-haley-government-worker-term-limits/.

Rawls, John. 1999. "The Idea of Public Reason Revisited." In *Collected Papers*, edited by Samuel Freeman, 573–615. Cambridge, MA: Harvard University Press.

Ray, Rashawn. 2020. "What Does 'Defund the Police' Mean and Does It Have Merit?" Brookings, June 19, 2020. https://www.brookings.edu/articles/what-does-defund-the-police-mean-and-does-it-have-merit/.

Reagan, Ronald. 1981. "Inaugural Address 1981." January 20, 1981. Ronald Reagan Presidential Library and Museum. https://www.reaganlibrary.gov/archives/speech/inaugural-address-1981.

Reagan, Ronald. 1986. "News Conference—I'm Here to Help." August 12, 1986. Ronald Reagan Presidential Foundation and Institute. https://www.reaganfoundation.org/ronald-reagan/reagan-quotes-speeches/news-conference-1/.

Reed, Betsy. 2023. "I Am Your Retribution: Trump Rules Supreme at CPAC as He Relaunches Bid for White House." *The Guardian*, March 5, 2023. https://www.theguardian.com/us-news/2023/mar/05/i-am-your-retribution-trump-rules-supreme-at-cpac-as-he-relaunches-bid-for-white-house.

Reich, Robert. 2023. "The Five Elements of Fascism: How Trump and Much of Today's Republican Party Embrace Them." Personal blog, June 15, 2023. https://robertreich.substack.com/p/the-five-elements-of-fascism.

Resneck, Jack, Jr. 2023. "This Could Be One of the Most Brazen Attacks on Americans' Health Yet." *New York Times*, April 20, 2023. https://www.nytimes.com/2023/04/20/opinion/abortion-pill-case-supreme-court.html.

Reuters. 2016. "House's 63rd Attempt to Dismantle Obamacare Fails Also." *Newsweek*, February 2, 2016. https://www.newsweek.com/houses-63rd-attempt-dismantle-obamacare-fails-also-422418.

Rhodes, Jesse, Raymond La Raja, Natishe Nteta, and Alexander Theodoris. 2022. "Martin Luther King Jr. Was Right. Racism and Opposition to Democracy Are Linked, Our Research Finds." *The Monkey Cage* (blog), *Washington Post*, January 16, 2022. https://www.washingtonpost.com/politics/2022/01/17/mlk-racism-democracy-opinion/.

Riccardi, Nicholas, and Joey Cappelletti. 2023. "Failing at Polls, Election Deniers Focus on State GOP Posts." *AP News*, February 26, 2023. https://apnews.com/article/politics-us-republican-party-colorado-6ab686410f80d67b4fe0950a54f16bdb.

Richards, Zoë. 2022. "Trump Intensifies Attacks on McConnell with 'Death Wish' Remark on His Social Media Platform." *NBC News*, October 1, 2022. https://www.nbcnews.com/politics/donald-trump/trump-intensifies-attacks-mcconnell-death-wish-remark-social-media-pla-rcna50293.

Richardson, Heather Cox. 2014. *To Make Men Free: A History of the Republican Party.* New York: Basic Books.

Richardson, Heather Cox. 2022a. "December 16, 2022." *Letters from an American* (blog), December 17, 2022. https://heathercoxrichardson.substack.com/p /december-16-2022.

Richardson, Heather Cox. 2022b. "December 31, 2021." *Letters from an American* (blog), January 1, 2022. https://heathercoxrichardson.substack.com/p/december -31-2021.

Richardson, Heather Cox. 2023a. "January 3, 2023." *Letters from an American* (blog), January 4, 2023. https://heathercoxrichardson.substack.com/p/january-3-2023.

Richardson, Heather Cox. 2023b. "September 6, 2023." *Letters from an American* (blog), September 7, 2023. https://heathercoxrichardson.substack.com/p/september-6 -2023.

Roche, Dara. 2023. "Donald Trump Calls for Protests Ahead of Potential Tuesday Arrest." *Newsweek*, March 18, 2023. https://www.newsweek.com/donald-trump -calls-protests-ahead-potential-tuesday-arrest-1788695.

Rogers, Katie. 2019a. "How Infrastructure Week Became a Long-Running Joke." *New York Times*, May 5, 2019. https://www.nytimes.com/2019/05/22/us/politics /trump-infrastructure-week.html.

Rogers, Katie. 2019b. "In Remarks to Young Supporters, Trump Falsely Calls Elections a 'Rigged Deal.'" *New York Times*, July 23, 2019. https://www.nytimes.com/2019 /07/23/us/politics/donald-trump-charlie-kirk-tsas.html.

Rohr, John A. 1986. *To Run a Constitution: The Legitimacy of the Administrative State.* Lawrence: University Press of Kansas.

Rosanvallon, Pierre. 2011. *Democratic Legitimacy: Impartiality, Reflexivity, Proximity.* Princeton, NJ: Princeton University Press.

Rosanvallon, Pierre. 2018. *Good Government: Democracy beyond Elections.* Cambridge, MA: Harvard University Press.

Rosenblum, Nancy L. 1998. *Membership and Morals: The Personal Uses of Pluralism in America.* Princeton, NJ: Princeton University Press.

Rosenblum, Nancy L. 2020. "Introduction: Paths to Witnessing, Ethics of Speaking Out." In "Witnessing Climate Change," ed. Nancy L. Rosenblum. Special issue, *Daedalus* 149, no. 4 (Fall): 6–24.

Rosenblum, Noah. 2023. "The Case That Could Destroy the Government." *The Atlantic*, November 7, 2023. https://www.theatlantic.com/ideas/archive/2023/11 /securities-and-exchange-commission-v-jarkesy-supreme-court/676059/.

Rubin, Jennifer. 2023. "There Are No Moderate House Republicans." *Washington Post*, January 11, 2023. https://www.washingtonpost.com/opinions/2023/01/11/house -republicans-no-moderates/.

Ruple, John C., and Kayla Race. 2019. "Measuring the NEPA Litigation Burden: A Review of 1,499 Federal Court Cases." *Environmental Law* 50 (2019): 479–522.

Ryan, Missy. 2020. "As Election Nears Pentagon Leaders' Goal of Staying Out of Elections Is Tested." *Washington Post*, October 14, 2020. https://www.washingtonpost

.com/national-security/as-election-nears-pentagon-leaders-goal-of-staying
-out-of-elections-is-tested/2020/10/14/cbf20c6a-0e2a-11eb-bfcf-b1893e2c51b4
_story.html.

Ryan, Missy, and Shane Harris. 2020. "Lt. Col Alexander Vindman Retires, Citing Campaign of 'Bullying' and 'Retaliation' by Trump after Impeachment Testimony." *Washington Post*, July 8, 2020. https://www.washingtonpost.com/national-security /lt-col-alexander-vindman-retires-citing-campaign-of-bullying-intimidation-and -retaliation-by-trump/2020/07/08/934bc6ba-c12e-11ea-864a-0dd31b9d6917 _story.html.

Sabel, Charles. 2012. "Dewey, Democracy, and Democratic Experimentalism." *Contemporary Pragmatism* 9, no. 2 (December): 35–55.

Salas-Wright, Christopher P., Mildred M. Maldonado-Molina, Augusto Pérez-Gómez, Juliana Mejía Trujillo, and Seth J. Schwartz. 2022. "The Venezuelan Diaspora: Migration-Related Experiences and Mental Health." In "Immigration," ed. Amanda Venta, Alfonso Mercado, and Melanie M. Domenech Rodríguez. Special issue, *Current Opinion in Psychology* 47, art. 101430. https://doi.org/10.1016/j.copsyc .2022.101430.

Samuels, Brett. 2022. "Trump in DC Speech Calls for Death Penalty for Convicted Drug Dealers." *The Hill*, July 26, 2022. https://thehill.com/homenews/campaign/3575157 -trump-in-dc-speech-calls-for-death-penalty-for-convicted-drug-dealers/.

Samuels, Brett. 2023. "Trump Suggests He Could Investigate Opponents If Reelected." *The Hill*, November 9, 2023. https://thehill.com/homenews/campaign/4303525 -trump-suggests-he-investigate-opponents-if-reelected/.

Sanchez, Yvonne Wingett. 2022. "Alone in Washington, Rusty Bowers Tells World What Happened in Arizona." *Washington Post*, June 21, 2022. https://www .washingtonpost.com/national-security/2022/06/21/rusty-bowers-jan-6/.

Savage, David G. 2020. "Supreme Court Sides with Trump on Building Border Wall with Diverted Military Funds." *Los Angeles Times*, July 31, 2020. https://www .latimes.com/politics/story/2020-07-31/supreme-court-trump-border-wall -construction.

Scalia, Antonin. 1989a. "Judicial Deference to Administrative Interpretations of Law." *Duke Law Review* 1989, no. 3 (June): 511–21.

Scalia, Antonin. 1989b. "The Rule of Law and a Law of Rules." *University of Chicago Law Review* 56, no. 4 (Fall): 1175–88.

Schifrin, Nick, and Dan Sagalyn. 2023. "Tuberville's Hold on Military Promotions Is Impacting Troop Readiness, Mullen Says." *PBS Newshour*, August 22, 2023. https://www.pbs.org/newshour/show/tubervilles-hold-on-military-promotions -is-impacting-troop-readiness-mullen-says.

Schlozman, Daniel. 2015. *When Movements Anchor Parties: Electoral Alignments in American History*. Princeton, NJ: Princeton University Press.

Schmidt, Michael S. 2017. "Comey Memo Says Trump Asked Him to End Flynn Investigation." *New York Times*, May 16, 2017. https://www.nytimes.com/2017/05/16 /us/politics/james-comey-trump-flynn-russia-investigation.html.

Schmidt, Michael S. 2022. "Trump Wanted I.R.S. Investigations of Foes, Top Aide Says." *New York Times*, November 13, 2022. https://www.nytimes.com/2022/11/13/us/politics/trump-irs-investigations.html.

Schmitt, Eric, Thomas Gibbons-Neff, and Peter Baker. 2020. "Trump Agrees to Send Home Troops from Washington, Easing Tensions with the Pentagon." *New York Times*, June 12, 2020. https://www.nytimes.com/2020/06/04/us/politics/trump-troops-washington-pentagon.html.

Schumpeter, Joseph A. (1943) 2008. *Capitalism, Socialism, and Democracy*. 3rd ed. New York: Harper Perennial Modern Classics.

Scott, Dylan. 2022. "Ron DeSantis's Vaccine 'Investigation' Is All about Beating Trump." *Vox*, December 15, 2022. https://www.vox.com/policy-and-politics/2022/12/15/23509091/ron-desantis-trump-2024-president-covid-vaccine.

Scowronek, Stephen, John A. Dearborn, and Desmond King. 2021. *Phantoms of a Beleagured Republic: The Deep State and the Unitary Executive*. Oxford: Oxford University Press.

Seligman, Joel. 2023. "The Judicial Assault on the Administrative State." *Washington University Law Review* 100 (6): 1687–724. https://wustllawreview.org/2023/08/09/thejudicial-assault-on-the-administrative-state/.

Selin, Jennifer L., and David E. Lewis. 2018. *Sourcebook of United States Executive Agencies*. 2nd ed. Washington, DC: Administrative Conference of the United States, Office of the Chairman.

Shear, Michael D. 2022. "Trump Asked Why His Generals Couldn't Be Like Hitler's, Book Says." *New York Times*, August 8, 2022. https://www.nytimes.com/2022/08/08/us/politics/trump-book-mark-milley.html.

Shklar, Judith N. (1964) 1986. *Legalism: Law, Morals, and Political Trials*. Cambridge, MA: Harvard University Press.

Shklar, Judith. 1989. "The Liberalism of Fear." In *Liberalism and the Moral Life*, edited by Nancy L. Rosenblum, 21–38. Cambridge, MA: Harvard University Press.

Skocpol, Theda, and Vanessa Williamson. 2012. *The Tea Party and the Remaking of Republican Conservatism*. New York: Oxford University Press.

Skowronek, Stephen. 1982. *Building a New American State: The Expansion of National Administrative Capacity*. Cambridge: Cambridge University Press.

Skowronek, Stephen, John A. Dearborn, and Desmond King. 2021. *Phantoms of a Beleaguered Republic: The Deep State and the Unitary Executive*. New York: Oxford University Press.

Smith, Alan. 2023. "Vivek Ramaswamy Wants to Trigger Mass Layoffs at Federal Agencies—and He Thinks the Supreme Court Will Back Him Up." *NBC News*, September 12, 2023. https://www.nbcnews.com/politics/2024-election/vivek-ramaswamy-wants-trigger-mass-layoffs-federal-agencies-thinks-sco-rcna104676.

Smith, Blake. 2022. "Only an Absolute Bureaucracy Can Save Us." Review of *For State Service*, by Paul du Gay and Thomas Lopdrup-Hjorth. *Foreign Policy*, November 13, 2022. https://foreignpolicy.com/2022/11/13/bureaucracy-state-public-service/.

Smith, Clint. 2021. "Why Confederate Lies Live On." *The Atlantic*, June 2021. https://
www.theatlantic.com/magazine/archive/2021/06/why-confederate-lies-live-on
/618711/.

Smith, Terrence. 2020. "Has Longstanding History of Calling Elections 'Rigged' if
He Doesn't Like the Results." *ABC News*, November 11, 2020.https://abcnews
.go.com/Politics/trump-longstanding-history-calling-elections-rigged-doesnt
-results/story?id=74126926.

Snow, Anita. 2022. "Group Can Monitor Arizona Ballot Drop Boxes, a U.S. Judge Has
Ruled." *AP News*, October 29, 2022. https://apnews.com/article/2022-midterm
-elections-arizona-voting-phoenix-44809c62794456afee434672da6efl15.

Snyder, Timothy. 2017. *On Tyranny: Twenty Lessons from the Twentieth Century*. New
York: Crown.

Solender, Andrew. 2020. "Biden Blames Trump 'Liberate Michigan' Tweet for Whitmer Kidnapping Attempt." *Forbes*, October 8, 2020. https://www.forbes.com/sites
/andrewsolender/2020/10/08/biden-blames-trump-liberate-michigan-tweet-for
-whitmer-kidnapping-attempt/?sh=35733778774e.

Sommerlad, Joe. 2019. "Did Joseph Stalin Really Want to Steal America's Hamburgers?" *The Independent* (UK), March 1, 2019. https://www.independent.co.uk/news
/world/americas/us-politics/cpac-hamburgers-stalin-cortez-gorka-a8802646.

Sonmez, Felicia. 2019. "Trump Says He's 'in No Hurry' to Replace Acting Cabinet
Members." *Washington Post*, January 6, 2019. https://www.washingtonpost.com
/politics/trump-says-hes-in-no-hurry-to-replace-acting-cabinet-members/2019
/01/06/afac5fea-11e4-11e9-b6ad-9cfd62dbb0a8_story.html.

Southern Poverty Law Center. 2022. "Family Separation—a Time Line." March 23,
2022. https://www.splcenter.org/news/2022/03/23/family-separation-timeline.

Specia, Megan. 2019. "From Friends to Frenemies: Trumps Relations with World Leaders." *New York Times*, December 3, 2019. https://www.nytimes.com/2019/12/03
/world/europe/world-leaders-trump-frenemies.html.

Spencer, Christian. 2021. "Trump Has Reportedly Rejected Multiple Pleas from Allies
to Promote Vaccination." *The Hill*, August 12, 2021. https://thehill.com/changing
-america/well-being/prevention-cures/567615-trump-has-reportedly-rejected
-multiple-pleas/.

Stallard, Katie. 2020. "Donald Trump's North Korea Gambit: What Worked, What
Didn't, and What's Next." *Asia Dispatches* (The Wilson Center), November 26,
2020. https://www.wilsoncenter.org/blog-post/donald-trumps-north-korea
-gambit-what-worked-what-didnt-and-whats-next.

Stanley, Jason. 2020. *How Fascism Works: The Politics of Us and Them*. New York:
Random House.

States United Action. 2022. "Secretary of State Races in 2022." December 7, 2022.
https://statesuniteddemocracy.org/wp-content/uploads/2022/12/sos_deniers
.html.

States United Democracy Center. 2022a. "Election Deniers in Governor Races."
December 7, 2022. https://statesuniteddemocracy.org/resources/governors/.

States United Democracy Center. 2022b. "Election Deniers in Secretary of State Races." December 7, 2022. https://statesuniteddemocracy.org/resources/secretary-of -state/.

Stavridis, James. 2020. "Trump's Firings at the Pentagon Put Our Nation's Security at Risk." *Time*, November 11, 2020. https://time.com/5910672/donald-trump -pentagon-firings/.

Stevens, Stuart. 2020. *It Was All a Lie: How the Republican Party Became Donald Trump*. New York: Knopf.

Stieb, Matt. 2020. "'Obamagate' as Explained by President Trump." *New York Magazine*, May 2020. https://nymag.com/intelligencer/2020/05/obamagate-as -explained-by-president-trump.html.

Stolberg, Sheryl Gay. 2023. "New C.D.C. Director Seeks to Foster Trust in a Battered Agency." *New York Times*, December 15, 2023. https://www.nytimes.com/2023 /12/15/us/politics/mandy-cohen-cdc-director.html.

Stoller, Matt, and David Dayen. 2023. "Moving Past Neoliberalism Is a Policy Project." *American Prospect*, June 27, 2023. https://prospect.org/politics/2023-06-27 -moving-past-neoliberalism-policy-project/.

Stone, Katherine V., and Robert Kuttner. 2020. "The Rise of Neo-Feudalism." *American Prospect*, April 8, 2020. https://prospect.org/economy/rise-of-neo -feudalism.

Strauss, Peter L. 2021. "How the Administrative State Got to This Challenging Place." In "The Administrative State in the Twenty-First Century: Deconstruction and/or Reconstruction," ed. Mark Tushnet. Special issue, *Daedalus* 150, no. 3 (Summer): 17–32.

Sulieman, Ezra N. 1974. *Politics, Power, and Bureaucracy in France: The Administrative Elite*. Princeton, NJ: Princeton University Press.

Sullivan, Andy, and Michael Martina. 2021. "In Recorded Call, Trump Pressures Georgia Official to 'Find' Votes to Overturn Election." *Reuters*, January 2, 2021. https://www.reuters.com/article/us-usa-election-trump/in-recorded-call-trump -pressures-georgia-official-to-find-votes-to-overturn-election-idUSKBN2980MG.

Sullivan, Eileen. 2018. "Trump Says 'There Is No Longer a Nuclear Threat' after Kim Jong-un Meeting." *New York Times*, June 13, 2018. https://www.nytimes.com/2018 /06/13/us/politics/trump-north-korea-nuclear-threat-.html.

Sunstein, Cass R. 2016. "The Most Knowledgeable Branch." *University of Pennsylvania Law Review* 164 (7): 1607–48. https://scholarship.law.upenn.edu/penn_law _review/vol164/iss7/13.

Sunstein, Cass R. 2019. "Chevron as Law." *Georgetown Law Journal* 107: 1613–83.

Sunstein, Cass R. 2020. "Post-Election Chaos: A Primer." Harvard Public Law Working Paper No. 20-25, Harvard Law School, Cambridge, MA, September 2, 2020. https://ssrn.com/abstract=3685392.

Sunstein, Cass R., and Adrian Vermeule. 2018. "The Morality of Administrative Law." *Harvard Law Review* 131, no. 7 (May): 1924–78.

Sunstein, Cass R., and Adrian Vermeule. 2020. *Law and Leviathan: Redeeming the Administrative State*. Cambridge, MA: Harvard University Press.

Sunstein, Cass R., and Adrian Vermeule. 2021. "The Unitary Executive: Past, Present, Future." *Supreme Court Review* 20 (1): 83–117. https://doi.org/10.1086/71486083.

Swan, Jonathan, Charlie Savage, and Maggie Haberman. 2023. "Trump and Allies Forge Plans to Increase Presidential Power in 2025." *New York Times*, July 17, 2023. https://www.nytimes.com/2023/07/17/us/politics/trump-plans-2025.html.

Tabon, Amir. 2019. "Trump Adviser Once Compared Carbon Dioxide to Jewish Victims of the Nazis." *Haaretz*, May 28, 2019. https://www.haaretz.com/us-news/2019-05-28/ty-article/.premium/trump-adviser-compares-carbon-dioxide-to-jewish-victims-of-the-nazis/0000017f-dc7e-df9c-a17f-fe7ee0180000.

Tamir, Yuli. 1993. *Liberal Nationalism*. Princeton, NJ: Princeton University Press.

Tamkin, Emily. 2023. "Why the GOP Fell in Love with Hungary." *New Republic*, September 23, 2023. https://newrepublic.com/article/175368/why-republicans-love-hungary-orban.

Tarrow, Sidney. 2021. *Movements and Parties: Critical Connections in American Political Development*. Cambridge: Cambridge University Press.

Teles, Steven M. 2009. "Transformative Bureaucracy: Reagan's Lawyers and the Dynamics of Political Investment." *Studies in American Political Development* 23, no. 1 (April): 61–83.

Teles, Steven M. 2012. "Kludgocracy: The American Way of Policy." New America Foundation, December 2012. https://static.newamerica.org/attachments/4209-kludgeocracy-the-american-way-of-policy/Teles_Steven_Kludgeocracy_NAF_Dec2012.d8a805aa40e34bca9e2fecb018a3dcb0.pdf.

Tennery, Amy. 2016. "Trump Accuses Cruz of Stealing Iowa Caucuses." Reuters, February 3, 2016. https://www.reuters.com/article/us-usa-election-trump-cruz/trump-accuses-cruz-of-stealing-iowa-caucuses-through-fraud-idUSKCN0VC1Z6.

Tenpas, Kathryn Dunn. 2019. "Who Is in the President's Cabinet?" Brookings, May 21, 2019. https://www.brookings.edu/articles/who-is-in-the-presidents-cabinet/.

Terkel, Amanda. 2023. "Trump Says He Would Pardon a Large Portion of Jan 6 Rioters." *NBC News*, May 10, 2023. https://www.nbcnews.com/politics/donald-trump/trump-says-pardon-large-portion-jan-6-rioters-rcna83873.

Texas Tribune (Austin). 2022. "No, Texas Can't Legally Secede from the U.S., Despite Popular Myth." June 20, 2022 (updated March 6, 2023). https://www.texastribune.org/2021/01/29/texas-secession/.

Toobin, Jeffrey. 2020. *True Crimes and Misdemeanors: The Investigation of Donald Trump*. New York: Doubleday.

Toobin, Jeffrey. 2023a. "Donald Trump Is Going to Get Someone Killed." *New York Times*, October 19, 2023. https://www.nytimes.com/2023/10/19/opinion/trump-gag-order-violence.html.

Toobin, Jeffrey. 2023b. *Homegrown: Timothy McVeigh and the Rise of Right-Wing Extremism*. New York: Simon & Schuster.

Toth, Csaba. 2014. "Full text of Viktor Orbán's Speech at Băile Tuşnad (Tusnádfürdő) of 26 July 2014." *Budapest Beacon*, July 29, 2014. https://budapestbeacon.com/full-text-of-viktor-orbans-speech-at-baile-tusnad-tusnadfurdo-of-26-july-2014/.

Trilling, Lionel. 1951. *The Liberal Imagination: Essays on Literature and Society*. Introduction by Louis Menand. New York: New York Review Books.

Trump, Donald J. (@realDonaldTrump). 2018. "Many Gang Members and some very bad people are mixed into the Caravan heading to our Southern Border. Please go back, you will not be admitted into the United States unless you go through the legal process. This is an invasion of our Country and our Military is waiting for you!" Twitter, October 29, 2018. https://twitter.com/realDonaldTrump/status /1056919064906469376?s=20.

Trump, Donald J. 2020a. "Donald Trump Election Night Transcript." *Rev*, November 4, 2020. https://www.rev.com/blog/transcripts/donald-trump-2020-election-night -speech-transcript.

Trump, Donald J. 2020b. "Remarks by President Trump on the Election." November 5. https://trumpwhitehouse.archives.gov/briefings-statements/remarks-president -trump-election/.

Trump, Donald J. 2021. "Transcript of Trump's Speech at Rally before US Capitol Riot." *AP News*, January 6, 2021. https://apnews.com/article/election-2020-joe -biden-donald-trump-capitol-siege-media-e79eb5164613d6718e9f4502eb471f27.

Trump, Donald J. 2023a. "CPAC Speech Transcript." *Rev*, March 6, 2023. https://www .rev.com/blog/transcripts/trump-speaks-at-cpac-2023-transcript.

Trump, Donald. 2023b. "Donald Trump Hosts First 2024 Presidential Campaign Rally in Waco, Texas Transcript." *Rev*, March 27, 2023. https://www.rev.com /blog/transcripts/donald-trump-hosts-first-2024-presidential-campaign-rally -in-waco-texas-transcript.

Trump, Donald. 2023c. "Speech at Turning Point Action Conference." *C-SPAN*, July 15, 2023. https://www.c-span.org/video/?529330-1/donald-trump-speaks-turning -point-action-conference.

Tudor, Maya. 2023. "Why India's Democracy Is Dying." *Journal of Democracy* 34, no. 3 (July): 121–32.

Tushnet, Mark. 2021. "Introduction: The Pasts and Futures of the Administrative State." In "The Administrative State in the Twenty-First Century: Deconstruction and/or Reconstruction," ed. Mark Tushnet. Special issue, *Daedalus* 150, no. 3 (Summer): 5–16.

United Nations High Commission on Refugees. 2023. "Emergency Appeal: Venezuela Situation." https://www.unhcr.org/us/emergencies/venezuela-situation.

Urbinati, Nadia. 2019. *Me the People: How Populism Transforms Democracy*. Cambridge, MA: Harvard University Press.

U.S. Department of Justice. 2022. "Recent Cases on Violence against Reproductive Health Care Providers." Last updated May 30, 2023. https://www.justice.gov/crt /recent-cases-violence-against-reproductive-health-care-providers.

U.S. House of Representatives Committee on Oversight and Reform. 2020. *United States Government Policy and Supporting Positions (Plum Book), 2020*. Washington, DC: Government Publishing Office. https://www.govinfo.gov/content/pkg/GPO -PLUMBOOK-2020/pdf/GPO-PLUMBOOK-2020.pdf.

U.S. House Select Committee to Investigate the January 6th Attack on the United States Capitol. 2021. "Interview of General Mark A. Milley." November 17, 2021. https:// www.govinfo.gov/content/pkg/GPO-J6-TRANSCRIPT-CTRL0000034620 /pdf/GPO-J6-TRANSCRIPT-CTRL0000034620.pdf.

U.S. House Select Committee to Investigate the January 6th Attack on the United States Capitol. 2022. *The January 6th Report*. New York: Celadon Books.

U.S. Senate Committee on Foreign Relations. 2020. *Diplomacy in Crisis: The Trump Administration's Decimation of the State Department*. S. Prt. 116-50. July 28, 2020. https://www.foreign.senate.gov/imo/media/doc/Diplomacy%20in%20Crisis %20--%20SFRC%20Democratic%20Staff%20Report.pdf.

U.S. Senate Select Committee on Intelligence. 2017. "James B. Comey, Statement for the Record." June 8, 2017. https://www.intelligence.senate.gov/sites/default/files /documents/os-jcomey-060817.pdf.

Vakil, Caroline. 2021. "Democratic Party Headquarters in Texas County Attacked by Man with Molotov Cocktail." *The Hill*, September 30, 2021. https://thehill.com /homenews/state-watch/574822-democratic-party-headquarters-in-texas-county -attacked-by-man-with/.

Valverde, Miriam. 2020. "Donald Trump Promised to Build a Wall and Make Mexico Pay for It." *Politifact*, July 15, 2020. https://www.politifact.com/truth-o-meter /promises/trumpometer/promise/1397/build-wall-and-make-mexico-pay-it/.

V-Dem Institute. 2023. *Democracy Report 2023: Defiance in the Face of Autocratization*. Gothenburg, Sweden: Author. https://www.v-dem.net/publications/democracy -reports/.

Verkuil, Paul R. 2017. *Valuing Bureaucracy: The Case for Professional Government*. New York: Cambridge University Press.

Vermeule, Adrian. 2016. *Law's Abnegation: From Law's Empire to the Administrative State*. Cambridge, MA: Harvard University Press.

Vermeule, Adrian. 2022. *Common Good Constitutionalism*. New York: Polity.

Villa, Dana. 2021. *Arendt*. New York: Routledge.

Villareal, Daniel. 2022. "Right-Wing Media Giants Say LGBTQ Bar Patrons Are Responsible for Their Own Murders." LGBTQ Nation, November 23, 2022. https://www.lgbtqnation.com/2022/11/right-wing-media-giants-say-lgbtq-bar -patrons-responsible-murders/.

Vives, Ruben, and Hayley Smith. 2021. "Maskless Protestors Storm a Grocery Store and Westfield Century Mall." *Los Angeles Times*, January 4, 2021. https://www.latimes .com/california/story/2021-01-04/maskless-protesters-grocery-store-westfield -century-city-mall.

Von Drehle, David. 2018. "The Two-Syllable Word That Summed Up George H. W. Bush." *Washington Post*, December 1, 2018. https://www.washingtonpost.com /opinions/george-hw-bushs-prudence-was-a-laugh-line-it-was-also-his-strength /2018/12/01/6440f81a-f52c-11e8-bc79-68604ed88993_story.html.

Wade, Peter, and Patrick Reis. 2023. "CPAC Speaker Calls for Eradication of 'Transgenderism'—and Somehow Claims He's Not Calling for Elimination of

Transgender People." *Rolling Stone*, March 6, 2023. https://www.rollingstone.com /politics/politics-news/cpac-speaker-transgender-people-eradicated-1234690924/.

Waldman, Paul. 2020. "Trump's Last Gasp: The Pandemic Isn't Real and Everything's Fine." *Washington Post*, October 26, 2020. https://www.washingtonpost.com /opinions/2020/10/26/trumps-last-gasp-pandemic-isnt-real-everythings-fine/.

Waldo, Dwight. (1948) 2007. *The Administrative State: A Study in the Political Theory of American Public Administration*. With new introduction by Hugh T. Miller. New Brunswick, NJ: Transaction.

Walker, Amara, Chris Youd, and Ray Sanchez. 2021. "Family of Georgia Secretary of State Was Still Getting Death Threats Months after Election, Report Says." *CNN*, June 11, 2021. https://www.cnn.com/2021/06/11/politics/georgia-raffensperger -family-death-threats-election.

Wallace-Wells, David. 2023. "The Myth of Early Pandemic Polarization." *New York Times*, June 28, 2023. https://www.nytimes.com/2023/06/28/opinion/covid -pandemic-2020-or-covid-pandemic-politics.html.

Wallison, Peter J. 2018. *Judicial Fortitude: The Last Chance to Rein in the Administrative State*. New York: Encounter Books.

Walzer, Michael. 1984. *Spheres of Justice: A Defense of Pluralism and Equality*. New York: Basic Books.

Walzer, Michael. 2023. *The Struggle for a Decent Politics: On "Liberal" as an Adjective*. New Haven, CT: Yale University Press.

Warburton, Moira, and Jason Lange. 2022. "Exclusive: Two in Five U.S. Voters Worry about Intimidation at Polls—Reuters/Ipsos." Reuters, October 26, 2022. https://www.reuters.com/world/us/exclusive-two-five-us-voters-worry-about -intimidation-polls-reutersipsos-2022-10-26/.

Ward, Alex. 2019. "Trump Met with Putin without Staff or Notetakers Present—Again." *Vox*, January 29, 2019. https://www.vox.com/2019/1/29/18202515/trump-putin -russia-g20-ft-note/.

Washington Post. 2016. "Trump: 'Knock the Crap' Out of Tomato Throwers." February 1, 2016. https://www.washingtonpost.com/video/politics/trump-knock -the-crap-out-of-tomato-throwers/2016/02/01/1d1fe1e2-c92b-11e5-b9ab -26591104bb19_video.html.

Washington Post. 2020. "Trump and Pompeo Have Overseen the Degradation of the State Department." August 15, 2020. https://www.washingtonpost.com/opinions /global-opinions/trump-and-pompeo-have-overseen-the-degradation-of-the-state -department/2020/08/14/7aaa1bca-d34e-11ea-9038-af089b63ac21_story.html.

Washington Post. 2021. "In Four Years, President Trump Made 30,573 False or Misleading Claims." January 20, 2021. https://www.washingtonpost.com/graphics/politics /trump-claims-database/.

Weber, Lauren, and Anna Maria Barry-Jester. 2021. "Republicans in at Least 26 States Have Rolled Back Public Health Powers amid Pandemic." *Los Angeles Times*, September 9, 2021. https://www.latimes.com/science/story/2021-09-15/republicans -roll-back-public-health-powers-amid-pandemic.

Weber, Max. (1921) 1946. *From Max Weber: Essays in Sociology*. Translated, edited, and with an introduction by H. H. Gerth and C. Wright Mills. Oxford: Oxford University Press.

Weisman, Jonathan, and Ashley Parker. 2013. "Republicans Back Down, Ending Crisis over Shutdown and Debt Limit." *New York Times*, October 16, 2013. https://www.nytimes.com/2013/10/17/us/congress-budget-debate.html.

Weiss, Brennen. 2018. "$1 Million in Private Flights and a $31,000 Table—Here Are the 6 Trump Cabinet Members under Scrutiny for Their Lavish Spending of Taxpayer Money." *Business Insider*, March 17, 2018. https://www.businessinsider.com/trump-cabinet-officials-spending-taxpayer-money-under-fire-2018-3.

Wheeler, Russell. 2021. "Trump's Judicial Campaign to Upend the 2020 Election: A Failure, but Not a Wipe-out." Brookings, November 30, 2021. https://www.brookings.edu/blog/fixgov/2021/11/30/trumps-judicial-campaign-to-upend-the-2020-election-a-failure-but-not-a-wipe-out/.

White, Helen. 2022. "As *Moore v. Harper* Takes Shape, a Broad Coalition Takes Aim at the Independent State Legislature Theory." *Just Security*, October 28, 2022. https://www.justsecurity.org/83831/as-moore-v-harper-takes-shape-a-broad-coalition-takes-aim-at-the-independent-state-legislature-theory/.

Wilentz, Sean. 2005. *The Rise of American Democracy: Jefferson to Lincoln*. New York: W. W. Norton.

Wilson, James Q. 1991. *Bureaucracy: What Government Agencies Do and Why They Do It*. New York: Basic Books.

Wilson, Kristi, Haley Talbot, Clare Foran, and Melanie Zanona. 2023. "McCarthy Visibly Frustrated after GOP Hardliners Put His Plan to Avoid a Shutdown on Ice." *CNN*, September 21, 2023. https://www.cnn.com/2023/09/21/politics/house-government-shutdown-negotiations-latest/index.html.

Wilson, Woodrow. 1887. "The Study of Administration." *Political Science Quarterly* 2 (2): 197–222.

Wise, Alana. 2002. "Trump Fires Election Security Director Who Corrected Voter Fraud Disinformation." *NPR*, November 17, 2022. https://www.npr.org/2020/11/17/936003057/cisa-director-chris-krebs-fired-after-trying-to-correct-voter-fraud-disinformatio.

Wolfe, Jan. 2020 "U.S. Judiciary, Appointed by Trump, Thwarts His Election Challenges." Reuters, December 1, 2020. https://www.reuters.com/article/us-usa-election-trump-judges/u-s-judiciary-shaped-by-trump-thwarts-his-election-challenges-idUSKBN28B60O.

Woodruff Swan, Betsy. 2022. "Read the Never-Issued Trump Order That Would Have Seized Voting Machines." *Politico*, January 21, 2022. https://www.politico.com/news/2022/01/21/read-the-never-issued-trump-order-that-would-have-seized-voting-machines-527572.

Wright, Lawrence. 2020. "The Plague Year: The Mistakes and the Struggles behind America's Coronavirus Tragedy." *New Yorker*, December 28, 2020. https://www.newyorker.com/magazine/2021/01/04/the-plague-year.

Yang, Maya. 2023. "Names and Addresses of Trump Jurors in Georgia Posted on Rightwing Websites." *The Guardian,* August 17, 2023. https://www.theguardian.com/us-news/2023/aug/17/georgia-grand-jurors-information-posted-rightwing-websites.

Yourish, Karen, Larry Buchanan, and Denise Lü. 2021. "The 147 Republicans Who Voted to Overturn Election Results." *New York Times,* January 7. 2021. https://www.nytimes.com/interactive/2021/01/07/us/elections/electoral-college-biden-objectors.html.

Zacka, Bernardo. 2017. *When the State Meets the Street: Public Service and Moral Agency.* Cambridge, MA: Harvard University Press.

Zacka, Bernardo. n.d. "Institutional Atmospherics: The Interior Architecture of the Welfare State." Manuscript in progress, on file with the authors.

Zaveri, Mihir. 2019. "Trump's NOAA Pick Barry Myers Asks to Withdraw Nomination." *New York Times,* November 21, 2019. https://www.nytimes.com/2019/11/21/us/politics/barry-myers-noaa-nomination.html.

Zelizer, Julian E. 2020. *Burning Down the House: Newt Gingrich and the Rise of the New Republican Party.* New York: Penguin.

Zhao, Alex, and Daniel Lippman. 2021. "Biden Races to Hire Senior Staff at Drained Agencies." *Politico,* August 10, 2021. https://www.politico.com/interactives/2021/biden-staffing-hiring-trump-turnover/.

A NOTE ON THE TYPE

This book has been composed in Adobe Text and Gotham.
Adobe Text, designed by Robert Slimbach for Adobe,
bridges the gap between fifteenth- and sixteenth-century
calligraphic and eighteenth-century Modern styles.
Gotham, inspired by New York street signs, was designed
by Tobias Frere-Jones for Hoefler & Co.

GPSR Authorized Representative: Easy Access System Europe - Mustamäe tee 50, 10621 Tallinn, Estonia, gpsr.requests@easproject.com

www.ingramcontent.com/pod-product-compliance
Lightning Source LLC
Chambersburg PA
CBHW011100280526
45785CB00009B/3051

* 9 7 8 0 6 9 1 2 5 0 5 3 3 *